Studies in Deprivation and Disadvantage 13

Hard To Place
The Outcome of Adoption and Residential Care

Studies in Deprivation and Disadvantage

Despite the Welfare State: A Report on the SSRC/DHSS Programme of Research into Transmitted Deprivation
Muriel Brown and Nicola Madge

1 **Cycles of Disadvantage:** A Review of Research
   Michael Rutter and Nicola Madge

2 **A Cycle of Deprivation?** A Case Study of Four Families
   Frank Coffield, Philip Robinson and Jacquie Sarsby

3 **The Health of the Children:** A Review of Research on the Place of Health in Cycles of Disadvantage
   Mildred Blaxter

4 **Disadvantage and Education**
   Jo Mortimore and Tessa Blackstone

5 **Mothers and Daughters:** A Three-generational Study of Health Attitudes and Behaviour
   Mildred Blaxter and Elizabeth Paterson

6 **Continuities in Childhood Disadvantage**
   Juliet Essen and Peter Wedge

7 **Housing Inequality and Deprivation**
   Alan Murie

8 **Families At Risk**
   Edited by Nicola Madge

9 **Policies, Programmes and Disadvantage:** A Review of Literature
   Roger Fuller and Olive Stevenson

10 **Parents and Children:** Incomes in Two Generations
   A. B. Atkinson, A. K. Maynard and C. G. Trinder

11 **The Money Problems of the Poor:** A Literature Review
   Pauline Ashley

12 **The Structure of Disadvantage**
   Edited by Muriel Brown

13 **Hard To Place:** The Outcome of Adoption and Residential Care
   John Triseliotis and James Russell

Studies in Deprivation and Disadvantage 13

Hard To Place

The Outcome of Adoption and Residential Care

John Triseliotis and James Russell

Heinemann Educational Books · London · Exeter (NH)

Heinemann Educational Books Ltd
22 Bedford Square, London WC1B 3HH
Heinemann Educational Books Inc
4 Front Street, Exeter, New Hampshire 03833
LONDON   EDINBURGH   MELBOURNE   AUCKLAND
HONG KONG   SINGAPORE   KUALA LUMPUR   NEW DELHI
IBADAN   NAIROBI   JOHANNESBURG
EXETER (NH)   KINGSTON   PORT OF SPAIN

© Crown copyright 1984
First published 1984

British Library Cataloguing in Publication Data

Triseliotis, John
  Hard to place.—(Studies in deprivation and disadvantage; 13)
  1. Children, Adopted—Scotland
  2. Child development—Scotland
  3. Children—Institutional care—Scotland
  I. Title   II. Series   III. Russell, James
  305.2 '3   HV875.7.G72S3

ISBN 0-435-82892-4

Typeset by Castlefield Press, Northampton.
Printed in Great Britain by Biddles Ltd, Guildford, Surrey

Contents

	Acknowledgements	vi
	Foreword	vii
1	Growing up Adopted or in Residential Care	1
2	Aims, Methods and Samples	15
3	The Families of Origin and the Respondents	24
4	The Growing-up Experience	37
5	Genealogical and Personal Information	92
6	Current Social and Personal Circumstances	108
7	The Respondents' Circumstances Contrasted with Those of Their Biological Families	159
8	Summary and Discussion	179
	Appendix – tables	202
	Bibliography	215
	Index	222

Acknowledgements

We would like to take this opportunity to express our deepest thanks and appreciation to the many people and organisations who helped to make this study possible. Our warmest thanks go first to those adoptees and residential people who volunteered to participate in the study, sharing their personal experiences and perceptions. Many thanks are also due to the Directors of Social Work and to those of voluntary agencies and their staff for offering us access to their records. Similarly, our appreciation goes to Professor A.D.B. Clarke and the Organising Group at the SSRC, and Professor M. Rutter and Dr B. Tizard for their continued support and constructive suggestions. Our deep gratitude also goes to Dr A. M. Clarke for her foreword to the book.

Finally, very warm thanks go to the secretarial staff and to David Goda for additional statistical advice.

Note: The Social Science Research Council (SSRC) changed its name on 1 January 1984 and is now The Economic and Social Research Council (ESRC). The functions of the Council are unchanged.

Foreword

In June 1972, Sir Keith Joseph, then Secretary of State at the Department of Health and Social Security, announced at once a problem, an hypothesis and a means of testing that hypothesis. The problem lay in the persistence of poverty and deprivation in our society despite general economic development and the growth of social services. The hypothesis was the existence of a cycle of deprivation whereby deprivations and maladjustments might be transmitted from generation to generation through patterns of parenting and other familial processes. The mechanism was to be a joint DHSS/SSRC working party, funded by the former, which would commission and monitor research in this area.

The ten-year programme supported some 23 studies and more than a dozen reviews of world literature bearing upon the theme of transmitted deprivation. It has been admirably evaluated by Muriel Brown and Nicola Madge (1982). Among the important conclusions, it seems apparent that the processes leading to disadvantage and to cycles of disadvantage are multifactorial, and that there is a natural 'escape' rate as well as fresh recruitment. Muriel Brown (1983) summarised the evidence very well in stating that

> Cycles of deprivation exist – but they do not inevitably exist . . . individuals do defy predictors and so continuities are never absolute . . . . The individual's experience of deprivation, and his response to it, are determined by the interaction of his natural endowment and family resources within the socio-economic structure of society, and the network of unequal opportunities and life chances that the structure maintains. The final report . . . documents the scale and impact of deprivation and demonstrates the futility of espousing simplistic explanations of social problems or adopting simplistic policy solutions.

One way of breaking a cycle of disadvantage is by removing children from deleterious environments and placing them in homes which are likely to promote normal intellectual and social development, a procedure not lightly undertaken where parents, however apparently unsuitable, are anxious to rear their own offspring. More often than not, adopted children have been illegitimate and placed in early infancy with parents who have sought to acquire children resembling as closely as possible those they could not have naturally. The study of the outcome of adoption is important for two major reasons. First, to provide information to social workers, magistrates, prospective parents and others concerning factors which appear to relate to success or failure; second, for the significance of this unusual family pattern in understanding the operation of nature and nurture during development.

There is a vast and expanding literature in which the characteristics of adopted children are compared to those of their adoptive and true parents. In turn these findings are contrasted with the relationship between parent–child characteristics in normal families. Most of these investigations, however, have not collected information on adoptees as adults, although there are some recent exceptions. The study of individuals towards the end of the major developmental sequence is of seminal importance, granted what is now beginning to be known about the interplay of biological and social factors across the years to adulthood.

Late adoption has for long been seen as second best, often to be avoided, partly because parents usually prefer to receive infants, partly because such children are often hard to place by virtue of background problems, and partly because there has been a strongly held belief in the critical significance for later development of early rearing practices which may have been less than ideal. For good reasons, therefore, there are comparatively few studies of late-adopted children, and it would take exceptional determination to gather a sample of 44 late adoptees as adults. Fortunately for social science this task has been undertaken in Scotland by John Triseliotis and James Russell, whose findings are of great significance both for theories of child development and also for social policy. They have in addition been able to identify and study a group of 40 similarly aged young adults who had been reared in institutions, providing evidence concerning the outcome of this alternative method of substitute care for children in need.

The authors faced formidable problems of which the most difficult was the assembly of a sample of adopted 'hard to place' children born in the 1950s. At that time late adoption was rare and was actually discouraged as unlikely to be successful. The further problem of tracing these children as adults was so considerable that only a little under half of those who met the criteria for inclusion could be found and interviewed. The ex-institutional adults were somewhat more easily traced, although only 59 per cent were located and interviewed. Sample loss is of course always selective, and raises the problem of unknown biases. Although those 'lost' did not differ in their early records from those 'found', the authors point out that

> it is certainly *possible* that our two sub-samples diverged earlier in life, and we have no way of knowing whether the 'lost' sample did better, worse or the same as the sample retained. It is also essential to avoid simplistic comparisons between the outcome for the adopted and residential sample. Rather, they are to be seen as reflecting the life histories of two groups, who have some similarities but also some important differences in background.

The late adoptees were settled into their adoptive homes between the ages 2 and 8, with a mean age of 3.5. They had been in care for an average of 2.5 years before final placement, preceded by between three and four moves between institutions or foster homes. Unsurprisingly, some 40 per cent displayed moderate to severe emotional and behavioural problems before adoption. The delay in adoption occurred mostly because of questions connected with the natural parents' social or emotional conditions or with the child's physical or psychological state. In effect, there were many doubts at the time as to whether these 'high risk' children should be adopted at all.

The young adults who had been reared in institutions were of approximately equivalent age to the late adoptees, an obviously important consideration if any contrasts between the groups are to be made. As already stated, comparisons between these groups should be treated with circumspection, since although they had in common very disrupted backgrounds, they also initially differed on a number of potentially potent variables (see the Appendix for these stark differences). The reader may judge the extent to which the common research methodology suggests useful contrasts.

Detailed findings are clearly presented. The main results, supplemented by sympathetic inclusion of some verbatim responses by the young adults, indicated that the adopted sample demonstrated definite discontinuities with the material, social and personal circumstances of their natural families. They were in the main much more likely to resemble in circumstances their adoptive families. It is, however, of interest that social mobility from the adopting parents has been high in both directions; only 14 of the 44 remained in the same social class as their adopted father. Eight were one class higher, seven were two classes higher and two were three classes higher. Eight were one social class lower, and five between two and four classes lower.

As might be expected, the outcome for those who had been institutionally reared was on average less satisfactory than for those who had been adopted. Nevertheless, only a minority displayed serious personal pathologies, others had escaped the cycle of disadvantage, and many had good educational achievements. The discussion of the factors in the different patterns of rearing which appear to have influenced the diverging life-styles of the two groups should be of great value to social workers and policy-makers.

There are clear indications from this study that later adoption of 'hard to place' children can in many cases work well. Suitable adoptive experiences have the capacity of eradicating or diminishing the effects of early adversity. As the authors indicate, the most important factor in outcome seems to be the quality of the rearing experience, rather than the characteristics of the child or of its natural family. These suggestions add considerably to the growing body of evidence that the effects of early adversity can be compensated for later, and that contrary to the traditional view, early adverse experiences do not set for the child a predetermined path unless followed by further adversity.

This book, then, contains some unique information which, as indicated, provides important guidance to those concerned with child care and also adds to our knowledge of human development. The authors' painstaking work is to be highly commended.

Ann M. Clarke
Reader in Educational Psychology,
The University of Hull
July 1983

References

Brown, M. (1983) 'Despite the welfare state', *SSRC Newsletter*, no. 48, 9–11, March.

Brown, M. and Madge, N. (1982) *Despite the welfare state*, London: Heinemann Educational Books.

1 Growing Up Adopted or in Residential Care

In 1974, a seven-year programme of research into what came to be know as 'the cycle of transmitted deprivation' was undertaken by the SSRC with financial support from the DHSS. The use of the term 'cycle of transmitted deprivation' arose from a speech by Sir Keith Joseph (1972), then Conservative Secretary of State for Social Services, who asked, 'Why is it that, in spite of long periods of full employment and relative prosperity, and the improvement in community services since the Second World War, deprivation and problems of maladjustment so conspicuously persist?' The persistence of such problems, it was claimed, prevents people developing their physical, emotional and intellectual potential.

The term 'cycle of deprivation' itself has come under considerable criticism mainly for its diffuseness and lack of specificity. It has been argued that different writers have used the term 'deprivation' to refer to quite diverse conditions and problems ranging from material to maternal or more general emotional and personal deprivations. Jordan (1974) criticised the concept of the 'cycle of transmitted deprivation' for equating poverty with maladjustment and special difficulties. Rutter (1972), whilst acknowledging that the term seemed to draw attention to some grave consequences of deficient or disturbed care in early life, concluded that it was too heterogeneous and the effects too varied for it to have any usefulness. He preferred the use of the concept of disadvantage to that of deprivation.

The basic question being asked is whether the cycle of deprivation or disadvantage exists and, if so, what kind of processes are involved in the transmission of aspects of behaviour, handicaps or difficulties from one generation to the next. Do people who were themselves deprived in one or more ways in childhood become in turn the parents of another generation of deprived children? Sir Keith Joseph (1972) maintained that various problems keep recurring because they are being passed on within sub-groups, including the family. The SSRC/ DHSS Joint Working Party (1975) rightly states that 'transmission can be at the individual or family level or at a level of institutions or society', and it stressed that transmission should not be interpreted simply as 'the role of the family in the recurrence of such problems as poverty, limited economic opportunities, bad housing, psychiatric difficulties and educational handicaps'.

Though the role of the family is not singled out as the sole agent for the transmission of such problems, the probability has been posed that some families, particularly at the lower end of the socio-economic scale, who are multi-disadvantaged, transmit their handicaps, ways of living, their characteristic values and behaviour, their attitudes and 'inadequacies' to their offspring, who go on to reproduce similar conditions, thus perpetuating the situation. On the other hand, the perpetuation of these conditions may be the result of societal and structural processes which keep successive generations in continued poverty and disadvantage. Townsend (1979), Wedge and Prosser (1973) and Field (1974) survey the extent of social disadvantage and poverty in Britain and other gross inequalities in the distribution of income, wealth and opportunities that can help explain the persistence of various social ills. Haggstrom (1964) describes the psychological impact of chronic forms of material disadvantage on individuals and families. Other writers, such as Burt (1943) and Eysenck (1973) concentrate on individual factors influencing behaviour, including poverty. For instance, they discuss the development of intellectual ability which they view as mostly genetically determined and how this strongly influences income levels.

Rutter and Madge (1977) warn against the futility of looking for any supposed 'basic' cause to explain disadvantage and emphasise the need for understanding the chain of circumstances and different mechanisms which operate and interact one with another. With each form of disadvantage or condition such as poverty, poor housing, crime and delinquency, occupational status, psychiatric disorder and parental behaviour, the relative importance of different mechanisms – genetic, biological, familial, extra-familial, institutional, structural and societal – must be considered. In other words, not only are different forms of disadvantage differently transmitted, but any single type may be related to more than one causal factor.

It was to be expected that, in the attempt to establish the mechanisms for the assumed transmission of certain forms of behaviour or of certain qualities such as intelligence, the discussion would be caught up with the issues about the relative importance of nature and nurture or of genetic versus environmental factors. The best opportunities for the control of the complex variables involved were mostly found in child development studies, particularly those able to study monozygotic and identical twins reared together or separately, or siblings reared apart. Other studies followed individual children removed from extremely limited and isolated environments in an attempt to establish the reversibility or otherwise of early adverse childhood experiences.

People who have spent most of their childhood lives in 'substitute' forms of care, including adoption, have, for the same reason, become the target of a number of studies. Most interest has focused on such issues as the relative influence of heredity and environment, e.g. the possible genetic transmission of forms of behaviour such as crime, alcoholism and mental illness, and the reversibility or otherwise of psychological trauma. One of the most hopeful aspects of work with damaged or multi-disadvantaged children is the belief that, given certain positive conditions, early adverse experiences can be reversed. There is a belief, supported by some studies, that development does not stop at any age and that it is a process of transactions between organisms and environment (see Clarke and Clarke 1976). Therefore, aspects such as social functioning and social behaviour are modifiable by experience.

This study was planned with some of the questions raised earlier in mind. It examines the current social and personal circumstances of a group of adults who were adopted when over the age of 2, and contrasts their conditions and experiences with those of a group of people who grew up in residential institutions. The circumstances of each group are then related to those of their families of origin at the time of the respondents' reception into care. Though there is no shortage of investigations of early adoptions, there are only a couple of studies available with a focus on the older placed child. This neglect is accounted for by the fact that until recently few, if any, such adoptions took place to make possible their study. This explanation cannot be offered, however, for the absence of any follow-up retrospective studies of people who grew up in institutions.

Studies in adoption outcome
Studies in adoption outcome can be broadly divided into two groups: those which investigate the outcome of early adoptions, and those which concern themselves with the adoption of the older or 'high risk' child. As a result of certain recent demographic and other social changes, interest in adoption work has switched from the placement of young, healthy infants to the adoption of the older or handicapped child. In response to these changes, adoption practice has been evolving from being a service mostly concerned with the interests of childless couples to becoming a child care or a child-centred service with the interests of children most in mind. Because of the change of focus from the healthy infant to the older or 'handicapped' child, issues connected

with the relative importance of nature and nurture, the possible transmission of behaviour and attitudes from one generation to the next, and questions about the reversibility or otherwise or early psychological trauma, are receiving fresh attention. Many child care workers have been turning to research, hoping to find answers about the wisdom of placing older or 'high risk' children.

Comparing outcome studies presents many problems, chief of which is the fact that different investigators have studied their samples at a different point, such as at age 7, 11 or 16. On the other hand, a couple of cohort studies are now available which provide information about the same group of adopted children at different ages contrasting them, at the same time, with children in the general population.

The outcome of early adoption
As already stated, there is no shortage of studies of early adoptions, and because of this reference will only be made to some recent ones. An important study in the United States by Witmer *et al.* (1963) investigated 484 children about nine years after placement. Data for the study were collected from adoptive parents, teachers and the administrators of psychological tests to the children. The researchers classified the adoption outcome of 67 per cent of the children as 'excellent to fair', that of 8 per cent as not 'definitely unsatisfactory' and of the remaining 25 per cent as 'definitely unsatisfactory'. No difference was found between agency and independently placed children.

Lawder *et al.* (1969) followed up 250 children 3 to 10 years after placement. On the basis of interviews with the adoptive families, 64 per cent of adoptions were classified as 'superior' or 'good', 26 per cent as 'fair', and the remaining 10 per cent as 'low'. Ripple (1968) followed up 160 children placed in infancy by the Illinois Children's Home and Aid Society. The children ranged from 7 to 10 years of age at the time of the research. Information was collected from agency records, interviews with the adoptive parents, and with the child. Forty-seven per cent of the children were grouped as being 'within the normal range', 29 per cent as having 'some problems in adjustment', and 24 per cent as displaying 'serious emotional or behaviour problems'.

Jaffee and Fanshel (1970), in a detailed and well-documented study, investigated 100 adoptions made by four agencies 20 to 30 years after placement. Information was collected from the adoptive parents. Thirty-three per cent of the adoptees were designated as 'low problem', 34 per cent were classified as 'middle range' and the remaining 33 per cent as 'high problem' adoptees, McWhinnie (1967), in a retrospective study of 52 adoptees aged 16–66 years after placement found that 40 per cent had achieved a 'good' or 'fairly good' adjustment in all areas, another 40 per cent a 'reasonable adjustment in some fundamental areas', and the remaining 20 per cent were classified as having achieved poor adjustment in many areas. Seglow *et al.* (1972) followed up the 145 available adopted children who formed part of the cohort of children born in one week in 1958 and found that 'in all aspects of ability and attainment examined, the adopted children did as well, or even better than the other children in the cohort.' Raynor (1980) in a follow-up retrospective study of adoptees aged about 25 at interview found that 80 per cent were either very satisfied or reasonably satisfied with the experience; the remaining 20 per cent expressed various shades of dissatisfaction. The researchers themselves rated 70 per cent of the adoptees as making a good or excellent life adjustment as adults, and 30 per cent as poorly or very poorly adjusted. In a study of trans-racial adoption in the United States, Grow and Shapiro (1974) also found that about 80 per cent of the children were making a good adjustment. A summary of a number of follow-up studies covering a total of 2236 adoptions provided by Kadushin (1971) showed that success rates varied from 74–85 per cent, depending 'on whether one included in the success group the intermediate group'; some 15 per cent were definitely unsuccessful.

Of greater importance to practitioners than the percentage of successful and unsuccessful adoptions is the kind of attributes and characteristics whose presence can be predictive of outcome. Such attributes may refer to the adoptive couple, to the child, or to his background. Jacka (1973), in a brief summary of adoption research, claims that 'the most certain thing that is known about the adoption process is that its "success" depends more than anything else on the adopting couple and on their having the right attitude to children.' The attributes that the majority of research studies suggest as being desirable and whose presence among adoptive couples can be predictive of 'success' include: being warm and accepting towards the child; a stable marriage and family; acceptance of the adopting role; an accepting attitude towards the family of origin; and helping the adoptee to develop his emerging personality on the concept of two sets of parents – a biological and a psychological set. These qualities refer mostly to the adoption of young infants and we still know very little about those involved in the adoption of the older or 'high risk' child. Knowledge also of these attributes does not tell us much about how to recognise them among would-be adopters and substitute parents.

As most adoptions, until very recently, involved the very young, healthy infant with a 'good' history, predictive outcome factors centring on the child or his natural family could not be studied and identified. A couple of exceptions to this understandable dearth of studies will be referred to later in this chapter.

Children with a 'poor' background growing up as fostered or adopted
The studies referred to so far concentrated on the outcome of adoptions involving the placement of young, healthy infants uncomplicated by an 'inferior' history or by poor, 'in care' experiences. Theis (1924) published a study of 18-year-old children who had been placed in long-term foster homes. Some, but not all of them, had been legally adopted. She found no significant difference in the social adjustment of children from 'good' and 'bad' backgrounds, though there was some difference in their educational achievements. Those placed in their early years tended to be better adjusted than those placed later. Eighty-six per cent of the children placed before the age of 2 turned out well, even though only 20 per cent of them had a good hereditary background. Meier (1962) followed up former foster children to assess their social effectiveness and its relation to childhood experiences. He interviewed 61 persons who were now aged 28–32 years. The study covered those who experienced over 5 years of foster care and who had not been returned to their families in childhood. His overall findings showed that the vast majority of his subjects had found places for themselves in their communities. They were indistinguishable from their neighbours as self-supporting individuals; were living in attractive homes and taking care of their children adequately; were sharing in the activities of the neighbourhood and found pleasure in association with others. The evidence, however, suggested a higher incidence of marital breakdown and illegitimate births than among the general population. The findings by Theis (1924) and Meier (1962) are supported by a number of other retrospective studies which tend to refute the suggestion that children growing up in 'substitute' forms of care will necessarily repeat or display their original parents' handicaps.

Salo (in Meier 1962), in a Finnish study, compared the adult adjustment of individuals who, as children, had been removed from neglectful surroundings, to that of persons who, as children, remained in neglectful surroundings. Some of the former children went into foster homes and others into institutions. Salo found that those who were removed showed consistently less maladjustment in adulthood than those who remained. Roe and Burks (1945) evaluated the adult adjustment of those of normal parentage and those whose parents were alcoholics or psychotics or both. They comment: 'The striking thing is that there are so few significantly intergroup differences . . . . In general, the distributions show that the normal parentage children have done a little better.' The researchers, however, further found that whereas 92 per cent of children of normal parentage had been subsequently adopted, this was true of only 57 per cent of those with alcoholic or psychotic parentage. Maas' (1963) follow-up study on the young adult adjustment of 20 wartime residential nursery children strengthens other evidence in suggesting the reversibility of early childhood trauma. In other words, that though children are easily damaged, they are 'also notably resilient'. Similarly, Witmer *et al.* (1963) found little difference in the adjustment of 56 children with 'poor histories' as contrasted with other adoptees placed at a similar age and in similar adoptive homes. Skodak and Skeeles (1949), who studied children with 'inferior histories' placed in infancy from institutions with adoptive parents, found that a favourable development in early childhood continued into adulthood. Hereditary factors, however, were seen to be at play as the IQ of children reared apart from their biological parents still correlated with that of their natural mother. Placement in a good environment, though, had led to a major increase in the overall level of intelligence. In some cases, the children's IQ was 20 points above that of their natural mothers.

Other studies point to a possible connection between certain parental characteristics and similar behaviour in their offspring which suggests a genetic transmission. Crowe's (1972) study involving adopted children showed that those with criminal parents were more likely to commit crime in later years than the rest. Similarly, Hutchings and Mednick (1974) claim to have found a significant correlation between criminality among adoptees and their biological parents. Bohman's (1978) studies, however, failed to establish such a correlation. A number of other studies, notably those of Goodwin *et al.* (1973, 1974), Cadoret and Gath (1978) and Bohman (1978), have found alcohol abuse among adoptees and similar behaviour in the biological families. Cunningham *et al.* (1975) investigated the incidence of 'behaviour disorders' among adopted children born to psychiatrically disturbed parents. Control adopted children from normal biological parents were matched to experimental adoptees. They claim to have found that a greater number of children from psychiatrically disturbed parents had shown behaviour problems. They conclude that behaviour disorders and hyperactivity – with their natural tendency to be precursors of psychopathy in adulthood – are to some degree under genetic control. Based on studies of adoptees and of their biological families, Kety *et al.* (1968) (in Denmark) and Rosenthal *et al.* (1968) concluded that heredity was a prominent factor in the aetiology of schizophrenic disorders, adding that environmental variations were also of importance for the display of such behaviours in the adult personality.

The outcome of late adoptions
As stated earlier, there are relatively few studies focusing on the outcome of late adoptions. One important investigation which bears close similarity to the present one was carried out in the United States in an attempt to determine the reversibility of early psychological damage in children who are subsequently placed in adoptive homes. Kadushin (1971) followed up a group of 91 children who were in early adolescence at the time of the investigation. The children were placed for adoption when they were at least 5 years of age or older and had suffered considerable trauma before adoptive placement. Kadushin based his findings on data obtained from the parents. Compared to other studies of early adoptions, the success rate was similar: 74 per cent successful, 15 per cent unsuccessful, and 11 per cent equivocal. In spite of the very bad experiences of the children, Kadushin concluded that 'there has been a tendency to over-estimate the importance and power of the past . . . . Agencies can take risks in placing older children with a high probability of success.'

Tizard (1977), reporting from her study of residential children, some of whom were later adopted when aged between 2 and 7½ years, concluded that the subsequent developments of the early institutionalised child depends upon the environment to which he is moved. The study also established that parents can be very happy with children placed with them up to the age of 7½ years (the highest age of any child in the study), and that neither a below average IQ nor very difficult behaviour need prevent satisfaction with adoption provided that mutual affection develops between parent and child. Flint (1978), reporting on a follow-up study of 25 children aged about 15 who were placed when under the age of 3 with adoptive parents directly from an institution, reported that 'as a group, the children have demonstrated a remarkable capacity for in-depth affiliation with their parents and families.' She described the adjustment of the group as a whole as healthy but 'immature'. Flint found no significant relationship between the length of time the children spent in the institution and any of the other variables investigated later (IQ, SQ, security rating, dependent trust, immature dependence, effort). She added that 'events which took place after placement in homes [families] were more powerful factors in the final outcome than were earlier experiences.' Similarly, Clarke and Clarke (1976) add that the effects of early experiences have immediate effects which, if not reinforced, will fade in time, they will not *per se* have long-term influences upon adult behaviour, other than as a link in the developmental chain. The persistence of early traumas and disadvantage, it is argued, is usually made possible because of the reinforcement of the adverse experiences. In contrast, an enabling environment, with caring, sensitive and affectionate parents, is likely to reverse the trend. Tizard (1977) came to the conclusion that 'the subsequent development of the early institutionalised child depends very much on the environment to which he is moved.' In effect, what all the studies in adoption outcome seem to say is that whether we talk about the placement of young white or black infants, or of older children, we can expect up to 80 per cent of them to work out satisfactorily. These more optimistic findings contrast sharply with the evidence provided by a number of studies summarised by Bowlby (1951) which claimed that adverse experiences in early childhood were irreversible and likely to damage the child permanently.

The residential care of children
The provision of communal care for children whose parents are unable or unwilling to care for them dates back several centuries, and until 1948 was closely associated with the Poor Law. Other forms of residential provision have also been provided in the form of special schools for children whose behaviour or psychological problems appeared to necessitate a period away from home. The present study concentrated on the first group of children, those who were received or committed to the care of local authorities because of their parents' social or material disabilities or inadequacies. The parents were unable or unwilling subsequently to resume parenting, resulting in the children growing up in children's homes. Brill and Thomas (1964) noted from their work experience that child care 'is almost entirely a "rescuing" service for a limited section of the child population and is thus associated in the public mind with negative concepts of ineffectiveness, rejection and failure.' Burgess (1981) added that 'the problem that affects many children in care is that it is itself a form of disadvantage as much as a response to individual disadvantages.'

The last major inquiry into child care provision in Britain dates back to the publication of the Curtis Report (1946) in England, and the Clyde Report (1946) in Scotland. The recommendations of these Committees have become a landmark in the history of child care in this country, and formed the basis for the Children's Act 1948 which brought about the final break in the links between the care of 'deprived' children and the Poor Law. Among other things, members of the Curtis Committee visited 451 insititutions of various kinds and spoke to staff and administrators as well as to people who were brought up in Homes. Both the Curtis and Clyde Committees were shocked by what they found and had some very critical words to say about institutions in general. The Committee members heard witnesses who drew a 'very dark picture' of their upbringing in Homes, but very optimistically the Committee remarked that such conditions were perhaps characteristics of the period 10 to 15 years earlier. They went on to suggest that 'a code of rules, regular inspection and continued watchfulness' would provide sufficient and adequate safeguards against future harsh treatment. The Committees indicated their preference for small family group-type Homes, preferably run by married couples who could offer a close caring experience to the children. As a result of recommendations made in these reports, some old and large institutions were closed, and smaller ones built. Some authorities and voluntary organisations responded by adapting large institutions into smaller units. Agencies also tried to respond by increasing the ratio of staff to children and by preserving some continuity in care. The Curtis Committee attributed part of the responsibility for the unsatisfactory standards of care to the fact that large sections of the staff lacked special training, a situation which has only partly improved since then, at least as far as residential services are concerned. Overall, much was expected of the new Children's Departments set up under the Children's Act 1948. The Home Secretary at the time (Mr Chuter Ede), when guiding the Bill through the House, told Parliament that 'in the future much happiness would be created and many promising lives preserved through the skill, affection and attention of those [children's] officers.' (The study outlined here obtained the perceptions of people who spent an average of 11 years of their childhood in Homes, mostly during the 1960s and early 1970s, or about 25 years after the publication of the Curtis and Clyde Reports.)

As a result of remarks made in the Curtis Committee's Report and certain provisions in the Children's Act 1948 it was assumed that, when considering the placement of children, foster care was to be preferred over residential care. Studies about the negative effects of institutional care for infants reinforced this view. Following the Children's Act 1948 and the setting-up of Children's Departments by local authorities, a concerted effort was made to place as many children as possible in foster care. Institutions came to be seen as 'bad', and child care authorities vied with each other to be at the top of the fostering league. The publication in the 1960s and early 1970s of studies by Trasler (1960), Parker (1966), and George (1970), showing that something like 50 per cent of all fostering placements arranged are likely to fail, made practitioners and administrators stop and think again about fostering. For a short period of time residential care was reasserting itself as a method of care for 'deprived' or 'delinquent' children. The reversal of the tide did not last for long. The publication of studies mostly in the criminological field showing the very high failure rates of institutions for delinquent children gave rise to renewed efforts to secure family placements for all types of children needing care for short or long periods. (See Mattinson 1974, who provides a review of the research literature. Also Cornish and Clarke 1975.) The de-institutionalisation of children and the closing of as many institutions as possible has become a major objective for many local authorities. Some early positive results achieved from the fostering of 'delinquent' adolescents by Kent County Council gave a fillip to these campaigns (Hazel 1981). What has largely been missing from many of the debates was some tested knowledge about the distinctive type of service required to be responsive to the particular needs of specific children. In effect, much greater distinctiveness is required for the residential needs of different groups of children. In the end services such as foster care, adoption and residential care may have to be seen as part of a continuum of resources that can be used for short or longer periods of time depending on the needs of each child at a particular time and point in his development, rather than as the sole answer to diverse needs. It is often not unreasonably argued that residential care is provided not as a first choice but as a last resort.

Outcome studies of the residential care of children
Most available studies have concerned themselves with the emotional and intellectual development of infants or young children in residential care or of older children being investigated at a particular age whilst still in the institution. Like adoption, comparisons between different studies of children in residential care is difficult because of the differing qualities of the institutions studied, the varying periods of time spent in them by the children, and the difficulty of establishing the 'before' and 'after'. When summarising a number of studies of residential care, Dinnage and Pringle (1967) commented that the two potentially most damaging aspects of residential care are that 'a psychologically, culturally and educationally restricted, impoverished at worst, even depriving substitute environment may unintentionally be provided; secondly, that unless special steps are taken, children may grow up without a personal sense of identity, lacking a coherent picture of both their past and their future.'

Studies of infants and young children
The decade following the end of the second world war saw the publication of a number of important studies whose concern was the

effect of institutional care on the emotional and intellectual development of infants and young children. Studies by Bowlby (1951), Goldfarb (1943), Spitz (1949), Roudinesco and Appell (1950) first drew attention to the effect of 'maternal deprivation' on young children living in institutions. A plethora of other studies followed in an attempt to validate these early studies and to assess further the consequences of residential care for children. 'Maternal deprivation' was seen to be the cause of many negative conditions ranging from delinquency to psychopathy. Dinnage and Pringle (1967) concluded from summarising research evidence that 'prolonged institutionalisation' during the early years of life leaves a child very vulnerable to later stress. When summarising more recent research, Prosser (1976) added that 'today there appears to be no new evidence which contradicts it.' Trasler (1960) found that the breakdown of foster care was associated with previous prolonged institutional care. Dennis and Najarian (1957) and Pringle and Bossio (1958) indicated that the longer the stay in an institution, the greater was the cognitive deficit and the more extreme was the emotional and behavioural disturbance. At least as far as infants are concerned, most studies are agreed that all children reared in institutions suffer permanent damage to their emotional health. The identification of institutions as places perpetuating depriving conditions resulted in efforts to direct young children away from them.

Other studies suggest that, at least as far as cognitive development is concerned, what matters is not whether the child is in an institution or not, but rather the type of care he or she receives. Flint (1967) concluded that the mental health scores on sixteen babies decreased significantly as age increased and institutional life was prolonged. When, however, the institution was fundamentally reorganised to promote 'healthy development' through paying attention to individuality, dependent relationships, opportunities for initiative in the children, and consistency of care and discipline, the children made marked improvements after the first year. Prosser (1976) adds that 'whereas earlier studies have documented the impaired language, poor intelligence and disturbed behaviour which frequently occurs in children who have been reared in institutions', these are not found in all children who have been reared in institutions. Tizard and Tizard (1971) for instance found that residential nursery children were significantly less friendly than children reared in their own homes and that while they had fewer social experiences and less contact with adults, there was no significant intellectual or language retardation at 3 years old. Dinnage and Pringle (1967) made a number of suggestions of how residential institutions could improve the quality of care offered, such as by 'drastically reducing the number of people concerned with the daily care and handling of infants, and by ensuring continuity of caretakers'. Francis (1971), reporting from an Australian study comparing the effects of own home and institution rearing on the behavioural development of young normal and mongol children, suggested that institution-reared normal children were behaviourally more retarded than their home-reared counterparts of the same chronological age.

Studies of older children in residential care
A number of studies have found a possible link between prolonged residential care and later maladjustment or failure to make use of family life (Trasler 1955; Conway 1957; Pringle and Bossio 1960). Wolkind and Rutter (1973), however, suggest that children experiencing short-term institutional care are 'at risk' of anti-social disorder, not so much because of the effect of the care *per se*, but rather because such children are liable to come from disturbed families. Wolkind (1974) also found important sex differences in the development of anti-social disorders among children in institutions. Yule and Raynes (1972) showed that children in care are more likely to be maladjusted than those growing up in their own homes. They found no evidence though that the age at which a child comes into care and the number of changes he experiences whilst in care are related to later behaviour. Similarly, only slight evidence was found to support the view that the longer a child stays in an institution the greater the likelihood of becoming maladjusted. Rosen (1971) maintains that children in long-term care are retarded not only in their emotional development but also in terms of social development, particularly in adolescence. Based on the records of one local authority's Children's and Education Departments, Ferguson (1966) studied 205 young people 2 to 3 years after leaving the care of Glasgow Corporation, and concluded that on a range of items, such as employment record, scholastic achievements and intellectual ability, the young people were 'poorer' compared to a group of working-class Glasgow boys not in care; and similarly, that the conviction rate of the 'in care' group was higher than that of the 'not in care' one. Unfortunately, Ferguson did not distinguish between the children who grew up fostered and those who grew up in Homes. For information about the comparative group he relied exclusively on the records of the Education Department.

Pappenfort and Kilpatrick (1969), reporting from a survey of over 2000 residential institutions in the United States, claim that three-quarters of all children in institutions were believed to be emotionally disturbed. The percentage of children being referred to psychiatrists ranged between 1–13 per cent, depending on the type of institution.

In summary, studies in adoption outcome seem to suggest as good an 'adjustment' for late adoptions, including that of children with early institutional experiences, as for children placed when under 6 months old. These studies also suggest that the effects of early experiences may disappear if not reinforced subsequently. In contrast, children growing up in care appear to be more likely than others to develop emotional, behavioural or psychiatric problems possibly as a result of their 'disturbed' family background or of their institutional experiences. There is also the view put forward by Dinnage and Pringle (1967) based on their review of the literature, that 'early entry into care and the absence of good family (or substitute family) contacts' are associated with 'poor' outcome for children in residential care. Rutter (1972) concluded from his thorough review of research in 'maternal deprivation' that most long-term consequences result from deprivation of care and stimulation and not separation.

2 Aims, Methods and Samples

Aims
The first aim pursued by the study was to establish whether aspects of behaviour, handicaps or difficulties are transmitted from one generation to the next in situations where children are separated from their families of origin at an early stage. In other words, whether a change of environment in children produces adults who are qualitatively different from their natural families in terms of personal and social functioning. The second aim was to establish possible similarities and differences between people who, after being separated from their parents at an early stage, experience contrasting forms of substitute care. A subsidiary objective was to examine how far discontinuities of care, early institutionalisation and moves from one institution to another have long-term effects. To achieve these aims the study contrasted two groups of people: one group who grew up adopted, but who were considered to carry high risks for adoption, and another group who grew up in residential institutions for an average of 11 years of their childhood.

It was expected that findings from the study might provide some guidelines to social policy-makers in the areas of social disadvantage and to practitioners, such as social workers, who are called upon to make decisions and provide services for children in their care.

Methodology
Methods were chosen that seemed appropriate for the collection of both quantitative and qualitative material. Data collection from files, semi-structured, tape-recorded interviews and formal questionnaires, including rating scales, were used depending on the type of information sought. Statistical concepts and comparisons were made where appropriate with regard to the frequency of certain factors, such as the presence of criminal activities and alcohol consumption. Besides the quantitative material the study obtained a considerable amount of qualitative information whose purpose was to help illuminate the phenomena being studied. It could be argued that the pursuit of both numerical and qualitative information eventually results in loss of both breadth and depth. However, we would like to think that the use of quantitative and qualitative data act as a check on each other.

Data collection from agency records

The records of the local authorities participating in the study were used to extrapolate certain information. Because the records were uneven in the areas and amount of information they provided, the study had to content itself by concentrating on those characteristics about which information was available in all the records. In other words, information referring to the characteristics of the family of origin at the time of the child's reception into care had to be mostly even in all records. Eventually standardised information was collected referring to the following:

(1) The personal, economic and social circumstances of the families of origin, covering composition of the family, age, status, occupation, economic situation, housing conditions, physical and mental health, quality of relationships, history of crime and/or alcohol abuse.
(2) Reasons for reception into care, including information about the child's circumstances before the final placement.
(3) The adoptive parents' material, social and personal characteristics and circumstances at the time of placement, which included age, status, other children in the family, occupation, economic situation and type of housing.
(4) In the case of the residential sample, information about the care experience as seen by the case social workers. The residential records span over a longer period of time and were therefore more detailed compared to the adoption ones which ceased with the issuing of the adoption order.

Data from respondents

Studies in adoption outcome have mostly relied so far on the accounts of adoptive parents or teachers. (See, for example, Bohman 1970; Jaffee and Fanshel 1970; Kadushin 1971; Seglow *et al* 1972.) Raynor (1980), on the other hand, obtained the views of both adoptive parents and adopted persons. No study has as yet sought the views of a representative sample of people who grew up in residential establishments.

Qualitative and other material was obtained through semi-structured, tape-recorded interviews with the people featuring in the study. The interviews covered a large lifespan area of about 500 items, mostly on the subjects' substitute care experience and on their current material, social and personal circumstances. The interviewers used a detailed questionnaire as a framework to ensure uniformity of information collected, but otherwise respondents were encouraged to describe and enlarge on key experiences. Most of the interviews were carried out between 1978 and 1980.

Formal interview schedule and self-rating scale

A formal interview schedule was used to check that all the desirable information was collected from the semi-structured interviews referred to above. In addition, a number of self-rating scales were administered, constructed specifically for this study. These tried to measure the subjects' own perceptions of their quality of life, past and present, in such matters as satisfaction with life experiences, past and present circumstances and behaviour, quality of relationships, sense of well-being and closeness to their substitute carers. These areas were seen as important to the lives of most people, and because they are not easily observable by outsiders, the subjects were asked to make judgements themselves. This approach was used by the SSRC Survey Unit in their quality of life surveys in 1975 and earlier (see Hall, 1976.) Ward (1980) comments that 'when the individuals are their own judges no two standards of judgement will be exactly the same, but the greater the degree of commonality of experience, the easier it will be to gain consensus on the appropriate characteristics of life and their quality.' He later adds that the subject's perception will be influenced by characteristics such as health and basic biological make-up, as well as the values developed over his life. Though the set of values or standards will be unique to the individual, the commonality of experience will ensure that this set does not vary dramatically between individuals within any one society. Bradburn (1969), writing about the structure of psychological well-being, remarked that feelings of well-being (psychological well-being) reflect directly the quality of a person's life and are the only valid referants for individuals.

Questions could obviously be asked about the respondents' verbatim descriptions when compared to the ratings they ascribed to their behaviour, satisfaction with their growing-up experiences, capacity to cope with life, and feelings of emotional well-being. Interviewers should not be surprised when this occurs. The respondent may rank various values in quite different ways from the interviewer. On the other hand, when the respondent ventilates particularly negative feelings about his life experiences he may possibly feel more generous and ascribe a somewhat higher rating. As a general rule, however, descriptions seemed to match the ratings the researchers expected.

The discrepancy between the ratings of a respondent and those of an 'objective' observer might also have occurred in the area of coping or satisfaction with current life situations. Sometimes observable conditions indicated a somewhat less optimistic situation compared to the ratings ascribed to it by the subject. Kadushin (1971: 15), who used measuring form-scales when interviewing the parents of adopted children rather than 'adjustment' comments:

Objectively, in terms of some commonly accepted levels of interpersonal and intrapersonal performance, he may be judged to be doing poorly. However, in his own disorganised way he fits the needs and complements the requirements of his role reciprocal – the wife to the husband, the parent to the child, the employee to the employer.

Fanshel (1962), in discussing the same problem of measurement of adoption outcome, adds that it would be a mistake 'to equate stress in living experience with the worthwhileness of the experience for those involved'.

Ratings in such areas as emotional/behaviour problems and states of well-being were again based on the subjects' 'overall global judgement' rather than on the count of symptoms. If the subjects identified themselves as moderately or severely emotionally disturbed, or as having behaviour problems, this was accepted as fact. When the residential people's self-rating of their emotional or behavioural or psychiatric problems whilst growing up in care was checked with the social workers' records, the discrepancy between the two accounts amounted to only 4 per cent. Questions could equally be asked about possible discrepancies between actual and reported behaviour, and doubts about the accuracy of retrospective besides very recent behaviour. Yet Triseliotis (1980a) found considerable agreement in the comments separately obtained from foster parents and foster children concerning past experiences and behaviour.

Serious thought was given to the possibility of using some form of psychological test that might elicit attitudes or measure personal/emotional adjustment, but the idea was abandoned for two main reasons. In the first place, and after a long search, no test was thought to be suitable for the age group under investigation. Second, experience from another somewhat similar study suggested the near impossibility of administering a formal test (Triseliotis 1980a). Most of the subjects were interviewed after extensive searches and at times under very difficult circumstances that would have made the use of tests near impossible.

The samples
Samples for the two groups of young people came from social work departments in Scotland and from one big voluntary agency which placed children in all parts of Scotland. For the adoption sample, the study covered five regional departments but as all the adoption placements took place before the local government reorganisation of 1976, something like 17 separate local authorities have been involved. The other Scottish regions which do not feature in this study had no samples meeting the study's criteria except for one big region which

refused to participate. Of three voluntary agencies which made their records available, only one had placed children who met the criteria. For purposes of economy in time and money, the residential sample was restricted to two regional departments representing six local authorities before reorganisation. Though the residential sample represented the practices of six separate agencies, the children were brought up in more than 40 Homes scattered in different parts of Scotland and run by statutory or voluntary organisations. They ranged from small- through medium- to large-sized institutions. A minority provided education on the premises. Some children were in various Homes at different times.

Basic selection criteria
The following criteria had to be met for inclusion in the sample:

(1) All respondents should, as far as possible, come from a very disadvantaged background, hence the concentration on people who had been taken into care.
(2) All adoptees in the sample should have been over 2 years old and under 10 at the time they were placed in the adoptive home. Because of the aims pursued, the study avoided all children under 2 placed for adoption. Similarly, all residential subjects should have gone to live in one or more residential establishments when under 10 and to have stayed there at least until the age of 16. Adopted subjects featuring in the study spent an average of 11 years 8 months with their adoptive families before they reached the age of 17. The residential group lived for an average of 11 years in one or more institutions.
(3) Respondents should as far as possible be in their twenties at interview. the mean age at interview was 24 years (s.d. 3.6) for the adoption group and 22.8 years (s.d. 1.2) for the residential sample.

The adoption sample presented most difficulties because the period under discussion was one when few, if any, children were placed for adoption when older than a few months. Adoption societies and local authorities children's departments did not believe then that 'older' children or children with a 'poor' history or those from a deprived background were suitable material for adoption. Professionals, such as social workers and doctors, often tried to dissuade would-be adopters from adopting the type of children referred to here. In fairness to adoption practitioners, the literature on the subject tended to dissuade them from placing older or 'high risk' children. On the rare occasions when older children were placed for adoption it was mostly either because of perseverance by adopting couples, or because the agency perceived the adopters as being equally 'marginal' as the child, in which case it was thought the family would not be too bothered with issues about heredity and adverse early experiences. Evidence of this practice can be found in the pages of the *Journal of Child Adoption* in the 1960s. One section of the *Journal* was devoted to reports from the adoption societies and many of these would say how many children were accepted for placement and how many 'refused'. The reasons for refusals were given by some societies. For example the Western National Adoption Society was unable to accept 27 babies in one year mainly 'because of the irregular and immoral life of the mother' and 'all babies regarded as subnormal physically or mentally' (*Child Adoption*, no. 49, 1966). Adoption of the child with special needs having been such a rare phenomenon, the study tried to cover children placed by agencies in almost all parts of Scotland.

The total sample: and numbers interviewed

Table 2.1   The two samples*

	Adoption N	%	Residential N	%
Interviewed	44	48	40	59
Willing but unable to participate (overseas)	2	2	—	—
Refused to participate	10	11	7	10
Unable to trace	35	39	21	31
Total	91	100	68	100

* Five respondents, three in the adoption and two in the residential sample, were interviewed after the main statistical computations were carried out and they do not appear in all the statistical tests.

The study succeeded in interviewing just under half of those who featured in the original adoption sample. Of the 44 subjects interviewed, 28 were male. The most discouraging aspect was the number of people (39 per cent) who could not be traced at all, in spite of several efforts. Raynor (1980), who also attempted to interview young people placed mostly in infancy, succeeded in obtaining interviews from only one-third of the original sample. The obvious question is how similar or different those interviewed were from the rest of the sample. A comparison by sex, status, age at coming into care, number of moves before the adoptive placement, behaviour or emotional problems and physical health before placement, and age at interview revealed no significant differences between those interviewed and the rest. When those interviewed and the rest were also compared on four items referring to the families of origin regarding crime, alcohol abuse, socio-economic status and type of relationships, again no significant differences emerged between the two groups. The next stage was to compare those interviewed with the rest by taking the age, social class and house occupancy of the adoptive family, but again no significant differences emerged between the two groups.

Taking the adoption group as a whole, no significant differences were found on a range of characteristics between those interviewed and the ones the study failed to see. In many areas there was remarkable similarity between them. However, it is well known that sample loss can bias results. In a sense, this is always selective in that some members can be located and interviewed, some refuse, and some cannot be found. The question then becomes whether the sample loss is likely to produce a bias relevant or irrelevant to the hypothesis. Most researchers, ourselves included, look at factors which might be relevant between located and non-located members; if there is no difference they then express the belief that the two sub-samples are matched. This procedure is essential, and it is difficult to better it. However, it ignores the fact that crude indices relating to the often remote past have been used, and not those more proximal in time to the follow-up. Thus we believe that it is certainly *possible* that our two sub-samples diverged earlier in life, and we have no way of knowing whether the 'lost' sample did better, worse or the same as the sample retained. It is also essential to avoid simplistic comparisons between the outcome for the adopted and residential samples. Rather, they are to be seen as reflecting the life histories of two groups, who have some similarities but also some important differences in background.

Of the 68 possible subjects who formed the residential sample, 30 (44 per cent) were male and the rest female. The male:female ratio of 44:56 is almost the exact opposite of that quoted by Parker (1980) concerning all children coming into the care of local authorities in the 1950s. Of the 40 (59 per cent) interviewed by the study, 15 (38 per cent) were male and the remaining 25 (62 per cent) female. Though more women than men were in the end interviewed, the difference did not amount to statistical significance when compared over a number of background characteristics. The study sample was also somewhat biased towards children who came into care between the ages of 5 and 9 rather than under 5. No other difference was identified between the total sample and those interviewed on the following items: status, the display of emotional, behavioural or psychiatric problems whilst in care, or the appearance before a Hearing (somewhat similar to the Juvenile Court system in England and Wales) or adult criminal court at the same period. Similarly, there was no difference between the two groups in terms of the characteristics of their natural parents, i.e. housing and economic conditions, the quality of relationships and the presence of alcohol abuse or of a history of crime. Again, however, one must stress the points made in connection with the adoption sample: there may be undetectable but important differences between non-located and located members of the sample. Hence the results can only safely be assumed to relate to the outcome of those who had this type of history and were traceable later. The others may have done better, worse or the same as those interviewed. It does not stretch the imagination to assume that some of those who underwent 'care' experiences might well wish to cover their tracks and put this less than fortunate past behind them. Equally, it might be the more feckless drifter who left no trace of his subsequent career. These possibilities endorse the writings of such authors as Labouvie *et al.* (1974) and Campbell and Stanley (1963), who give clear evidence of the potentially distorting effects of sample loss. We had evidence about people from either sample whom we were unable to interview and whose current circumstances appeared to be either 'precarious' or 'unsatisfactory'. For example, one adoptee phoned to say his adoptive mother was so disappointed in him that he had better not have anything to do with the study. One residential person with a long criminal history asked for his fares in advance and then disappeared. On the positive side, we had letters from both adopted and residential people claiming to be leading a 'happy and adjusted life' and not seeing the point of being interviewed. And again, one must remind the reader of a second point: the differences in the background of the two samples make a straightforward comparison of the outcome of adoption and residential care unwarranted.

At selected points in the report, reference will be made to the experiences and conditions of former foster children. The information is extracted from published material and also from reports submitted to the SSRC in 1979 and 1980. The foster care group was made up of people aged 21 at interview. They lived with a single foster family from at least the age of 9 to the age of 16. The mean period they spent with the same foster family before the age of 16 averaged 11 years.

The statistical analysis
Most of the statistical computations carried out were with 41 adoptive and 38 residential respondents. With a nominal level of measurement

only tests of the probable existence of relationships between two variables have been used (chi square). With ordinal and interval levels of measurement (or dichotomies) appropriate tests indicating the strength of possible relationships have been used (τ C or τ B) depending upon the shape of the table. In a number of tables where extra cases were added after computing, the value of χ^2 was calculated by hand and the level of significance given corresponding to the degrees of freedom allowed by the table.

3 The Families of Origin and the Respondents

The families of origin

Data for this part of the study were obtained from the records kept by the social work agencies. As information on all desirable characteristics was not evenly available, the study had to content itself with those about which there was comparable information for both samples. It is recognised that the gathering of information contained in records not collected for a specific research purpose has serious limitations in the uniformity and detail of the material provided. The alternative, however, would have been a longitudinal study over 20 years. It is widely recognised also that, with few exceptions, the families whose children are received or committed into the care of local authorities are some of the most disadvantaged in the community. Packman (1968) concluded that the conditions most likely to produce the need for reception into care were: 'Illegitimate children, unemployed fathers, the lowest social classes, poorly housed and overcrowded families, newcomers and foreigners were all prominent.' The natural families of children featuring in this study conform to this view. Chronic disadvantage associated with poor housing, low income, long periods of unemployment, dependence on social security benefits along with disruptive relationships which were either the cause or the result of the disadvantages, necessitated in most cases the reception into care of the sample children.

Social workers used some of the following comments to describe the social and personal circumstances of the families of origin of the residential group:

'Mother is down and out. I have never seen such neglectful conditions before. Family known as problem family.'

'A history of child battering. Mother is a very helpless, inadequate person.'

'Parents homeless. Evicted before. Mother deserted father. Lives in Salvation Army Hostel.'

'Mother treated for depression after child's birth, later certified. No one to care for the child.'

'Mother drinks excessively and on many occasions picked up for

prostitution. Children left unattended.'
'Mother has been frequenting various soup kitchens and Salvation Army Hostels to get food and board for the child and herself.'
'Mother borderline ESN. Nowhere to take the child.'
'Father disappeared and mother killed herself. No one to care for the children.'
'Mother unable to care for her children because she is an alcoholic.'
No judgement is intended here on the accuracy or otherwise of the social workers' comments. They are reproduced as an illustration of the hardships faced and the behaviour exhibited by the parents which necessitated the children's reception into care. They serve also as an illustration of the possible experiences that the children went through before their reception into care.

Though the majority of natural mothers in the adoption sample were single at the child's birth, these were not the usual parents surrendering their young infants for adoption. Single parents asking for their children to be placed for adoption through local authority Children's Departments in the 1950s and 1960s in Scotland were either from a lower socio-economic background than the rest or were those whose child presented a complicated history (e.g. physical or mental handicap). Single mothers holding non-manual or professional occupations and those with an uncomplicated personal or background history were usually referred to voluntary adoption societies. It was assumed that voluntary agencies were more suited to deal with middle-class-type applicants compared to local authority ones, and that this would enable the former to match adopters with children of a similar background. In fact some adoption societies when faced with an unusual situation would refer the child to the local authority Children's Department. The Guild of Service (an adoption society in Edinburgh) wrote in its report for 1963 that the society was 'most grateful to the children's officer for taking two other children in care also because of special difficulties' (Guild of Service, Edinburgh Annual Report for 1965).

Local authority Children's Departments were expected to place the children of low social class mothers with adopters from a somewhat similar background. Of course, the rules of supply and demand did not always operate in this way because the number of available infants with a middle-class background was not sufficient to meet the increasing demand by middle-class couples. Another argument for this 'selective' process of referral was that voluntary adoption societies had few resources and therefore were unable to handle young infants with complicated personal and background histories who could not be placed almost straight away or after a short period of pre-adoption fostering. Evidence for such practices comes from a study of 376 children referred to twelve adoption agencies in Scotland in 1965. Eight of the agencies were local authority ones and the remaining four voluntary societies (Triseliotis 1969). That study showed that significantly more mothers from a higher socio-economic background were referred to voluntary adoption societies compared with local authority Children's Departments. These referrals were usually made by hospital social workers or by family doctors. Judging from the descriptions and comments made by social workers, the natural parents of the children featuring in this adoption group were overwhelmed by personal and social problems. They were not run-of-the-mill mothers asking for their children's adoption. The following are some of the comments made by social workers about the natural mothers of adoptees:

'Mother was in a Remand Home when the child was born.'
'Mother who is an ex-child protection herself had a prison record for theft and breach of the peace.'
'A very inadequate, helpless person from a very deprived background.'
'In trouble with the police for drink and vagrancy.'
'A history of prison sentences for theft and petty crime.'
'Known as a problem family and to drink heavily.'
'Mother had been violent to child.'
'A prison record for soliciting, drunk and disorderly and petty thefts.'
'Mother with very low intelligence, promiscuous and poor conditions in a deprived area.'
'Suspected ill-treatment of child.'
'History of violence and deprivation, child had to be removed after RSPCC report.'
'Mentally-retarded, promiscuous, drank excessively.'
'Unstable personality, history of vagrancy, Salvation Army Hostels.'

The fact that children from such 'high risk' backgrounds were later adopted against the 'theories' and climate of the period says something about the perseverance of some social workers and of the open-mindedness of some adopters. One adoptive father said to the interviewer: 'Because we were older at the time we wanted to adopt an older child. We were being discouraged by all sorts of people. They couldn't understand that where there is plenty of love the child's background is no problem.'

The information that follows concentrates on an identification of the personal and social characteristics and conditions of the families of origin at the time of the children's reception into care. They include age, marital status, social class, history of crime, psychiatric history or 'psychological instability', mental handicap, and alcohol abuse. They are based on factual information provided in the files. The classification of the families' economic situation, housing circumstances and the quality of relationships equally rely on descriptive information abstracted from the records. This information had to be interpreted for the purposes of classification after agreement by the two researchers. If anything, the severity of the social conditions was played down because of some gaps in the records. It is also recognised that, unlike the residential group, most of the information on the natural parents of adoptees refers to the mother only and it may underestimate the incidence of certain conditions such as crime and alcohol abuse.

Age, marital status and social class of the natural parents
Overall, the adopted group had parents who were more likely to be younger at the child's birth, also to be single and have fewer children born to them compared to the parents of the residential group. About a third of the natural parent(s) of the adoption group were classified in non-manual occupations compared with none in the residential group. The parents of the residential group mostly held semi-skilled or unskilled occupations.

Housing conditions
The housing conditions of about half the natural parents of both groups were described as 'precarious' or 'very precarious' at the time of reception into care. However, significantly more of the parents of the residential group were in the 'very precarious' classification. Homelessness, repeated evictions and 'problem family' conditions were described for both groups. The somewhat better housing circumstances of the natural families of the adoption group were rather deceptive. Whilst many of the single mothers who feature in the study had secured some kind of accommodation for themselves with their own families, in hostels, or in living-in jobs, the arrangement was often temporary and precarious.

Economic situation of the families of origin at the time the children came into care
As stated earlier, local authorities usually concentrate their attention on children whose parents are facing extreme material, social and personal handicaps. Many of the parents in the two samples, but more so in the residential than in the adoption one, were on social security benefits for lengthy periods of time resulting mainly through the breakdown

of relationships, unemployment or illness. Economic dependence was not the only characteristic of what often appeared to be a situation compounded by other social handicaps. In almost no case could the economic situation of the families of origin be described as stable. It was in recognition of this fact that the economic conditions of the families were eventually classified as 'fairly stable', 'precarious' or 'very precarious'. On this basis, the economic situation of over half the families of origin was assessed as 'precarious' or 'very precarious' at the time of the child's reception into care. Seven of the residential families and three of the adoption group came into the 'very precarious' category. The main explanation for the somewhat less complicated and less precarious financial situation of the families of origin of the adoption group compared to the residential one was that the pressures had not yet been compounded by the presence of more than one child.

Quality of relationships
Looking at the quality of relationships among the families of origin, the term 'disruptive' is used to describe situations of chronic conflict between the parents, or spouses, leading to separation, divorce, abandonment, cohabitation, etc. The disruptive relationships present in the majority of the families of origin were often given as the immediate reason for the child's reception into care. The chronicity of these problems led to many separations and desertions by one parent, possibly accounting more than any other single factor for the children's reception or committal into care.

Disruptive and disturbed relationships among the families of origin featured extensively in both groups. Some of these conditions had a chronic aspect about them. Most of the children, especially in the residential sample, were exposed to these disruptions before they were eventually received or committed into care. The worst conditions and the most chronic ones were again to be found among parents of the residential sample. The families of origin of the adoption group, possibly because they were younger, appeared to have had significantly fewer serious relationship problems compared to the residential group ($p < 0.001$). Their main relationship conflicts were with spouses or cohabitees and often with their own parents.

Alcohol abuse and history of crime
Severe problems of alcohol abuse with its related personal and social problems featured significantly more among the parents of the residential than the adoption group ($p < 0.001$). In two-fifths of the families of origin of the residential group and in about one-fifth of the

adoption group serious problems seemed to result from excessive alcohol consumption. Apart from relationship and other personal difficulties, other problems included 'assault following drink', 'child neglect', 'breach of the peace', and being 'drunk and disorderly'.

Convictions for criminal offences featured significantly more among the families of the residential group than among the parents of the adoption group (p < 0.005). Convictions were mostly about stealing, soliciting, breach of the peace, drunk and disorderly, manslaughter and the ill-treatment of children. Just over half of the parents of residential people had a criminal conviction compared to under a fifth of those of adoptees.

Psychiatric history or 'psychological instability'
Four of the parents of the residential group had received psychiatric treatment and another seven were described as 'unstable' or 'inadequate' or having a 'drug problem'. None of the natural parents of the adoption group appeared to have had psychiatric treatment, but six were described as 'helpless and inadequate', 'violent and aggressive' or 'immature and unstable'. These conditions would possibly fit the broad classification of 'personality disorders'. Whilst recognising the limitations of this classification it is being used in some subsequent correlations.

Mental handicap
Nine (21 per cent of the natural mothers of those adopted) were described as being 'severely' or 'borderline' mentally handicapped (of limited intelligence). The social workers in their records used descriptions such as 'retarded', 'educationally subnormal', 'borderline ESN', 'limited intelligence' or 'possibly retarded'. It is recognised that the social workers' judgements concerning the natural mothers' mental handicap may not have been accurate. However, questions about the mothers' intellectual limitations were on occasions the main reason for delaying the child's placement for adoption. Six (16 per cent) of the mothers of children who grew up in residential care were also described as mentally 'handicapped'.

Summary
The families of origin of both samples shared a number of indices of deprivation and social handicap. Wedge and Prosser (1973) in *Born to Fail* identify three important factors as constituting social disadvantage: first, a large family of children or only one parent figures. Thirty-four (42 per cent) of the families in the total sample had never married. Separation and disruption leading to single-parent conditions

existed in most of the remaining families. Second, low income. The economic situation of half the natural families featuring in the samples was described as precarious or very precarious and of the rest as only fairly stable. Many of the families were on social security benefits. Third, poor housing is the last important factor constituting social disadvantage. With few exceptions, almost all of the parents of origin were facing serious housing difficulties at the time the children came into care. Some of the parents had been evicted several times and others were living in temporary lodgings.

Put in another way, either the financial situation or housing circumstances of over half of the families of origin were precarious or extremely precarious. Disruptive relationships featured in almost all of these families to create a very close association between the three characteristics of inconsistent and low income, poor housing, and disruptive relationships. In many of the same families, there was heavy drinking and/or a history of criminal convictions. The natural families featuring here, and especially those of the residential group, were probably some of the most disadvantaged and perhaps 'disturbed' in the country. The next step was to identify the most 'disturbed' and the most materially handicapped families.

The most 'disturbed' families

To identify the most 'disturbed' natural parents, four indices signifying some form of social or personal disturbance were considered. These were a criminal history, severe alcohol abuse, severe disruptive relationships and 'psychological instability'. Parents who shared two or more of these four indices were classified as 'disturbed'. (A reminder again that this classification is based on the social work records and occasionally on additional information supplied, especially by residential people, at interview. In the case of the adoptee's natural parents, most of the information refers to the mother.) In the end twelve (27 per cent) of the natural families of adoptees and eighteen (45 per cent) of those of residential people were classified as 'disturbed'. The difference between the two groups did not amount to statistical significance. However, when three or more indices signifying disturbance were taken together, the residential parents emerged as considerably more 'disturbed' than the natural parents of adoptees. In effect only three of the families of adoptees came into this category compared with fourteen of the families of residential people ($p < 0.005$). One explanation for this bias is that information on the natural parents of adoptees refers mostly to the natural mother whilst for the parents of residential people it refers to both parents. Another explanation is the younger age group of the adoptees' parents compared to the residential ones.

The most 'materially handicapped' families

Families facing moderate to severe financial and housing problems simultaneously at the time of the child's reception into care were classified as the most 'materially handicapped'. Fourteen (32 per cent) of the natural parents of adoptees and fifteen (38 per cent) of those residential people came into this category. However, infinitely more residential families were facing serious housing problems. Again, it was the chronicity and severity of the residential parents' situation that distinguished them from the parents of adoptees.

The 'quality of life' of the two groups of families

In an attempt to present an overall picture of the 'quality of life' of the families of origin at reception into care, the two sets of families were compared on six characteristics indicating material, social or personal handicaps. The characteristics were moderate to severe financial or housing problems; severe drink problems; moderate to severe relationship difficulties; a history of crime; and 'psychological instability' or some degree of 'mental handicap'. Nine (20 per cent) of the natural parents of adoptees shared from four to six indices indicating material, social or personal handicaps, compared to sixteen (40 per cent) of those of residential people. The adoptees' natural parents had a mean of 2.1 (s.d. 1.6) handicaps compared to 3.1 (s.d. 1.6) of those of residential people. In effect, the families of residential people shared a higher number of handicaps. It may seem surprising that eleven of the families of adoptees and three of those of residential people appeared to have no handicaps. The main explanation lies in the fact that the handicaps were either of a not pronounced enough condition to merit their inclusion, or, in the case of the parents of adoptees, they had asked for adoption but were referred to the local authority instead of a voluntary agency because of the complicating factors presented by the child. These biases will be taken into account as far as possible in future comparisons. The differences between the two groups suggest that the natural parents of adoptees were less 'deprived' compared to those of the residential sample. A significant overlap was found between material deprivations and 'disturbance' in the residential families but not in the natural families of adoptees, a further indication of the worse conditions of the residential families.

Characteristics of the two samples of children

Two-thirds of the adoption sample came into care when under a year old compared to only one in every eight of the residential sample. In fact only one adoptee was received into care when 5 years and older compared with eighteen (45 per cent) of residential subjects. Overall, those who grew up adopted came into care significantly younger compared to those who grew up in residential Homes. This also meant that the residential group experienced their families of origin over a lengthier period of time than the adoption one. A minority of children were at times looked after for short periods by members of the extended family. Whilst 85 per cent of those adopted were illegitimate at birth, this was true of only 31 per cent of those who grew up in residential establishments. In effect, illegitimate children were more likely to be 'surrendered' for adoption compared with legitimate ones.

Age at final placement
An important stage in adoption parenting is the age at which the child joins his new family. Table 3.1 sets out the age at placement of the adoption group and also the age at which the residential group were seen as moving into a permanent Home.

Table 3.1   Age at final placement by group

Age	Adoption		Residential*	
	N	%	N	%
Under 2 years	—	—	8	20
2–3 years	30	68	10	25
4–5 years	11	25	6	15
6–7 years	3	7	7	18
8–9 years	—	—	9	22
	44	100	40	100
Mean age in months at placement	41 (s.d. 16)		77 (s.d. 29.5)	

* Final placement for the residential group was deemed to be the time they entered long-term residential care.

Almost 70 per cent of those who grew up adopted were placed with their adoptive parents between the ages of 25–47 months old and the rest (32 per cent) between the ages of 48–93 months. The mean age at final placement was 41 months (s.d. 16). Two-fifths of those who grew up in residential Homes went to their long-term residential placements when aged between 6 and 10 years. The mean age at final placement of the residential group was 77 months (s.d. 29.5). The mean period between reception into care and their long-term residential placement was 24 months. In this respect those who grew up in Homes were considerably older when they started their long-term residential placement compared with those who joined adoptive families. Adopted people featuring in this study were unusual compared to other adoptees because they were placed when older and after experiencing a period of care in different establishments. Some studies in child development suggest that such experiences may give rise to emotional and psychological problems. Bowlby (1951) claims that the possibility of psychological damage increases with the absence of a stable nurturing environment in the very early years of life, which was the case with adoptees featuring in this study. This, and some other factors to be highlighted later, puts such children into the 'high risk' category.

The mean gap between reception into care and final placement was 30 months for those adopted and 24 months for those who grew up in Homes. All the children were exposed to a number of moves between different institutions or institutions and foster homes before their final placement. In contrast, Kadushin's (1971) sample experienced moves only between foster homes. In this study the adopted sample averaged 3.5 moves and the residential sample 3.3 moves before they went to what was to be their final placement. The residential sample though had an average of 6 moves before eventually leaving care. The adopted sample had a mean period of 25 months in residential institutions. Because of the number of moves experienced by both groups of children, continuity of care, which most literature on early child development stresses as important, was interrupted at frequent intervals. In fact, one child experienced 11 moves before finally being placed for adoption. The rather lengthy gap between reception into care and final adoptive placement seemed to be related to the 'high' risk that the children appeared to present. Apart from agency reservations concerning the children's parental background, other fears arose from the fact that some of the children had either a physical 'disability' or, perhaps as a result of their experiences, had begun to develop emotional difficulties. Comments such as the following from the records would support this suggestion: 'only fostering, as child is very disturbed and demanding'; 'adoption postponed because of child's background. decided to wait and see how the child develops'; 'abnormally large head'; 'adoption postponed because of the mother's background, mother was an unstable character.' It can be assumed that other children who did not satisfy the child care workers on these counts were not eventually placed for adoption. In one child's records the comment was made that he was not 'suitable for adoption because of his background'. This child spent the rest of his childhood in a Home. Reference was made in Chapter 2 of the policy followed by many adoption agencies of rejecting physically or mentally handicapped children. In their annual reports, some agencies would make reference to delays in placing children on the 'advice of the paediatrician' (see Guild of Service Annual Report 1961). By 1965 the same society started placing babies with 'slight medical difficulties and several who appeared to have an unpromising start'. At the time this was seen as a real breakthrough.

Siblings
Thirty-four (85 per cent) of those in the residential sample had siblings in care and in 31 cases the siblings were in the same establishment. The difficulty in finding families for sibling groups may have been one of the reasons why some of these children were not placed in foster or adoptive homes. As already pointed out, residential people came from larger families compared to adoptees. Only one adoptee and her twin brother were adopted by the same family.

Physical health before final placement
Approximately two-fifths of those adopted and one-quarter of those who grew up in institutions experienced one or more physical illness or condition before going to their final placement. Some of them had to spend brief periods in hospital for these conditions. However, the evidence from the records suggests that the seriousness of the physical condition of sixteen (36 per cent) of the children in the adoption group possibly contributed to their being held back from early adoption placement. Conditions described in the records included:

'Mild asphyxia at birth – impossible to say if child will be mentally normal. Possibility of collapsed lung.'
'Sickly child. Underweight at birth. Kept in hospital for seven months. Residual weakness remains.'
'Suffered from a lot of chest trouble from birth. A weak child. Very susceptible to infection.'
'Excitable child. Had strange fits. Put on phenobarbitone. Latent epilepsy could be present.'
'Late in attaining developmental milestones. An enormously fat child. Cannot walk and makes no attempt. Speech impediment – started school late because of his problems.'
'Very slow development from birth. Adoption postponed.'
'Disproportionate growth of the child's head. Very slow development from birth. Adoption postponed to see if the child could develop normally.'
'Slight assymetry of child's face – damaged foot from birth – had to wear a caliper.'
'This child suffered from pneumonia, rubella and influenzal meningitis.'

THE FAMILIES OF ORIGIN AND THE RESPONDENTS 35

This left him weak and susceptible to infection. Postponed adoption.'
'A premature baby – continued to be very small and somewhat sickly.'
'Suffered from fairly severe dermatitis.'
'Squint in one eye.'
'Abnormally large head – adoption postponed.'
'Severe eczema.'
'Broken right arm.'
'Chronic infantile eczema.'
'Slight malformation of his pelvis.'
'Physical condition reason for postponing adoption.'

Considering that this was the period when only 'gilt-edged' or 'perfect' babies were thought to be suitable for equally 'first class' adoptive families, it is surprising that these children were eventually placed with families at all.

Emotional or behaviour problems before final placement
In the course of this study the presence or absence of emotional or behaviour problems will be examined at different stages, i.e. before final placement, during the placement (in childhood), and at interview. Almost two-fifths of those adopted were described as presenting from moderate to severe emotional problems before being placed with their adoptive parents compared with only one-fifth among the residential group before going to what was meant to be their final placement. In effect, significantly more of those who were adopted than of those who grew up in Homes were identified as displaying moderate to severe emotional problems before their 'final' placement.

Problems identified in the records included 'temper tantrums', 'serious bed-wetting', 'withdrawal', 'unresponsiveness', 'destructiveness', 'extreme passivity', 'clinging to adults', 'attention seeking', 'excitable', 'stealing'. In some cases more than one condition existed at the same time. In addition, three adoptees, but none from the residential group, had already been referred for psychiatric help or assessment before their final placement. It is open to speculation how far the adoption group's earlier reception into care compared to the residential one contributed to these problems. It is also of importance to note that emotional problems in some residential children did not appear until about a year or so after their reception into care. This may be surprising considering the 'disturbed' backgrounds from which many of them came. Neither can it be argued that the social workers failed to notice possible problems because broadly the same workers were making such observations for children who were eventually adopted. This observation raises the question (to be examined in greater detail later) whether children growing up in residential care become 'disturbed' because of their residential experience or for having a 'disturbed' family background.

Summary
The sample consisted of two groups of people who as children were received into the care of local authorities. These were placed before the age of 10 either in adoptive homes or were left to grow up in residential establishments up to their late teens. Each group spent an average of 11 years in their respective substitute 'homes'. The shortest period possible was 8 years and the longest 17 years. Compared to those who grew up in institutions, the adopted group were significantly younger at reception into care but at the time of adoptive placement they were identified as having more emotional and physical disabilities. Those who grew up in institutions experienced their families of origin over a lengthier period of time compared to those who were adopted. The adopted group spent an average of 30 months in various places between reception into care and final placement. Both groups had an average of just under four moves between reception and final placement, though the residential group experienced further institutions after what was thought to be their long-term placement.

In final summary, adopted people came from families which faced somewhat fewer social handicaps at reception compared to those who grew up in residential care. However, adoptees, before going to their adoptive families, displayed more emotional and behaviour problems compared to the residential group. Similarly, there were many more questions concerning their physical condition at birth compared to the residential group. The adoptees' background and their emotional and physical condition appear to have contributed to their being held back from early adoptive placement. Some residential people may have been held back from being placed in foster or adoptive homes because of the presence of siblings and/or continued interest by some parents.

4 The Growing-Up Experience

The first part of this chapter concentrates on the quality of the growing-up experiences with adoptive parents or in residential establishments. Respondents in each group were asked to describe and rate their experiences on a range of items, including the degree of satisfaction with, and the strength of attachment they felt towards, their carers. The detailed focus on the childhood experiences is a recognition of the importance of this period of life to the development of personality. Personal and social factors during this period seem to contribute significantly towards the establishment of self. The process assimilates new learning, qualities of being cared for, feelings of being wanted and a knowledge of one's personal history and genealogy. Studies in child development may disagree about the exact stage in childhood when personality and identity begin to be formed, but most of them agree that warm, caring and satisfying emotional experiences are important ingredients in the development of a secure self. Though the evidence as to the lasting effects of separations and discontinuities is conflicting, it is generally accepted that negative experiences, such as discontinuity of care, emotional and physical neglect, anxious parenting and faulty learning can undermine the emerging personality. For example, Tizard and Hodges (1978) conclude that children who experience multiple and changing caretakers are most likely to develop emotional and interpersonal difficulties. Such experiences would fit the adopted group before they joined their new families and were also true of the residential group from the moment they entered until they left care in their late teens. But emerging evidence also suggests that, provided the child has the opportunity to form new attachments, there may be no long-term consequences arising from earlier privations and the loss of early attachments (Kadushin 1971; Rutter 1972; Clarke and Clarke 1976). In this and the remaining two chapters three basic experiences, among others, which are important in the development of identity will be examined: first, the quality of caring and attachment experienced by respondents; second, knowledge about their genealogy and personal history; and third, how respondents perceived the attitudes of the wider community towards them, and how they placed themselves in relation to the rest of society.

The quality of caring and attachments experienced by respondents

Significantly more of those who grew up adopted expressed a greater degree of satisfaction with their carers compared to those who grew up in institutions (Table 4.1) (τ C = 0.34, p < 0.03). Overall 38 (86 per cent) of those who grew up adopted described their relationships with their adoptive parents as 'very good' or 'fairly good' compared to only 24 (60 per cent) of those who grew up in Homes. A major difference between the two groups was the proportion of adoptees (45 per cent) who described these relationships as 'very good' compared with only 15 per cent of residential people. Respondents in both groups seemed to opt for the rating 'mixed' rather than 'poor' when critical of their growing-up experiences. Because of this, and for purposes of overall assessment, the study considers 'mixed' outcome as signifying fairly negative experiences. The wish of most respondents not to appear destructively critical was a general characteristic among members of both groups. For example, one residential person who argued that all residential Homes should be 'erased' still opted for a 'mixed' rating. In a study of long-term fostering (Triseliotis 1980b) it was found that almost seven out of ten former foster children rated their experience from 'fairly good' to 'very good' (see Table 4.1). At the opposite end, about one in every five rated it as 'poor' to 'very poor' which may appear rather higher compared to those growing up adopted or in residential care. The main explanation that can be offered for this is that when a disruption occurred in fostering, former foster children were still likely to 'mourn' the loss of foster parents. Somehow the loss of a foster family, even in late teens, was experienced as most upsetting. In at least half of these situations the breakdown in relationships which was more recent was not entirely irretrievable. It needs to be remembered, though, that over half of those fostered registered great satisfaction with their fostering experience.

Respondents were then asked to rate their total experience of growing up adopted or in residential care. In this instance they were expected to take everything into account including their immediate relationship with their carers. Little difference emerged between the two stages except that there was a slightly more negative position taken by a minority of respondents in both groups (Table 4.2). The 22 adoptees and five residential people who rated their experience as very positive and satisfying talked about it with enthusiasm. Those who rated it as fairly positive made a number of qualifications, but the overall view was that it was a positive experience. Overall 82 per cent

Table 4.1 *The quality of relationships between respondents and their carers*

	Adoption N	Adoption %	Residential N	Residential %	Foster care* N	Foster care* %
Very good	20	45	6	15	21	53
Fairly good	18	41	18	45	6	15
Mixed	4	9	14	35	4	10
Poor or very poor	2	5	2	5	9	22
	44	100	40	100	40	100

* Figures obtained from report to the SSRC (Triseliotis 1980b)

Table 4.2 *Overall satisfaction with the total care experience of growing up adopted or in residential care*

	Adoption N	Adoption %	Residential N	Residential %
Very positive	22	50	5	13
Fairly positive	14	32	17	42
Mixed	4	9	13	32
Fairly negative to negative	4	9	5	13
	44	100	40	100

of those adopted and 55 per cent of those who grew up in Homes expressed very positive or fairly positive feelings. Kadushin (1971), who also carried out a retrospective follow-up study of 'high risk' children, found that 74 per cent of adoptive parents rated the experience as 'unequivocally successful' 11 per cent as 'fairly successful' and the remaining 15 per cent as 'unsatisfactory'. The satisfactory outcome of 80 per cent 'high risk' adoptions in this study is similar to that found by a number of studies concentrating on early and 'uncomplicated' adoptions. A recent study by Raynor (1980), which looked at children placed for adoption in their early years (nearly all the children entered their adoptive families in their first year of life), reported that 85 per cent of the parents rated the experience of adoption as having been 'very satisfactory' or 'reasonably satisfactory'.

With no other comparable study available in long-term residential care, it is difficult to say whether these findings are normal or unusual. Depending on how these findings are viewed, the situation may not seem as grim as it was feared. Caution of course is required as so few residential people expressed real enthusiasm for this type or rearing.

Positive and satisfactory experiences had to do with being cared for, loved, wanted, closeness to parental figures, feeling secure, flexible enforcement of rules, openness about adoption and discussion around the circumstances of being adopted or being in residential care. Generally, positive feelings implied a satisfactory and good experience but were sometimes qualified by remarks concerning emotional closeness or distance from parental figures, some rigidity in the exercise of controls and some evasiveness concerning the truth about the subjects' circumstances and about their background. Mixed or negative or generally negative feelings had to do with the absence of caring and love, with harsh discipline, high expectations in the case of adopted people, impersonality of care and lack of individuality in the case of those who grew up in Homes. Residential people also resented the frequent changes of staff, particularly of those they had become attached to, and found this most upsetting.

The adoption group

Satisfaction and the adoptive family
The adoption worker is constantly faced with the difficult task of identifying 'good' families that will provide a certain standard of care for the child in his agency's care. This job becomes more uncertain when it is recognised that there is no guide or agreement as to what constitutes a 'good' or a 'bad' family. At the time the adoptions featuring here were arranged, research studies offered little help on what characteristics or attributes contributed to successful outcome and were therefore to be sought out in applicants. Later studies, as stated in the introductory chapter, were to suggest a number of attributes that were found to be predictive of success. These included: warm and accepting attitudes towards the child; acceptance of the adoptive role; a stable marriage and family; accepting attitudes towards the family of origin; and helping the child to develop his emerging personality on the concept of two sets of parents – a psychological and a biological one. The latter requires what Kirk (1964) has described as an acknowledgement, at a feeling level, that adoptive parenthood is different from biological parenthood. The 'acknowledgement of difference' posited by Kirk, and confirmed in McWhinnie's (1967) and Triseliotis's (1973) studies, 'facilitates

empathy with the child's circumstances. Empathy in turn would firm up the bond between them' (Kirk 1981).

Until very recently most adoption agencies followed, and some still do, a form of investigative approach in their search for 'suitable' couples. A number of tangible and intangible characteristics were looked for, though it was unclear how judgement was reached on the intangible attributes. Tangible characteristics investigated included the applicants' economic comfort or at least economic stability, age, years of marriage, health, and perhaps religion. Intangible attributes included: psychological motivation, emotional maturity, personality, quality of marriage, attitude to infertility and attitude towards the adoptee's family of origin.

The changing nature of adoption and the different types of children now available have brought about not only a change in thinking as to who is an adoptable child, but also who can adopt, which has implications for the selection procedures. Many of the children who need adoptive homes now are atypical and for this reason perhaps it takes atypical people to take them into their homes. The qualities required therefore may fall outside traditional and often biased views of what is a 'suitable family' to adopt. As a result of these developments would-be adopters are no longer viewed with suspicion about their motives, but are seen as people offering a service. Different families, it is again argued, bring qualities that can respond to the needs of different children. The move in the last five or so years has been away from selection towards the preparation of couples for the adoptive role. At the same time it is recognised that adoption, as it is practised now, is not the kind of parenthood for all.

Perceptions of growing up adopted
It was stated earlier that over 80 per cent of those adopted expressed positive or generally positive feelings about their experience of growing up adopted. What they valued most was the security of a family, the love, kindness and affection they said they got from their parents and especially of being accepted as members of the family. In fact, most of them never thought of themselves as being anything other than full members of their adoptive families. Adoptees overall enjoyed 'the love, care and kindness shown to me', 'being brought up as their son', 'the whole experience was satisfactory', 'having good parents and a good home', 'well cared for', 'home life, concern and interest of my parents in my life', 'being treated as one of the family', and 'getting together with relatives'.

Negative perceptions were associated with strictness, too many expectations, absence of loving and caring feelings, emotional distance and depreciative comments concerning adoption. Relevant comments were: 'My parents were a bit too strict', 'not loved for myself', 'unhappy about everything', 'that as an adopted person I was very much a second choice', 'not knowing enough information about my adoption', and 'the high expectations and ambitions of my parents'.

Positive to fairly positive experiences. Though four out of every five adoptees expressed satisfaction or a fair amount of satisfaction with their experience of growing up adopted, it did not mean that it was all a bed of roses. But any shortcomings, differences or conflicts were perceived as minor or insignificant compared to the total experience: 'The one I live with is my real mum and dad to me . . . I loved my mum like any kid would do . . . I loved my father too . . . adoption was good. I am glad I wasn't put into a Home, fostered out . . . I'm very glad I'm with a family.'

Another one placed at 4 years said: 'I wouldn't swap them for the world – kindness, loving, that is all I can say.' C. added:

> I was older than other kids [aged 7 at placement] and they must have tried hard to get my love. It makes me feel as if I was more wanted . . . it makes you feel great to feel you were wanted as much . . . I have had a good life. I couldn't have asked for a better life.
>
> She [adoptive mother] picked me out because she wanted me. There was a feeling of security and I did really have a happy childhood . . . couldn't imagine calling anyone else mother . . . there was nothing I felt could have been better.

A. like others commented that when he thinks of parents it is the people who cared for him that are in his thoughts:

> It is one thing to give birth but it is another to go through the struggles of bringing a child up – they never neglected me. I got my share before anyone else [meaning the natural children of the family].

M.'s experience was also typical of others:

> Basically I had a parent who wanted a child as opposed to it just happening . . . once I got into this new family [aged 4½] I didn't want to go back to the Home. I didn't want to leave it . . . I have got parents who wanted children.

Another adoptee placed at 3½:

> My mum and dad treated me so well . . . they didn't give us everything we wanted, but everything we needed . . . they did without things so that we got some things . . . I was lucky, I had a very happy life.

K. added that his mother and father were the only parents he ever had (placed at 4 years) and that he had been very happy as a child and that had seemed the most important thing. He had felt close to his mother and father and known that 'both loved me a lot' which made him feel very secure.

Mrs L. who grew up with the family's natural children felt that she was 'always treated as an equal . . . there was also lots of love . . . I have no real reason to think that I would have been better somewhere else . . . all families have their problems.' A coloured girl was placed at the age of 4 with a family who had four of their own children. Soon after she was placed another child was born to the parents: 'They treated us all the same. No difference at all. I was brought up as their own. I got on very well with my brothers and sisters . . . there was always lots of love. It was fun . . .' Another respondent who was adopted along with her twin brother by a couple who had a young child of their own, found that her adoptive parents' attitudes to her and her brother were no different to that of their own son. 'If I had to live my life over, I wouldn't want to change it a bit.' Somewhat similar sentiments were expressed by others who grew up with the adoptive family's natural children. C. at 11 years, had to go into short-term care because his adoptive mother was temporarily very ill and there was nobody else to look after him. He described his distress:

> I really missed them . . . I could hardly wait to see my mother and father. I didn't know any other parents . . . when my mother [adoptive] died I was really torn apart . . . my parents looked after me as if I was their own . . . no regrets at all.

K., who rated her experience of being adopted as 'generally positive', attached importance to the love she was given: 'My parents have never been wealthy but with love . . . I always had to work for anything that I got, but then I enjoyed it all the more.' M., who also rated her overall adoption experience as 'generally positive', felt very close to her adoptive father because he made her feel she was 'a very worthwhile undertaking', and that what she had given him in the way of love and companionship had been of much more value than anything else he could have had. On the other hand, her mother expected a 'perfect daughter' and was 'critical of my achievements', making her at times feel as if she had to be eternally grateful to her for having adopted her. Overall, however, she said she had been 'very lucky' really in terms of the parents she had and the life she had, especially when she thought of what it would be like growing up in a Home.

Quite a number of other adoptees who knew, or had some memories of, living in a Home would usually make the comparison between family life and living in a residential establishment, showing no preference for the latter: 'Never missed out on anything; better than being in a Home.'

Mixed view of adoption. Four adoptees (9 per cent) expressed mixed views about their experience. There were both good and bad things about it, though they did not go so far as to say that it was unsatisfactory. The bad things were somewhat similar to those referred to by the three people who rated the experience as negative, i.e. lack of love, no closeness, too much strictness and pressures or the expression of regrets by some parents for having adopted them.

M., who was placed at 5 feels close to his parents now, but was also critical of the experience:

> I got hit a lot . . . they didn't look at your point of view . . . they were very restrictive. My mother was always taking in foster kids and I think really we were deprived sometimes to make way for other children . . . I had to share a room with others for 6 to 7 years. You couldn't have privacy.

B., who described his adoption as 'sometimes good and sometimes bad', also focused his dissatisfaction on the parents' strictness 'as if you were a dog on a lead all the time. I felt as if I was in a prison all the time. All discipline and no play or give a little.' He felt he was adopted as a replacement for the family's lost son. He attributed his going to see a psychiatrist to his experiences at home and getting 'muddled' when he was told about his adoption when he was over 10. E., whilst recognising good parts in her adoption, stressed her parents' strictness, their high ambitions for her, long hours spent doing school work, and the feeling of not being loved or treated as an individual: 'I felt as if I was in a prison all the time . . . all discipline and no play or give.' Her underachievement resulted in her being referred to a Child Guidance Clinic. Her parents, she maintained, made her feel that she was a 'second choice' and that they were 'ashamed' for adopting her. Both parents were working and very active in local community affairs and they had little time for her. She often felt she lacked love and that she was in their way.

Fairly negative or negative perceptions. Three of the adoptees who expressed a definite disappointment with their adoptive experience explained it as being mostly due to the strictness of their parents, their high expectations of them, the absence of sufficient love and caring, and frequent reference to their adoption in a way that conveyed the parents' disappointment and regret. (A fourth adoptee who rated his relationship with his adoptive parents as 'fairly good' insisted on rating the overall outcome as 'poor', but gave no reasons for this.)

Two of the three adoptees were adopted by the same professional couple. When W. went to live with them she was about 8 years old. She came into care at the age of 7 months and had seven placement changes before the final one. One of the placements was with prospective adopters but it was terminated after 4½ years because of reported ill-treatment. She was then seen by a psychiatrist who recommended boarding out, but it was about a year later and three more changes before she was placed with her future adoptive parents. W. talked a lot about the unhappiness in the adoptive home which she mostly attributed to the high expectations of her adoptive parents:

> I suppose they expected a lot of me and I did become very withdrawn. They were not my parents . . . I couldn't ever be like them however hard I tried . . . if there was any trouble they would say, 'We didn't have to adopt you' . . . this would be rubbed in quite a lot . . . sometimes they were good but not until I had left home did I really feel they had improved a bit. I can't say I was ever particularly happy . . . I am closer to my mother since I left home.

The Children's Officer in the area whose help was sought by the adoptive parents at one stage described W. as 'moody' and the parents as 'expecting too much of W.'. At one stage, when W. was 16 years old, she and her parents did not talk to each other for about 4–5 months because of an argument. A psychiatrist who was consulted at the time could not find 'anything deep causing the trouble'. At his suggestion W. went to live in a hostel and visited the family at weekends. After this she was described as much happier.

When the adoptive mother was interviewed (as part of a pilot experiment) she said that W. and her adoptive brother were terribly jealous of each other and that the two would 'gang up' against the parents whilst also fighting each other. When the adopted boy married the mother refused to go to his wedding and W. did not invite the parents to her own wedding. The adoptive mother attributed W's 'wicked' behaviour to her earlier experiences and added: 'I couldn't ever really, deep down, feel the same about them as I used to feel.' At the same time she was proud of both children's careers and achievements.

W's adoptive brother T. described his adoption as 'a bad thing'. He was placed with his adoptive parents when he was 30 months old and had come into care at the age of 19 months. After living in a Home for 11 months he was placed with his adoptive parents. When T. was 13 his parents referred him to a psychiatrist because he was causing trouble at home and at school. The social worker who became involved at the time commented: 'The parents have less patience especially as he does not do well at school and this lack of success annoys them.' At the psychiatrist's suggestion T. was taken into care and placed in a Home, visiting the parents at weekends. T. did not think he was 'psychiatric'.

He saw himself as 'bad' and as 'emotionally insecure', wetting his bed till the age of 20. He talked about his 'hate' for school and the beltings he had from his father. The parents had high ambitions which he could not match:

> They wanted me to be what they wanted . . . I was slow in learning. I had a speech impediment until I was 11. I always used to get, 'We dragged you out of the gutter and gave you a name and this is what you do . . . we should just put you back in the gutter where we got you.'

T. thought his mother was trying to be caring but his father was harsh and punishing. He always felt 'on trial' and was always afraid of saying the wrong thing. He agreed that he and his adoptive sister never got on well together but expressed considerable contentment and 'happiness' with his current life.

H. was the third adoptee who expressed dissatisfaction with his growing-up experience. He described his mother as a 'strict disciplinarian' who wanted things to be done always her way. H. was taken into care at 10 days old. He first lived in a Home and then in a foster home but the arrangement broke down. He was placed with his adoptive family at 47 months. A year earlier he was described as having 'behaviour problems', including 'impairment of concentration' and very slow speech development: 'This child', said the notes, 'is difficult to control and requires constant attention.' At the age of 7 he was referred by his parents to a psychiatrist for being 'difficult' and was then sent to a school for the maladjusted. Later he was sent to an approved school and from there straight to Borstal. Whilst at the approved school his parents moved house without telling him where they had gone. He explained their restrictiveness to the advanced age at which they were allowed to adopt and to their refusal to let hime mix with other children because the others were inferior in 'social class'. 'They would then add', he went on, 'that as I had no one to play with there was no reason why I couldn't do lessons.' He maintained that his parents adopted him to replace their dead son, adding that he could have done 'with a better experience'. Describing his adoption as a 'mistake' he added, 'there is no room for pity with my mother.'

Satisfaction related to the family's economic situation
As already stated, adoption practice at the time when these adoptions took place was to select families who were economically comfortable. These were usually to be found among the middle classes but even when families of a lower social class were selected, economic stability was of primary consideration. However, agencies were always prepared to make exceptions and consider 'marginal' families for what were seen

to be 'marginal' or atypical children.

Almost half the adoptive families in this study were described as 'economically comfortable' and the rest as average, implying stability and continuity of income. The economic comfort or stability of most adoptive parents contrasted sharply with the economic conditions of the child's family of origin at the time of reception into care. No matching could therefore be claimed by the agencies between the economic circumstances of natural and adoptive parents.

Adopted people who grew up in families described as 'economically comfortable' experienced their families as having significantly more ambitions on their behalf compared to other adoptive parents. Similarly there was a close association between being reared by an 'economically comfortable' family and the non-sharing of background genealogical information ($p < 0.01$). Those reared by this group of parents also said that they were made to feel 'different' by their immediate community. More important, the adoptive family's increased 'economic comfort' was associated with a decrease in closeness between the adoptee and the adoptive mother. Those from better-off families also tended to say that faced with a crisis they would rather rely on themselves than on their adoptive parents. The same people would add that their past life still worried them. Greater satisfaction with the overall adoption experience tended to be associated with families whose economic circumstances were described as 'average', and greater dissatisfaction with those families described as 'comfortable'. Though the trend was unmistakable, some caution again is required not only because the association is rather weak, but also because of the very small percentage of adoptees who expressed mixed feelings or dissatisfaction with their adoption experience (18 per cent). (This is a point which needs to be borne in mind throughout this study when reference is made to mixed feelings or dissatisfaction among adoptees.)

Satisfaction with the adoption experience
In the post-1945 period, adoption, from being a predominantly working-class institution in Britain, became fashionable among the middle classes to the point where it became increasingly difficult for those from the lower social classes to adopt (Triseliotis 1970). This was because they could not usually meet the agencies' tangible criteria of economic and housing conditions.

About one-quarter of adoptees were adopted by professional or managerial parents and another quarter by parents holding semi-skilled and unskilled occupations. The proportion of adoptive parents classified in social classes I and II was higher than in the general population, but those classified in social classes IV and V were fewer.

Compared, however, to the findings of studies concentrating on early adoption, the proportion of couples from social classes I and II adopting here was much lower and those from a semi-skilled or unskilled background much higher. Triseliotis (1970) found that almost two-fifths of those adopting in Scotland in 1965 were classified in social classes I and II and only 14 per cent in IV and V. Raynor's (1980) study of the placements of one agency covering roughly the same period as the present one, but concentrating mostly on young infants placed from the start for adoption, classified almost two-thirds of the adopters in social classes I and II and only 3 per cent in IV and V. Similarly the majority of those adopting older children in Tizard's (1977) study were of a professional and managerial background. Of a total of 30 adopters only three were manual workers and none semi-skilled or unskilled. Seglow *et al.* (1972), reporting on the adoption of mostly young infants, found that the proportion of children living in social class I homes was more than twice as large among the adopted compared with the whole cohort or the population as a whole. The implication is that those adopting in this study were significantly of a lower social class when compared to the studies cited above. The explanation for this difference may lie in the kind of children placed. In effect whilst agencies, especially voluntary ones, would go for higher social class adopters for children coming from 'uncomplicated' backgrounds, in the case of 'marginal' children (i.e. older or handicapped or with a 'poor history') they would equally accept 'marginal' adopters. Evidence for this practice again comes from Triseliotis (1969) who found that couples adopting 'hard to place' children in Scotland in 1965 differed from other adoptive parents in the following ways: older at placement; lower socio-economic background; more of their own children; a greater percentage had suffered or were suffering from an illness; a smaller percentage were house owners. The evidence from this study suggests an attempt to place children of professional and white-collar workers with families of a similar background, but because at the stage of placement the children had acquired their specific characteristics (i.e. older age, institutional experience, etc.) the agencies appeared glad to consider any family.

No relationship was found between the social class of the adoptive parents and the presence among adoptees of emotional or behaviour difficulties. However, the higher the social class of the adoptive family the more likely they would have ambitions and expectations on behalf of the child, though this association was not strong. Mandell (1973) points out that adoptive parents have been noted to have high aspirations, which can induce stress in a child. Seglow *et al.* (1972) found from their study of 7 year olds that adoptive mothers were over-concerned with education, but Tizard (1977) also studying children at about the same age found no evidence of undue pressure. She refers though to the fact that the majority of the parents regularly helped their children with school work. Lambert and Streather (1980), commenting on Tizard's findings, remark that such activities indicate a 'child-centred' approach which may be linked with the middle-class background of the families.

When the adoptees' degree of satisfaction was related to the social class of their parents, the picture to emerge, though not statistically significant, indicated that adoptees reared in families classified in social classes I and II were more likely to express 'mixed' feelings or dissatisfaction compared to the rest (Table 4.3). A more detailed examination revealed a connection between a middle-class background, high parental aspirations and the expression of an element of dissatisfaction or of 'mixed' feelings by adoptees. The parents' high aspirations were often said to be responsible for inducing stress in the adopted person.

Table 4.3 Adoptees' satisfaction with their growing-up experience, related to social class of adoptive father

	Social class of adoptive father								
	I & II		IIINM		IIIM		IV & V		Total	
	N	%	N	%	N	%	N	%	N	%
Satisfactory	7	58	5	83	15	100	9	82	36	82
Unsatisfactory	5	42	1	17	—	—	2	18	8	18
	12	100	6	100	15	100	11	100	44	100

Housing. almost two-fifths of the adoptive parents owned their own house, another two-fifths lived in council housing, and about one-fifth in tied-type accommodation. Compared to the precariousness of the housing circumstances of most of the children's natural families, the housing situation of the adoptive families was very stable. House occupancy by the adoptive parents broadly followed the pattern for the rest of the population, except that fewer adoptive families were living in local authority or privately-rented accommodation. Home owners tended to have more ambitions on behalf of their children compared to the rest. No connection, however, was found between the mode of the adoptive parents' house occupancy and the adoptees' current adequacy of housing or overall housing satisfaction.

Other children in the adoptive family

About two-fifths of the adoptees were brought up as only children and broadly a similar proportion were brought up with another child. The mean number of children in each family was 2.00 (s.d. 1.4). Only one-fifth of the children were reared in families with three or more children. Seglow *et al.* (1972) found from their cohort study that 82 per cent of the adoptive families were constituted of only one or two children, roughly the same as in this study, though the type of child adopted here was different. Seven out of ten couples were childless at the time of the adoptees' placement. A quarter of the families had from one to six own children, one-third had other adopted children, and two had foster children. Leaving aside the 18 who grew up as only children, another 15 grew up as the youngest in their families. Overall, being an only or the youngest child in the adoptive family was a common feature in this study.

Adopted children who had emotional problems before placement were placed in almost equal proportions with childless families and with families with own or other adopted children. No relationship was found between the presence of own or other adopted children and the development of emotional or psychiatric problems during childhood. Neither was any link found between the development of emotional and psychiatric problems and being an only child or being placed with a childless couple. Similarly, closeness to the adoptive mother during childhood was not affected by the total number of children in the family. Equally, the subjects' perceptions of their growing up adopted was unaffected by the presence or absence of other children, whether natural or adopted.

Age of adoptive parents at placement

Half of the adoptive fathers and two-fifths of the mothers were 41 and over at the child's placement. Compared to non-relatives adopting in Scotland in 1966 (Gray and Blunden 1971), the children in this study were adopted by older people, but they were also older at placement. Kadushin (1971), whose study is comparable to this, found that the mean age of adoptive mothers in his study was 40 years and of fathers 41.3, very similar to the findings of this study. However, more mothers and fathers in this study were aged 45 and over at placement compared with Kadushin's study.

When summarising their perception of growing up adopted, subjects tended to express less satisfaction if placed in families where the parents were aged 46 and over at placement. Similarly, adoptees placed with families where the mother was aged 46 and over were likely to complain of some emotional distance from her. Whilst in their descriptive accounts some adoptees found older parents to be understanding and flexible, others felt somewhat 'embarrassed', or found that they could not understand them or join with them in youthful activities: 'They seemed, or were, a lot older and they didn't have as much energy to take us out and play games with us . . . that is what I missed.' Another adoptee placed at 3½ years with parents who were in their late forties at the time expressed the views of a couple of others, saying: 'my mother and father were older than my friends' parents and I found this quite embarrassing.' The presence among adoptees of emotional or behaviour or psychiatric problems was also more likely when placed with adoptive mothers who were aged 40 or over at placement. Caution is needed, however, because 11 of the 17 children who presented emotional or behaviour problems also displayed them before placement. Similarly, 3 of the 6 who displayed psychiatric problems had psychiatric 'referral' before placement. This means that children displaying disorders were more likely to be placed with mothers aged 40 and over than with any other age group. Otherwise there was no association between the development of emotional or behaviour problems during childhood and the adoptive mother being 40 or over. Again the presence of emotional or behaviour problems at interview was not linked to the adoptive mothers' age group at placement. The only firm conclusion that can be drawn from this is that there is an element of risk in child placement when the adoptive parents are beyond their mid-forties as it tends to decrease the amount of satisfaction felt with the adoption experience.

The residential group

Perception of growing up in residential establishments

As already stated, 60 per cent of those who grew in residential Homes rated their experiences from 'positive' to 'fairly positive', and the rest expressed mixed or negative feelings about it. Those who expressed positive or fairly positive views valued individual caring, personal interest, continuity of care, flexible rules and having outside contacts. They enjoyed 'the general life of the place', 'security', 'freedom to play', the 'companionship of other children' and 'going on holiday'. They appreciated establishments that offered them educational opportunities, somewhere to stay, freedom to make up their own minds, choice in meals, a chance to mix with the outside community, and help in the house without being expected or 'forced' to do hard work, such as scrubbing floors or looking after younger children at the expense of their studies. They liked house-parents and other staff who were 'caring', 'flexible', 'kind', 'had time to listen', 'took a personal interest'. They usually associated changes for the better with the arrival of trained staff. Knowing why they were there and what was happening to their own families was of great importance to almost all of them.

Negative experiences and perceptions included corporal punishment, rigid rules, lack of individuality and privacy, absence of individual caring and love, total 'female' influence (i.e. female residential staff only), the keeping of files on them to which they were not allowed access, not knowing the reasons for being in care or in the Home, and lack of interaction with staff except when things went wrong. They resented the lack of opportunities to choose some of their personal things such as clothes, they disliked passed-down toys and clothes and the fact that, whilst in the Home, the social services administration or other professionals did not talk to them but only to the staff. Specific dissatisfactions included 'alway being wrong because we were in care', 'lack of intimacy', 'staff not having enough time for individuals' 'just being in a Home', 'going to bed early' (stressed repeatedly), 'stupid regulations', 'rigid regulations', 'lack of care', 'the way the children were being treated', and 'staff changes'.

Commenting on the nature of the residential task Winnicott (1964) points out that the residential worker has a responsibility to provide real experiences of good care, comfort and control: 'These good experiences are not only the stuff of life, but the stuff that dreams are made of, and have the power to become part of the child's psychic reality correcting the past and creating the future.' Beedell (1970) argues that physical care involving good food, drink and bodily comfort has psychological implications. Burns *et al*. (1980) add that deprived children who have built up defences to protect themselves from further pain, still have a need for someone to devote time and attention to them – the concern of a member of staff becomes one of the most important parts of the total helping process. The Advisory Council on Child Care, in *Care and Treatment in a Planned Environment* (1970) which sets out a model for a community Home, suggests a warm, accepting environment, less stress on organised systems of rewards and punishments, and a greater attempt to modify the routine and approach of the Home to the needs of individual children. Berry (1975) claims that residential treatment need not require highly qualified psychiatrists or psychologists, but more attainable treatment can be attained by ordinary staff in the way they attend to daily routine events.

Though the sentiments expressed in the literature concerning the residential task appear sound, it would be naive to underestimate the difficulties and problems posed to the staff who have to carry out the caring role. Caring for a group of mostly unrelated children with heterogeneous needs and frequently displaying 'disturbed' behaviour and not always responsive presents considerable difficulties to staff.

Positive perceptions. As already stated, at least five (13 per cent) residential people expressed positive feelings. Most of the positive perceptions had to do with the perceived caring and flexible qualities of the house-parents. A change of Home or house-parents could involve a change for the better or worse. To B. being brought up in a Home meant:

> a home, a place to stay, all the things a home gives, love, care, etc. And I genuinely treated it as a home . . . obviously you can never get as close to people as a family but I still would have liked to know what it is like to have parents and to live in a family.

Another positive experience which was mostly attributed to the qualities of the house-parents was:

> being as young as I was when I was taken away, it sort of came natural and it was not too bad . . . being in a Home sort of created more friends for me. It became my way of life. Mr and Mrs G. seemed like parents, sort of. I have pretty good memories . . . it helped me in my job, the discipline I had; I am a very tidy person.

I. also talked in a similar way:

> Naturally I would prefer to be home with my mum and dad. But it [the Home] was good. It was a good upbringing. There were always plenty of people around you . . . there were more likes than dislikes . . . there was nothing I was unhappy with in the Home. I didn't regret it.

D. had mixed feelings early on, but came to like the Home with the passing of time. Early on he felt 'very sad': 'It was the saddest period of my life – you knew you had nobody else to look after you . . . you were just left . . . it was an empty world.' Later he came to like the housemother who acted 'like a mother' to him. He added: 'Overall I would say it was a happy time I had . . . you were shielded and things were so happy it was just like dreamland . . . nothing made me unhappy.' Children generally resented the frequent changes of staff and particularly of staff they were fond of or had become attached to: 'There was always so many faces, always changing.' They would equally welcome and get attached to a new 'kindly' house-parent replacing a hard one. Though many would have preferred growing up in 'an ordinary family' or to 'be part of a family' or 'family atmosphere', some had no illusion about their own families of origin. One person, in spite of memories of harsh discipline and regimentation, contrasted her current life with what it might have been if she had stayed with her own parents, brought up in one of the 'rough' areas of Edinburgh: 'I don't really think I would have had much of a life in P. and with seven of us in a family . . . I would have turned out a bad one, a real bad one . . . to be honest, I am glad I was brought up in a Home.'

Similarly, C. felt good about growing up in a Home. He understood that his parents had separated and could not look after them. The staff 'were looking after us and doing their best . . . bringing us up as their own kids.' At the same time he felt very unhappy about the prospect of staying in a Home for all his childhood. One person summarised the views of others in this group by saying: 'C. was a good place. It was as good a Home as you could get. On the whole no regrets of being in residential care.'

Fairly positive experiences. A group of respondents, though predominantly describing 'fairly good' experiences, also made quite a number of qualifications concerning its quality. F. like others referred to the harsh punishments he suffered and described rigid rules. Things improved, however, towards the end of his stay in the Home when new staff came 'who had been to child care courses':

> They were all for smaller groups, more discussion, more open instead of 'You will do this . . .'. I was happy at times and I would also be very unhappy. I have looked back at it with resentment and embarrassment but not now I don't . . . . there was no individuality, you were always classed as a group.

Whilst maintaining that residential care had done him no harm, he felt he had missed 'a lot' of his childhood, but was grateful to one housemother who acted like a mother substitute: 'She was the person who cared most for me.' Others blamed the absence of 'understanding and caring' to the lack of trained staff.

R., whilst rating her experiences of growing up in residential care as 'fairly good', also referred to how everything was a rule and there was a lack of mixing with people outside: 'I felt unhappy about the reason why I was there. I didn't like the place . . . I didn't like the whole idea.'

Another person who went through a stage of wondering why she had to be in the Home, realised as she grew older that she had to make 'the best of it' and went on: 'I was quite happy, I enjoyed life there but it could have been a lot better.'

P., though rating her overall experience as 'fairly good', sounded more uncertain and mixed from her description:

> I think you felt you were all alone. You wanted an awful lot of love, but there wasn't any. Not like parents give their children . . . I didn't have any of that.

> There was no physical contact, like a cuddle or things that kids really love. I used to get rather upset about it . . . the only person who helped me was the woman who used to come in to clean and serve the meals . . . .I would have liked to have the choice of being fostered.

Another subject, though rating her experience as 'fairly good', spoke in similar terms: 'I used to think the people in the Home cared for you because you were under their care, but I didn't honestly think so . . . . they cared for you because they had to . . . . I cannot really say that anyone cared for me . . . it was all right but I have no big feelings about it.'

Some respondents spoke of the fright, anxiety and sadness of the early stages of residential living. As time passed they became more used to it:

> It was more frightening than bad because there were so many children there . . . . the atmosphere was completely different from what I had been used to. When I first entered the children's Home having to get my hair cut and thrown in the bath and getting clothes that were too big for me . . . all this sort of thing was frightening and impersonal . . . . people around didn't seem to understand what you were going through at the time.

Mixed feelings. Almost a third of the subjects rated their experiences as 'neither good nor bad'. C., who had memories of being 'terrorised a bit', including punishments for bed-wetting, remarked: 'Nobody really feels happy about being brought up in a Home . . . I was there for 9 years. I used to count the years when I was going to get out. Overall you were just a nobody.' Though feeling that she doesn't know where she 'fits', never having experienced a real family life, she added: 'I think I am a better person for it, but I would have liked to have been a normal kid, like everyone else, with a mother and father.'

P., who was also punished for his bet-wetting, expressed similar mixed feelings. He spoke of how he 'hated' growing up in a residential Home and that if it wasn't for the fact that he had nowhere to go he would have run away: 'I have learned a lot but I have never lived in normal circumstances . . . I don't know what I have missed.' His views were reiterated by another person who felt that he had lost 'a lot of love' from his life because of being brought up in a Home. He didn't blame his house-parents 'as there were so many of us to love'. 'Looking back', said another, 'I hated it, every minute of it. There were no happy days. It is bound to affect you in some ways.' E., referring to the frequent changes of staff, said:

> There were always different people looking after you . . . there were so many staff they never got very involved with you . . . they didn't seem to have enough interest . . . . the person I would go to was the cleaner . . . when
> we were moved to D. the couple there cared an awful lot.

E. 'cried her eyes out' when later the house-parents who took an interest in her left. Another one commented:

> What made it difficult for me was the absence of a permanent figure in the background. I learnt very, very quickly not to feel too close to house-parents. They came and went so often . . . . if I loved them too much I was going to be let down, they were going to leave.

A., who had seen a number of psychiatrists since she was about 9, could only say that life was 'bad and what people were doing around me was bad . . . . No one in any of the Homes I was sent to was ever interested in me . . . . At first I relied on my brother for everything but they separated us and I had to rely on myself . . . . I just feel institutionalised.'

Fairly negative to negative perceptions. More decidedly negative views were expressed by a group of five respondents. One subject who experienced many 'beatings' and who felt unable now to feel close to or trust people blamed her current situation on being brought up in a Home:

> I think I can remember when I used to cry myself and nobody cared for me . . . when my son was crying it put something back in my mind with me when I was younger . . . . I think when you are in a Home you have a lot more difficulty in bringing up your own family. Adults who have never had any love or care shown to them when they were younger . . . . I would have liked to have been adopted . . . . I don't have nobody to turn to.

The overall impression of M. was of a harsh regime:

> we were just like cattle in a field, watered and fed at the same time – no individuality – we were all the same. A kid wants to run away because he probably knows it is not the right place or he thinks he shouldn't be there . . . . there was only one person I took to in the first Home, but I cannot honestly say I was cared for . . . . I was unhappy. I felt I was missing on something plus the reason I didn't know the reason why I was there.

Another added: 'I wanted parents like all other children . . . . I didn't like being in a Home . . . . I didn't think any of them did care for me.'

A., who talked about regular 'battering', said:

> you were terrified. You could never speak up for yourself . . . it's terrible. It's no place for kids. It's mental cruelty if you ask me . . . no home at all, just a jail. . . . I hated it. . . . the minute you go in you know there is no escape . . . they would never talk to you. All you got was your meat and veg. and that was it. . . . well if they had discussed it with you and showed a wee bit of loving towards you . . . but to them you were just one of the furniture. . . . we called them mum and dad because we were forced to. I didn't love them, I had no feeling for them, I hated them. . . . they never did anything for you.

Recollection of 'rigid rules', or 'routinised activities', of 'getting the belt' and 'punishments for bed-wetting' were recorded by another with equal bitterness and sadness:

> we were never mothered or fathered – only very few and far between you could say that you were happy . . . the only people who cared for us were the two visitors . . . but being in a Home was very bad. I really mean that. At 13 we had new house-parents who treated us more like a family. . . . I would have liked to have been mothered because I think if I had my mother I wouldn't be in the situation I am now. [i.e. she felt she had made a mess of her life]

Summary

There was no doubting the sincerity and reality of the experiences described by subjects in both groups. Those who grew up with families particularly enjoyed the personal interest, love and care of their parents and equally disliked the absence of these qualities and parents who expected a lot or who were harsh and distant. Those who grew up in Homes also liked the same things and particularly disliked too much routine, lack of care, harsh physical punishment, rigid rules and the absence of individuality. Berry (1975) argues that children living in residential care require 'benign daily experiences' over a long period of time to counteract previous 'harmful' experiences. The accounts given by many respondents in this study appeared to reinforce possible early harmful experiences. Did respondents in their accounts concentrate on a particularly distressing event which coloured all their perceptions? The suggestion is that they were expressing the overall impression left on them by this form of rearing. Perceptions of this type appeared on a range of other items about residential living and they were not isolated expressions of disappointment.

Though the number of adoptees who expressed mixed or negative feelings was small ($N = 8$) nevertheless the presence of emotional problems during placement in both the adoption and residential group tended to correlate with mixed or negative perceptions about the 'substitute' care experience. Similarly, the presence of psychiatric problems during placement in both groups was associated with mixed or negative perceptions of the growing-up experience. Obtaining psychiatric help in the 12 months prior to the interview also tended to correlate with mixed or negative feelings about growing up in institutional care. Equally, mixed or negative feelings about the growing-up period were also associated with a poor sense of emotional well-being at interview.

Satisfaction or dissatisfaction with the growing-up experience, as perceived by the subjects, did not appear to be affected by the subjects' age, sex, status (i.e. legitimate/illegitimate), age at reception into care, age at placement, and number of moves before final placement or having a 'disturbed' family background. Satisfaction with the adoptive experience, however, was adversely affected where adoptees grew up in families described as economically 'very comfortable' as opposed to 'average'.

Emotional closeness to parents and carers
Respondents were asked to rate how close they felt towards significant people in their environment who were charged with their care. Over two-thirds of those who grew up adopted felt very close towards their adoptive mothers and 18 per cent fairly close (Table 4.4). In all, 38 (86 per cent) of those adopted felt very close or fairly close towards their mothers. In contrast only 60 per cent of those who grew up in residential Homes felt 'fairly close' or 'very close' to a house-parent at some stage. At the other end, significantly more of those who grew up in institutions experienced 'in-between' states, or felt 'fairly distant', or 'very distant' from their carers compared with those who were adopted. Adopted people experienced their adoptive fathers somewhat less intensely than their mothers, but as will be seen later the situation sometimes changed in adult life. A change of house-parents for those brought up in Homes could bring them closer or put them at a distance from new carers. Occasionally, adoptees would establish very close relationships with relatives of the adoptive family, such as uncles, aunts or grandparents, whilst some of those who grew up in

Table 4.4 Closeness to carers during childhood

	Adoption				Residential group	
	Adoptive mother		Adoptive father		House-parent	
	N	%	N	%	N	%
Very close	30	68	17	41	14	35
Fairly close	8	18	16	38	10	25
In-between	5	12	6	14	10	25
Fairly distant	1	2	2	5	3	7
Very distant	—	—	1	2	3	8
	44	100	42	100	40	100
Missing			2			
			44			

Homes would experience closeness with ancillary staff and peripheral staff, such as gardeners, cooks and cleaners.

In the study of long-term fostering referred to earlier (Triseliotis 1980b), almost 60 per cent of former foster children felt very close to their foster mothers, but there was a tendency among those brought up in group-type foster homes to express in-between states of closeness. The number of adoptees who experienced 'distant' or 'in-between' relationships was too small (6, 14 per cent) to draw conclusions from, but the presence or absence of the family's own or of other adopted children or the subject's place in the family did not appear to affect the degree of closeness to parental figures. There was, however, a tendency among those who grew up in what were described as economically 'very comfortable' homes to convey somewhat less closeness to maternal figures compared to the rest. Those subjects who expressed mixed or negative feelings about growing up adopted or in residential care were also likely to say that they felt 'distant' or 'in-between' forms of closeness to their adoptive mothers or house-parents. The adoptee's age at reception into care and at placement was unrelated to the degree of closeness felt towards the adoptive parents. The presence of emotional/behaviour problems and psychiatric referral during the growing-up period tended to go together with a decrease in the intensity of closeness with the adoptive mother. Among the residential sample close association existed between the presence of psychiatric problems and distance from house-parents. It is hard to say how far the lack of closeness caused the emotional/psychiatric problems or the reverse.

Adoption group
Almost 90 per cent of those adopted made unqualified or only somewhat qualified comments concerning their close attachment towards one or both adoptive parents during their growing-up period. Some felt equally close to both parents, others felt closer to their mothers than fathers and vice versa. Comments about adoptive parents ranged from: 'I loved her like my mother and the same with my father', to 'I was close to my mother but I was a lot closer to my dad – I was a daddy's girl.' Another typical comment was: 'I was very close to my mother and fairly close to my father', or 'I was as close to my mother as any mother and daughter is. She was always the one I went to if I had any problems.' A few would refer to a very close relationship with their adoptive mother and a somewhat more distant one with their father, or they would say: 'My mother was easier to talk to.' Strict parents, whether mothers or fathers, were rated less favourably than more flexible and less demanding ones: 'I was closer to my dad. He used to

play with me, buy me all my toys, help me build things. . . . I was close to my mother but she was strict. That put me against her.'

The six (14 per cent) adoptees who expressed 'in-between' states of 'closeness' or 'distance' from their mother and the nine (21 per cent) who expressed similar feelings in relation to their fathers, concentrated their criticisms on the parents' strictness, high expectations, or the holding-back of feelings. W. felt only fairly close to her parents as both were demanding and too 'pushy' and when disappointed in her they would bring up her adoption. T. said he was never comfortable in the presence of his parents who always demanded a lot: 'You were always terrified of saying the wrong thing. . . . I was happy when at 13 they put me in a Home.' Another adoptee added about her parents: 'They were just sort of there . . . emotional relationships didn't really come into it.'

Residential group
Residential subjects appreciated the opportunity to feel close to a member of staff, particularly a house-parent. They retained good and fond memories of house-parents who made themselves available in this way. At least 60 per cent experienced a degree of closeness to a house-parent in at least one of the Homes they had been in. As already stated though, only exceptionally was continuity of closeness maintained because of the change of staff or of Home or the staff's preoccupation with routine tasks. Sitting down and talking to children which could help develop relationships and closeness was seen as 'not getting on with the job'. H. remarked on how close she felt towards the Matron in the Home who cared for her 'like a mum'. Another spoke in a similar way, saying: 'I suppose the house-mother was a sort of mother image. I felt quite close to her, not very close', or 'Sister B. was the best of them. I would say very close to her.' 'There was just the one. . . . I really took to her . . . but I felt no close to to anyone in the new Home. . . . I would say very distant.' Some felt closer to house-parents as they grew older and there was more sharing of some tasks and of information. Closeness to a house-parent was mostly associated with 'taking an interest in you', 'caring', 'flexible', 'understanding', and 'having time to listen'. Distance was associated with 'strictness', 'rigid enforcement of rules', 'changes in staff', 'lack of interest', 'impersonal caring'. Comments that went with rating of relationship as distant included: 'I wasn't close to anybody. . . . I felt nothing for them [staff]. . . . I hated them more than I loved them.' J. added: 'I learnt very quickly not to feel close to house-parents. . . . they came and went so often.' One young person who was moved seven times between institutions added how in one of these she became attached to a nun: 'But she left. After

that I was afraid of being rejected. I kept myself to myself. I was frightened of letting anyone get close to me.' Another residential person also remarked about being 'quite happy' at one of the Homes as it was the only Home he was familiar with: 'I adapted to the way it was run and I had begun to know the people in the village fairly well. When I was moved all this changed. I felt unhappy, confused and took a dim view of life.' Others would simply say 'very distant' or 'distant' or 'far from close'.

Closeness to siblings
Over a quarter of adoptees grew up with the natural children of the adoptive family. With only two exceptions all the others expressed considerable satisfaction about the closeness between them and the family's biological children. One black person who grew up with the family's five children commented: 'We all grew up together. They accepted me as part of the family and treated me as one of their own. I was brought up as their own. We were all very close.' Another one: 'My adoptive mother's own son is like a real brother to me. I feel I was part of the whole family, not an outsider.'

The closeness of attachments between adoptees and the family's natural children continued into adult relationships. No adoptee experienced unfavourable discrimination in relation to the family's own or other adopted children. What appeared to matter was the atmosphere of the home and the quality of the parenting rather than the 'status' of the child. In a couple of cases where older siblings were about to move out of the parental home, relationships with the adoptee were not always as close. With two exceptions, all the other adoptees said that they had been accepted by their parents' wider family. Some of them became very attached to grandparents or to aunts and uncles. They generally valued the opportunity of widening their circle of relatives. Many relationships which started in childhood seemed to continue in adult life and were often a source of mutual support.

The residential group. Thirty-three of the 40 subjects in this group were in residential establishments with at least one other sibling. This they generally valued very much and in a situation which was often distressing they found the presence of siblings comforting. Older siblings often took responsibility for younger ones. Almost 90 per cent of this group described very close relationships with their siblings. Typical comments indicating closeness included: 'There was a lot of joy because I had a sister' and 'we were very close'. 'We had always been close – it helped. We would have felt isolated if we were in different

Homes. We would probably have drifted away. . . . we are still very close.' Another one: 'We were awfully close . . . we still are and visit each other', and 'I grew up with my brother . . . we were and still are very close.' One person who had no siblings remarked: 'Sadly I was the only person in the Home who didn't have a brother or sister. I was on my own . . .'

Some subjects referred to the fact that their brothers and sisters were the only family they had and the only people they could rely upon in adult life: 'My brother S. I felt always close to. He was the only one I ever had, the only sort of family. . . . I still feel very close to him.' Another one said: 'My brother and three sisters were my family. We were quite close.' 'I love my sister', said G. 'she was the only thing I had . . . the only person who had been through everything with me from being with our parents to being in care and even now we have a very close relationship.' Another one talked with similar feelings: 'We were very close and very attached. You felt a strong bond between one another. . . . they were yours and it was something that you wanted to keep and hold onto.'

Some described the way they took care of younger siblings or the way they were taken care of by older ones: 'my brother and I grew up together. He sort of fathered me and I sort of mothered him because that was all we could do.' Another one: 'My older brother looked after all of us. He was special. Any problems I have I go to my older brother.' One person who went into a Home at the age of 6 described how her sister aged 4, who went with her, would cry for 'weeks and months' wanting their mother: 'I was the only one to comfort her.'

Subjects resented being split from siblings and were very critical of policies and practices that brought this about: 'I hated being moved from E. Home and from my brother because he was all I knew . . . my brothers were fostered but I was left. I couldn't understand it because I didn't know why I was there'; 'My brother was very protective towards my sister and I, then my brother moved to another Home . . .'; 'I was very close to my brother but we were separated. I don't know why.' Another subject regretted being split from her sisters who had to live in the infants' place because of their age. Others commented on how the policy of separating siblings pushed them apart from their brothers and sisters: 'My two sisters were sent to a different Home because of our sex . . . that is something I thought was wrong. I see my sisters all the time and I know they are my sisters but we are strangers. I think it was bad separating us.' Another one added: 'With my younger sister, I don't have such a close relationship because she was taken away at 4 months and we never saw her for 5 years.'

A lot of surprise and criticism was also voiced by a fair number who discovered after many years that they had other siblings in care: 'I didn't know I had brothers until I was told I had two younger ones coming.' Even then these siblings were kept apart because of their different sexes and were only allowed to mix on holidays: 'I used to look forward to my brothers coming for their Christmas dinner. . . . you only saw your brothers at school and your birthday, Christmas party and Easter.' One person who one day was told that her brother lived down the road in another Home remarked: 'I never even knew I had a brother . . . you couldn't understand how he could be a brother and you hadn't seen him in your life before.' When C. was brought together with siblings he had never met before he remarked: 'We were like total strangers. There was no relationship between us at all.'

Most, if not all, of the sibling relationships that were maintained in the Homes continued in adult life and seemed to offer a lot of security and a sense of comfort to many who felt they had 'no family'.

Methods of discipline and controls

Subjects in both samples were asked a number of related questions concerning the methods of discipline and the kind of controls used by their carers. The residential group were in addition asked specific questions concerning rules, what they were punished for, and their reactions to punishment.

Methods of control in both the adoptive families and the residential units ranged from appeals to reason, withdrawal of privileges, withdrawal of food, seclusion and physical punishment. Privileges that were likely to be withdrawn included play, watching television, visits to friends and pocket money. Corporal punishment as a method of control ranged from an occasional smacking to severe beatings and other forms of physical restrictions or punishment, particularly in the residential units. Physical punishment as a main method of control was used with about a quarter of those who grew up adopted and with over half of those who grew up in residential units. Yet physical punishment itself did not affect the amount of satisfaction felt during the growing-up period.

In over half of the adoptive homes and two-thirds of the residential units it was the mother or house-mother who mostly enforced discipline. Adoptive fathers, however, were usually the ultimate source of control. Some of the adoptees were quite explicit that their parents did not believe in corporal or other forms of physical punishment. In residential units headed by couples, house-fathers carried out most corporal punishment. Corporal punishment and other methods of control in residential units would sometimes change with the arrival of a new head of the establishment.

When interviewed, both adopted and residential subjects were able to distinguish between 'fair' and 'unfair' methods of punishment. Even some types of punishment that were experienced as 'unfair' at the time, in retrospect respondents would take some of the blame for being 'disobedient' or 'too obstinate'. Many forms of corporal punishment and physical cruelty, however, were still seen as 'unfair' and 'unwarranted'.

Almost two-thirds of those who grew up in Homes felt that when punished it was often or almost always 'unfair'. Reasons for being punished included behaviour problems, being troublesome and disobedient to staff, running away, breaking specific rules, bed-wetting, and three remarked 'for almost everything'. Seven out of ten felt that the Home rules were rigid and only five subjects found them flexible. Feelings of 'fairness' or otherwise concerning discipline did not affect the overall rating concerning satisfaction about the growing-up period.

Discipline and control in the adoptive home

In about 60 per cent of the adoptive homes appeals to reason, withdrawal of privileges and sometimes threats were said to be the main methods used to discipline and control the children. In the rest, light forms of physical punishment (clip on the ear, occasional smacks) were used but in a minority of cases physical punishment was experienced as rather harsh.

Overall four-fifths of adoptees described what they perceived as benevolent forms of discipline and control. One of them, typical of others, commented that when he was disobedient or cheeky his mother would sometimes give him the odd smack. If it was anything severe this would be reported to his father and he remembered his father smacking him only once. Another one said that discipline in his own family had always been fair and though his father would threaten to smack him, he never did. Another one added: 'I was never hit, it was more getting sent up to my room.' One adoptee remarked how he got the belt 'more often at school than at home'. Not being hit or belted as a child was generally valued: 'My dad rarely belted me. He was fairly good. I was a luckier kid getting parents like that than if you were born with them.' Another one commented: 'Basically I had good parents and when I did something wrong they sent me to bed or went without tea . . . or prevented me from playing football.'

Others also commented on appeals to reason or withdrawal of rewards or privileges: 'If I didn't do things they probably appealed to my reason, give me a row, or try to put some sense into me or keep some of my pocket money'; and 'I would be locked in my room or go without tea or TV.' A few adoptees used to think that if it was their real parents they wouldn't be punished for things, but realise now that this was quite an unrealistic thought: 'My parents never abused me but if we had an argument I would think if she was my real mother she wouldn't do that to me.'

Approximately a quarter of adoptees experienced forms of physical punishment that went beyond the occasional smacking, though it did not always lead to dissatisfaction with the adoptive experience: 'My mother', said one subject, 'would use anything that was handy to hit – the slipper or her hand.' Another one: 'I used to get a good spanking from my mother when I was at fault.' Heavier forms of punishment were very few, but they were generally resented. One woman who attributed her nervous breakdown to the harsh punishment she had both at home and at school remarked: 'What I felt I needed was understanding but I got hit. Giving somebody the belt doesn't always cure them. It didn't cure me.' Another person adopted by a professional couple said: 'Their main method was hitting though there were occasions when they would try to talk me round.'

Rigid forms of control were experienced by some adoptees as rejecting and uncaring:

> It was all discipline and no play or give a little. . . . I had to do things this way and that way. . . . Once I stole a sixpence from my mum to buy a comic and my dad took me to a police station and I was showed a cell. . . . when eventually I found I was adopted I started getting all muddled up. Looking back now, I feel they were a wee bit too strict in some ways and it held me back from growing up as quickly as I might.

Even among the few who felt they were heavily punished there was a tendency to forgive their parents and take the blame on themselves. One adoptee, who on one occasion was so badly bruised by his father that he could not do physical exercise at school, remarked that at the time he thought his father was harsh, but now he thinks he was quite right in what he did. A couple of them were unforgiving: 'She lost her temper because I actually talk a bit. She hit me and my nose bled . . . there was a silence when I wouldn't talk. Then she pulled my hair, that was a terrible thing, she always used to do that.'

Only a tiny number of adoptees reported comments that could be construed as being psychologically damaging. One adoptee remembered with bitterness being frequently reminded by his parents that they did not mean to adopt him but were pushed into it. Others also resented the threat of being sent back to the Home and found it most upsetting. 'There was always, "If you don't behave you will be put back in the Home." You were unhappy because you didn't want to go back in the Home.'

Discipline and controls in the residential units
Most of those who grew up in residential establishments were aware of the problems and difficulties of staff in disciplining and controlling large numbers of children and they seemed prepared to make many allowances. The main criticism centred on forms of physical punishment, on the rigidity of rules, and on forms of punishment that were seen as excessive and not warranted by the situation. They tended to associate some forms of harsh punishment with a particular member of staff and with the enforcement of rules. Whilst about 40 per cent thought that any punishment they had was fair, the rest experienced it as 'mostly or always unfair'. Things for which they were punished included: 'bad table manners', 'making noises', 'not polishing shoes', 'not going to church', 'bed-wetting', 'stealing apples or cakes from the Home', 'coming in late', 'untidiness', 'cheek to the staff', 'swearing and fighting'.

Withdrawal of privileges. Like the adoptive homes, withdrawal of privileges was used as a frequent method of control and subjects did not generally resent it. Pocket money would sometimes be withdrawn for long periods of time.

Physical punishment. Almost every person who grew up in a residential Home experienced some form of corporal punishment, and over half maintained that this was the main form of control. In quite a number of cases it was experienced as 'harsh' and 'cruel' and respondents were unforgiving. Typical comments were: 'They just belted you'; 'I used to get beaten and that was it. No pocket money for 3 months. There was quite a lot of punishment really'; 'if you did something wrong most of the time you got hit'; 'if they started hitting there's no chance of them stopping. They would go on and on and on. I got battered on the backside when I was 6 for standing on a heap of soil'; 'people at this Home beat up the children and it was quite a nasty experience. I became really confused and didn't know what to do. That is when I think I started rebelling the most – then they sent me to a psychiatrist.' Another person remarked that the more she was hit 'the more I would retaliate by doing what she hit me for in the first place.' One person who tried to complain about the harsh treatment meted out on everybody found that eventually none of the staff would speak to her: 'I hated the kids getting punished, really battered . . . so I took this member of staff to the M. [head of the Unit].' K. remarked:

> There was one woman there who used to pull our hair and I mean pull your hair . . . a lot of it was to be put to bed early for a week. Get home from school at 4 o'clock, have your tea and that was you away. . . . a few times you got a thrashing.

And 'I had a few thumps when I was in residential care. I had bruises for a day or so after it sometimes. I can specifically remember one across my back.'

The comment was often repeated how there wasn't much explanation or reasoning: 'They just hit you, no explanation of what you did, and sent you to bed. . . . We didn't ken what we were doing. . . . They didn't sit down and explain. . . . I got leathered a lot of times.' S. thought it 'unfair' that he would be punished for not eating all his meat: 'as I couldn't eat the fat because it made me sick and I was forced to eat it or else I would be finished . . . eventually I got round it by giving it to the dog.'

Respondents seemed to have clear memories of staff who predominantly hit them and of others who tried to use argument and persuasion: 'The ones that were not so nice hit you. Other ones gave you a row and if you just got too much cheek they resorted to hitting'; 'the first one was a real terror, she used to hit me a lot. . . . I don't think they had any training. They just took it upon themselves to hit us. Others were more gentle, they wouldn't hit you so bad. I wouldn't say they knew any better, they didn't have any qualifications in child care. . . . I think they hit you when it pleased them.'

One subject who agreed that he was a bit 'mixed-up' and not easy to control said, 'they used to batter me like hell . . .' A very 'disturbed' young woman commented that because of her upbringing and unhappiness she used to run away often: 'If I wasn't hit I was put on tranquilisers. I was allowed only pyjamas, no proper clothes, so as not to run away. On one occasion I was put in solitary detention for seven days in a row. . . . Not surprising I am a bit barmy . . . staff never listened to my point of view.'

A change of Home or staff would often introduce a different approach: 'The first Home was physical punishment. The second used rewards, rows, threats, etc.' Another one described how when a particular person was in charge everybody had to sit in rows with their arms folded: 'We never played or anything . . . all changed when Miss M. came, it was a bad place when I first went.' One woman who experienced three Homes said that in two of them there was an attempt to explain things, 'but in K. things were not talked over with you . . . the main way they could control me was if they talked and reasoned with me, instead they tried hitting me and putting me to bed . . . they weren't too keen in looking after bairns . . . . it wasn't no fun I can tell you.'

Bed-wetting: Bed-wetting was often seen by staff as a deliberate act, sometimes one of defiance: 'I used to get the belt for bed-wetting because they maintained it was laziness. I tried to tell them I couldn't help it but they wouldn't accept it. . . . if they had smacked me for something like stealing I would have understood.' Another one commented: 'If you wet your bed they would cut your pyjama bottoms . . . it was like a sort of humiliation. It never used to work because it couldn't stop you. . . . as time went on they used to hit you . . . if they spoke to you at the same time as hitting you, you maybe got some sort of response but they never used to do it.' Another one added: 'She [house-mother] had a cane which scared us . . . to be caned for bed-wetting was unfair, but for coming in late I suppose that was fair.'

Another person would be punished for stuttering as this was viewed as 'being cheeky'. One young person commenting on how things were changing when in his late teens observed:

> When I went there at first the forms of punishment were rather severe – you got a stick over the back of the hand. When I did leave the boys used to just get perhaps a clout round the leg. . . . on one occasion early on a boy was made to kneel all night long at his bedside until he fell asleep for saying something about religion.

A few others remarked that things were improving towards the end of their residential experience, either because they were getting older or with the arrival of more trained staff.

Not surprisingly residential staff appear divided in their attitude towards corporal punishment in children's Homes. White (1977), whilst acknowledging that 'if taken to excess corporal punishment is cruel and harmful, ugly and thoroughly inexcusable', at the same time considers lighter forms of corporal punishment as necessary. Echoing sociological studies, he argues that working-class children in particular expect corporal punishment, and that if the staff fail to understand this they will 'possibly confuse a child, as well as condemning implicitly that child's background and upbringing.' Others maintain that controls and sanctions should be at a minimum in areas where these are necessary. There was no evidence from this study that either adoptees or residential people enjoyed being hit. A circular sent out in January 1981 by the Department of Health and Social Security defined corporal punishment as 'physical assault by staff on a child as punishment'. The circular went on to add that it was not compatible with the principles on which control and discipline in community Homes should be based, and should be banned. The circular also said that under no circumstances should corporal punishment be administered on girls. The Society of Teachers Opposed to Physical Punishment in a survey of 130 local social services authorities found that 38 of them were ignoring government advice that corporal punishment should be banned in community Homes (*The Times* 20 May 1981).

Mental forms of cruelty. Mental forms of cruelty were experienced in about a fifth of the cases. They ranged from 'You are just going to be like your mother', to the 'social work department don't give us enough money to keep the likes of you here.' Subjects greatly resented the denigration of their parents by the staff, and because of this they didn't like staff to know much about their families. Other attacking references to parents included: 'How would you like to be back with your mother and father?'; 'How would you like to be amongst them? [i.e. parents].' Other staff would refer to their poor pay, adding that 'they were not in the Home for the good of their health'; or that 'they didn't get paid enough for what they did.' Some respondents said that the staff would always remind them that they were doing them 'a favour', commenting 'Look what I have given up for you'; and 'Oh, I have a good mind to leave this place, you are just a bunch of little brats.' Not letting other children talk to the one in 'trouble' was equally perceived as cruel: 'They would hit me up to a certain age. From then onwards the punishment was to keep me in quarantine like, or send me to Coventry . . . they would stop other kids from talking to me.'

More benevolent regimes. A small number of residential people experienced more benevolent regimes with a considerable flexibility of rule enforcement. Even in cases where physical punishment, restrictions and other forms of deprivation were used, subjects recognised the necessity for some rules and controls and they harboured no bitterness. Their attitudes towards discipline and controls appeared to be largely shaped by the amount of punishment they received, and the qualities of the individual(s) administering it and attempts at explaining. Appeals to reason were certainly valued above everything else, even if not very widely used: 'We were told what was right and what was wrong. Some days the matron would sit down and if you were worried she would talk to you about it. She was quite good that way.' Another one said: 'I think they reasoned with me. O.K. you are doing this wrong, this is why you shouldn't do it like this.' 'They were fairly reasonable . . . they would hit you only occasionally.' 'The houseparents were a good couple. It would be mostly reasoning and they were flexible. We also had the slipper but not often. . . . you would know when you were in the wrong, you accepted it . . . it was fair.' On a somewhat similar note another respondent added: 'They never hurled abuse at you . . . they always tried to point out things . . . If I got hit for anything then I deserved it . . . but they would always point out why you were getting hit. . . . At the time I thought it was all wrong but not now.' 'We used to get the slipper just when we deserved it, or we would get a clip round the ear or something . . . rules were not enforced strictly but we had to abide by them.'

The handling of conflict

Most conflict situations seemed to develop in the early or middle teens. It was a period when subjects in both samples seemed to be trying to establish their individuality and difference. Whilst most conflict arose mainly as a reaction to forms of control and restrictions, some, especially in the adoptive sample, were over education and schooling. Approximately a quarter of adoptees and two-fifths of those who grew up in residential Homes reported considerable conflict between themselves and their parents or house-parents.

Conflict between adoptees and their parents. Most conflicts between adoptees and their parents in early childhood were minor and related to everyday things such as: 'me not getting my own way', 'arguing a lot', 'coming in late', 'not doing what I was told', 'being cheeky', 'not helping enough' and 'occasional disobedience'. More open conflict developed in adolescence around such issues as: 'controls' and 'too much strictness', 'over boyfriends' and 'girlfriends', 'staying out late', 'keeping bad company' and 'getting into trouble'.

The attempt by adoptees to establish their individuality and separateness was not restricted to any particular group. Where relationships were good the conflict generated would eventually evaporate, but where the situation was already explosive it could lead to additional bad feeling: 'At 14 or 15 I wanted to go to record shops, dancing, wanting to stay out late that much longer. It seemed to me that I was very hard done by but looking back I wasn't really. It was just the normal growing up bit that you go through.' Some thought at first that difficulties developed because they were adopted, until they discovered through their non-adopted friends that they had similar arguments with their parents.

A typical comment summarising other views was: 'Most of the conflicts were during my adolescence, between 12 and 16 there was always arguments . . . probably about the time I came home at night, what I was going to wear and so on – they were old-fashioned and they didn't understand me.' Another one remarked:

> I went through a difficult patch with dad when in my late teens. Laying down laws 'You must not go out with boys, no eye make-up' . . . his little girl growing up and demanding independence. . . . eventually I decided it would be better for home peace if I did move out. It did work . . . everything was as best as it had ever been.

A young man trying not to feel out of step with peers described his mother as 'quite Victorian' in her outlook, and described how they fell out 'an awful lot over that – going out late, smoking. . . . she would say, "You just don't care about me and your father" which wasn't true.' A fair amount of conflict arose out over-protectiveness on the part of some parents: 'If I was going to be out late my mother would wait up and worry . . . she would get herself into a panic and sometimes telephone the police'; 'at 13 to 15 I couldn't wait to leave home. Just frightened of being tied to my mother – make my own life and decide my own future.'

The adoptees who perceived their adoption as having been rather an unhappy experience said that most of the conflict was focused on their reluctance or inability to respond to their parents' expectations and ambitions. In a minority of cases and when conflicts got a bit out of hand, some parents, as already stated, would threaten to send the adoptee back to his 'right mother' which was experienced as very hurtful since, as one put it, 'the adoptive mother was the only mother I had'.

The management of conflict in the residential establishments. Causes for conflict with house-parents were said to focus on such areas as: 'wanting my own way', 'coming home late', 'breaking the rules', 'wanting more control over my life', 'disobedience', 'being outspoken', 'giving cheek to staff'. Predictably, most conflict in the residential units centred on rules and how these were enforced or interpreted. Almost three-quarters of the subjects found the rules too rigid, inflexible and sometimes unreasonable which almost made it inevitable that they would be broken. Rules about going to bed, getting up, eating, cleaning, playing, visiting friends, coming in during the evening were a constant source of conflict: 'Get up at certain times, be in bed at a certain time. I have spent a whole Saturday in bed as punishment for not doing certain things . . . stuck in bed all day with nothing to read.' Another typical comment: 'If your toothbrush, etc. were not in spotless order you got beaten up for it. It was awful. I just didn't like the place at all. Everything was a rule.' Another subject, commenting on how 'regimented' the Home was, described the series of things that had to be done in the same sequence when arriving back from school, and added: 'If you didn't say grace the right way you had to say it backwards.' Rules about eating were equally rigidly enforced in some Homes:

> Mr and Mrs ____ was behind you when you were eating and you weren't allowed to turn round – you were so afraid and scared. You never got a chance to misbehave. If they started hitting you there was no chance of

stopping. You were terrified. . . . sometimes they would promise a cake, if you were good, but if you asked for it later you got leathered.

Berry (1975) suggests that the apparent carelessness over personal hygiene exhibited by children after leaving residential care is because possibly 'they were drilled in a manner which subsequently feels incongruous in the ordinary world.' She goes on to stress the importance of routine events, such as washing, dressing, bathing, eating, being used as opportunities for friendly supervision and the communication of affection and personal interest in the children. She found this approach in what she called the 'relaxed units' in contrast to the 'strict units' which placed unnecessary importance on routine and the rigid observation of rules.

The situation appeared to be exacerbated as the children got older and were looking for greater freedom and independence. The wish to separate and be more independent had some similarities with the strivings of adopted subjects in adolescence. However, many of those who grew up in institutions felt the pressure of too many rules as restrictive and limiting their independence. Particularly at this stage was the recurrent wish of being able to mix more freely with peers from outside and to be more like them. The constraints which limited opportunities for interaction were viewed as furthering the difference between them and the outside community: 'You weren't allowed to go dancing and at 15 or 16 you had to be home before the thing finished'; 'If you didn't come in at a certain time you got hit. . . . the main one was you got belted or stopped pocket money or no TV or no supper.' S. commented on this issue: 'Other children of our age were allowed [by their parents] to stay out later and we had to tell them we had to be home early. If we weren't, then we would not be allowed out for a week and had to be in bed every night after tea. I found this unfair.' Some respondents felt embarrassed having to explain to peers that they could not go out or that they had to be back early because they lived in a Home. It was felt that this set them apart from the rest.

Rules could be rigidly enforced:

> If someone didn't have a toilet roll – the last person who used the toilet roll and didn't replace it, every one of the kids was running up and down stairs about 50 times with a toilet roll until they got so sick of seeing the thing that they never forgot the next time. . . . there is no wonder some of the children come out a bit barmy. . . . there was a little 3-year-old girl and she was made to do it.

As part of the rules all children were expected to carry out housework some of it very heavy according to them (washing-up, drying, cleaning tables, sweeping floors, polishing floors, cleaning bedrooms). Housework had to be carried out properly otherwise punishments could follow: 'If things weren't done properly the house-mother used to pour treacle all over the floor and we had to clean it up again.' One person who, against the rules, left her coat in a cupboard where it shouldn't have been mentioned that as a punishment she had 'her head backed on to the radiator and to stand in the corner for the rest of the day'.

The rigidity of rules seemed to stick in most subjects' memories:

> They never bent the rules. If they said you weren't getting out to play you weren't getting out to play and that was it. Punishment would be the belt for a start. Sometimes they would say, 'Look, if you behaved a bit better you would get a bit more', and you would try and tell them that if they treated me more like a person you would behave a bit better.

A number of respondents experienced as a serious form of deprivation not to be allowed to play with their friends outside the Home: 'My pet hate was they wouldn't let you mix with the other normal kids. Maybe your father is missing, but I think you ought to be allowed to mix to make you as normal as possible. . . . Give the kids something they are missing, but they never used to do that.' Rigid rules were seen to add to too much routine, predictability and boredom: 'Each day was exactly the same as the next.'

In overall summary, the institutional experience appeared to offer limited opportunities for individualised caring, or for closeness and attachment to staff. To use a sociological term, most staff appeared to pursue 'instrumental' rather than 'expressive' goals. In this respect they were less responsive to the children's need for comfort, attention and care which would require greater emotional investment. Staff appeared to spend more of the time on administrative and domestic functions than on child-oriented activities. To the children, staff often appeared too busy to stop and talk or listen. The fall-back on routine, ritual, rigid rules and discipline with no risks being taken, could be viewed as a defence against the anxiety of having to operate daily under emotionally taxing and demanding situations. By allowing themselves to be more sensitive to the children's feelings and pain would possibly make them feel more vulnerable and inadequate. Harris (1979) draws attention to the emotional, physical and mental strains on staff and residents within confined environments and adds that not everyone can survive it. He goes on to say that in residential living 'caring and nastiness can so easily become entwined'. Caring for severely handicapped people or 'rejected' children can be most distressing for staff and they may then try to cope in ways which are not always helpful. Similarly, the making of rules governing almost every aspect of residential living may not be unconnected with fears among staff of residents getting out of control. The lack of adequate support systems and caring for the carers is frequently given as the main reason why residential staff do not pursue more 'expressive' goals and need to feel in total control, taking only limited risks.

The conditions described by most residential people would satisfy the criteria identified by Barton (1959) for producing 'institutional neurosis'. Barton's criteria are: loss of contact with the outside world; enforced idleness and loss of responsibility; harshness and browbeating; bossiness of professional staff; loss of personal friends, possessions and events; loss of prospects outside the institution. Barton adds the use of drugs to which only a minority of respondents were exposed, usually as a result of psychiatrically-defined difficulties. 'Institutional neurosis', according to Barton, is likely to occur 'when the original purposes of an institution are ignored, displaced by, or subordinated to increasing preoccupation with the rituals or symbols of administration or wealth of that institution.' Goffman (1961) referred to the concept of the 'total institution' as a place where loss of identity, lack of privacy, lack of choice and humiliation take place.

Conflict with the law before the age of 16
One-quarter of those adopted and half of those who grew up in Homes had received a police warning before the age of 16 because of some misdemeanour they had been involved in. Police warnings were usually for small thefts from shops or houses. Four of those adopted (9 per cent) and three (8 per cent) of the residential subjects appeared before a Hearing charged with offences, such as stealing, damaging property, breaking and entering (including one adoptee who was charged with breaking into his parents' home), assault and 'shooting' of house-parents. All three of the residential subjects and two of the four adoptees who appeared before a Hearing, later appeared before an adult court as well. Raynor (1980) reported that 13 per cent of her sample of adoptees had been known to the police at some time. The National Children's Bureau (1976) cohort study of Britain's 16 year olds found that 4.4 per cent were closely identified as having been taken to court because of (alleged) involvement in crime. The study adds, however, that 8 per cent of the parents failed to answer this question.

Leisure activities
Nine out of ten of those adopted and three-quarters of those who grew up in residential establishments belonged on average to two clubs at some stage during their growing-up years. These would be Brownies, Cubs, Scouts and occasionally a youth or sports club. Adoptees

generally reported more outside activities compared with those who grew up in Homes. These included cycling, horse-riding, walking, bowling, dancing, swimming, netball, squash, etc. Residential subjects reported swimming, cross-country running, sports and 'playing around'. Reading as an indoor activity was mentioned by more residential subjects than adoptees.

The educational experience
The importance of education and the acquisition of educational qualifications as a means for economic advancement and social mobility is widely recognised. For instance Allen (1975) maintains that 'full-time post-school education is the crucial avenue for entry into a non-manual or professional career.' Educational attainment is frequently used by employers as a screening device to determine suitability for different types of employment. Burgess (1981) claims that the educational records of children in care show that some of them might have difficulty in reaching even the minimum levels of competence in literacy and numeracy expected by employers in certain sectors. Based on his study of young males in institutions, he concluded that for the great majority, 'work opportunities will be restricted to the unqualified sector of the job market when they leave school' (p.12). The Plowden Committee (1967) claimed that interest taken by parents is the most important single factor, apart from natural ability, influencing a child's progress. Many of the adoptive parents and house-parents seemed conscious of the importance of education and they tried to encourage the children to stay on beyond the statutory school leaving age and make the most of their education. Interest, however, can be a double-edged instrument. Whilst some adoptees experienced too much pressure in this respect, some of those who grew up in Homes experienced total indifference. The general ethos, however, prevailing in many adoptive families and residential Homes appeared to be one of attaching importance to education and related activities, but institutions appeared more successful in their pursuits with girls than with boys.

Schools attended and age at termination of formal education
Half of those adopted and a third of those who grew up in Homes attended a single primary school and the rest two or more. Four-fifths of subjects in each group attended a single secondary school. Differences between the two groups concerning number of school changes were minor. Residential people in this sample did not experience the extent of changes and instability in their secondary education found by Burgess (1981). Burgess in fact considers such

instability as a causal factor in reducing the young people's motivation to achieve while at school. All those interviewed in his study (all males) gave up school at the earliest opportunity, a trend found among males in this study. Overall, 70 per cent of those adopted and 50 per cent of those who grew up in Homes continued their education beyond the compulsory school leaving age, compared with a national average of 47 per cent in the late 1970s. Halsey *et al.* (1980) and Mortimer and Blackstone (1982) comment that leaving school at the earliest possible opportunity with no qualifications gained is a handicap for those trying to overcome the effects of a deprived home background. Layard *et al.* (1978) demonstrated from the 1975 General Household Survey data that additional years of full-time education and qualifications both substantially increased pay. Whilst this was true of those featuring in this study, the presence of emotional problems, irrespective of qualification, were sometimes contributory to the interruption of earnings in residential people. Those leaving school early were more likely to change jobs and to have received police warnings.

Raynor (1980) found that a similar percentage of adopted people (73 per cent) continued their education beyond the statutory school leaving age. The National Children's Bureau (1976) cohort study on Britain's 16 year olds quoted 62 per cent of the children as saying that they were most likely to leave school at the age of 16. A significantly higher proportion of adoptees and of residential people continued their education beyond the statutory school leaving age compared with those growing up fostered (Triseliotis 1980a). An explanation which might account for this is the different socio-economic background of foster parents compared to that of adoptive and house-parents. The latter generally seemed to attach more importance to the acquisition of educational qualifications compared to foster parents. Foster parents generally encouraged the children to be more like themselves and their own children. In effect, the social climate within which foster children grew up was different in this respect from that of many adoptive families and Homes.

Educational qualifications acquired
Both the adopted and residential groups obtained somewhat similar qualifications, though adopted people did slightly better (Table 4.5). Raynor (1980) found that something like 34 per cent of her sample of adoptees had acquired a degree, diploma or certificate. Though this proportion is significantly higher than that found in this study, it needs to be remembered that Raynor was investigating very 'selective' adoption practices when the predominating ethos among voluntary societies was the attempt to place the 'perfect' child with the 'perfect'

couple, rejecting children and couples not measuring up to a number of selection criteria based mostly on social class and economic comfort. It was this type of practice that produced many 'reject' children and 'reject' couples.

Views about the outcome of the adoption or residential experience seemed unrelated to educational qualifications acquired, but a number of other variables appeared important. Very regular school attendance by adoptees was closely associated with the acquisition of higher educational qualifications. The acquisition of higher qualifications by the residential group was adversely affected by the presence of psychiatric referrals. Lack of qualifications by the residential group also increased the possibility of appearance before an adult court. More females than males who grew up in institutions were likely to obtain higher qualifications.

Educational and vocational ambitions of adoptive parents and house-parents

Almost 60 per cent of respondents in each sample experienced their parents or carers as having ambitions on their behalf. The effect of this was mixed. Whilst subjects in both groups liked unobtrusive interest

Table 4.5   Educational qualifications obtained

	Adoption N	%	Residential N	%
None	18	42	21	52
Lower	10 ⎫	28	10 ⎫	28
Higher	2 ⎭		1 ⎭	
City & Guilds	5 ⎫		3 ⎫	
Ordinary National Certificate	1 ⎪		— ⎪	
Higher National Certificate	2 ⎬	30	4 ⎬	20
Higher National Diploma	4 ⎪		1 ⎪	
Degree	1 ⎭		— ⎭	
	43	100	40	100
Not known	1			
	44			

Note: 'Lower' and 'Higher' similar to 'O' and 'A' levels

and encouragement, they disliked 'pushy' or indifferent parents or house-parents. Whilst a greater proportion of adoptees, compared with residential subjects, referred to unreasonably high expectations on the part of their parents, more of the latter commented on the total indifference of some of the staff to their future. Encouragement and support appeared more consistent with adopted people and more sporadic towards those who had grown up in residential care. Subjects in both groups liked encouragement and interest which left decisions and choices to themselves: 'I was encouraged in what I liked doing'; 'I was left to decide for myself.' Whilst ambitions by house-parents were usually perceived as a demonstration of interest, ambitions by adoptive parents were at times experienced as unrealistic or accompanied by undue pressures. The absence of ambitions by residential staff on behalf of the residents was generally seen as lack of interest, but their absence by adoptive parents was mostly seen as parents leaving the decisions to the adoptees. The most important experience for both groups was the feeling that their parents or house-parents would back them up in whatever they chose to do. Though no direct relationship was found between the subjects' upward occupational mobility and their parents' or house-parents' ambitions, the important factor appeared to be the fact that many respondents in both samples were socialised within such a climate.

The ambitions of adoptive parents. Over half of those adopted experienced their parents as having explicit ambitions on their behalf; the rest said they felt their parents either had no definite ambitions for them or that they were left to make up their own minds. Owner-occupiers and families described as economically 'comfortable' (rather than average) were more likely to have ambitions for their children compared to the rest. Provided the parents were not too ambitious and 'pushy' adoptees reacted favourably: 'Yes, my mum had ambitions but she never threw them at me'; 'They [parents] wanted me to get on well. I could stay on at school as long as I liked. . . . At one time I wanted to be a mechanical engineer but changed into quantity surveyor.'

More subjects appreciated a subtle interest and encouragement which allowed the decision to be left to them: 'My parents had no special ambitions as long as I tried my best. . . . they encouraged me in what I liked doing. I was pleased with their attitude.' Another one said that his parents encouraged him to study and do well at school but the fact that he did not achieve much made no difference to his parents' feelings towards him: 'They just wanted me to be happy and they did everything in their power to make me happy.' A university student remarked that he was never really pushed to do anything, but that his mother was always keen for him to do well at school. Others too appreciated the emphasis on 'happiness' and contentment: 'They only wanted me to be respectable and turn out well'; 'just to keep out of trouble, get a job and marry'. M. thought that his parents would be happy if he had been happy and well. 'My mother', he said, 'was not materially minded – she just seemed pleased with any success I had.'

Other adoptees talked of their parents' ambitions which didn't work out because they themselves were not similarly inclined. They held no resentment towards their parents except where parental ambitions were too forcefully put across, sometimes followed by expressions of disappointment:

> They wanted me to get on, that I know. I am afraid I just wasn't that type. I was unhappy about their ambition. . . . they were pushing you. . . . all I wanted was to get away and try to be myself.

Another one also referred to pressure: 'They wanted me to be what they wanted. I was a slow learner. I had a speech impediment . . . what they wanted me to be I just wasn't interested in being. . . . I was unhappy about their ambition.' One adoptee resented her parents' ambitions for her because she seldom felt praised and often criticised. Her parents, who were quite keen that she should succeed academically, expected her to study for long hours every evening. The higher the social class of adoptive parents the more likely that they would entertain ambitions on behalf of their children, and the same was true of those who were described as financially 'comfortable'. As stated earlier, however, it was among these groups that dissatisfaction was felt because of undue pressures and high expectations. 'Hate' for school, for example, was more likely to be expressed by adoptees coming from economically 'comfortable' backgrounds than from the rest. Adoptees who felt 'too hard' pushed by their parents to achieve were also likely to express less satisfaction with their growing-up experience. Overall, family life had its rewards in the shape of support and interest, but in a minority of cases it was soured by the high aspirations of a few parents, mostly from a middle-class background (social classes I and II).

The ambitions of house-parents. Residential subjects were very appreciative of staff who showed an interest in their educational and vocational careers but, like adoptees, were equally resentful of those who tried to 'mould' them. Sad and bitter comments were made by those who felt that no one took any interest or had any ambitions on their behalf. Positive reactions to individual house-parents were expressed in a number of ways: 'Matron wanted me to take 'A' levels and go to university but she left and so I didn't have anyone to boost my morale.' Others were pleased about being encouraged to stay on at school, or take music or art lessons, or do well in some sport to distinguish themselves: 'They just wanted you to get on at school; get as much out of the school as you could'; 'the house-parents and the agency', remarked another one, 'wanted me to go to art college to study painting. I was glad they had ambitions for me, it gave me a bit of pride in my work.'

A small number (N = 4) were rather resentful for what they thought were other people trying 'to shape their lives' or 'make them do things': 'Everyone had big ambitions for me. I wasn't very pleased because I felt I was being pushed. . . . somebody wanted me to be a nurse and somebody to go to university. I just didn't want to do them.' Another one added: 'She [matron] set her ambitions too high for me. It wasn't what I really wanted. . . . I was unhappy. . . . I didn't think I could have lived up to the expectations'; 'I didn't want to stay on. . . . I didn't think anyone had the right to make my mind up. I was unhappy because I was being pushed. My own ambitions were to get out of the Home.' M. referred to her struggles to be allowed to become a cook against the house-mother's insistence that she should train as a nurse.

Whilst some disliked house-parents who pushed them too hard, others were regretful or bitter that no one had shown any interest: 'I was more or less on my own. No one had real ambitions for me'; 'Mr and Mrs ___ [house-parents] never gave you a chance . . . no ambitions for you, no, nothing.' Another one remarked sadly: 'Can't remember anyone having ambitions for me. . . . I can't say anyone discussed my career with me whilst I was growing up.' A few found some encouragement from ancillary staff, such as gardeners and cleaners: 'The lady who used to work in the kitchens wanted me to go into cooking. . . . I did. . . . I am very pleased about it.' A few had their own ambitions which they tried to carry out: 'I just went out to secretarial college to get some decent job'; 'my ambition was to stand on my own feet because I had so much done for me. . . . I wanted to prove that I could stand on my own two feet and be successful. . . . I think they have worked out very well.'

Comment
Both adoptees and residential subjects indicated their dislike and resentment of parents or carers who tried to push them too hard to achieve educational success or to fulfil the parents' or house-parents' ambitions. A possible explanation for this dislike is that the parents and house-parents in question put the emphasis mostly on instrumental goals such as 'educational success', prestige and good behav-

iour and much less on 'expressive' areas such as caring, closeness and warmth in relationships and the fostering of individuality and independence. Raynor (1980), as stated in a previous chapter, claims that successful outcome in adoption is very significantly associated with a feeling of a family likeness on the part of both parents and their child. The adults and also their adoptive parents were much more often satisfied when they were able to perceive or imagine likenesses between them, and a major cause of dissatisfaction was an absence of this link. Raynor goes on to support the concept of 'matching' a child to his prospective adoptive parents. She argues that the adoptive parents' need for their child to 'get on' and be a credit to them was so marked that it clearly needs to be taken into consideration when selecting a home for a child. The author indicates that of those adoptees having advanced educational attainment, almost half were known to have had one or both birth parents or a maternal grandfather employed in social class I or II occupations, and nearly all also had a similarly employed adoptive father.

Considering that of the five adoptees in this study who complained of over-ambitious and 'pushy' parents, four also expressed dissatisfaction about the outcome of their adoption, the question posed is how far their parents would have been happier if they had had placed with them children of a supposedly 'higher' intellect who could fulfil their aspirations. Conversely, would the children be happier if they had been placed with families of a lower social class? This will never be known. A comparison of adoptees in social classes I and II with the social class of their natural and adoptive parents showed that almost all adoptees in social class I or II experienced upward occupational mobility compared to their natural families, and that eight out of thirteen of these did better than their adoptive parents. The lower social class of the natural parent(s) and most of the adoptive fathers did not stop adoptees from achieving upward mobility through educational achievements. At the same time, of twelve adoptees reared by parents classified in social class I or II only five achieved the same class, with the remaining seven experiencing downward social mobility. Two adoptees who were the offspring of professional women and who were reared by professional couples experienced downward social mobility.

What these findings may suggest is that a policy of matching by intelligence will guarantee neither upward social mobility nor 'happiness'. Variables such as the general ethos in the family about education, and encouragement without undue pressure, may prove to be more important.

Turning to the residential sample, the findings suggest that children irrespective of their intellectual endowment resent 'moulding' approaches, but that the attainment of upward social mobility can result from certain socialising influences, including reasonable aspirations on behalf of children which are based on a personal interest in them. The appalling disadvantages of many of the parents of origin did not stop a fair proportion of the residential group making good use of educational opportunities. Five out of six residential people who said that their house-parents had 'high ambitions' on their behalf and 'pushed' them hard, resented the fact and expressed negative or mixed views about their growing-up period in the institution. The fine balance between encouragement and indifference, along with such qualities as caring, personal interest and reasonable controls, indicated by this study may not always be easy to implement.

Social functioning at school
Respondents in both samples were asked, among other things, to rate the regularity of their school attendance, their enjoyment or otherwise of school, and the degree of difficulties or problems experienced at school.

The majority of people in both groups enjoyed school but about a quarter of those adopted and a third of those who grew up in Homes reported truanting at regular or fairly regular intervals. There was no significant difference between males and females. Burgess (1981) found that something like 60 per cent of the boys in his study truanted frequently or refused to attend school altogether. The Plowden Committee (1967) reported that 30 per cent of primary school children were likely to truant. The National Children's Bureau study (1976) of Britain's 16 year olds puts the figures on the answers supplied by teachers to 20 per cent and on answers supplied by the respondents to 52 per cent. The writer of the report sees the latter figure as including some trivial absences. Not unexpectedly, truanting was linked by most respondents in this study to a 'dislike' of school. Four adoptees associated their attitude of dislike and 'hate' with the unreasonable demands and aspirations of their parents. Dislike of school among residential people was mostly attributed to the attitude of other children and sometimes of teachers towards them, particularly the 'labelling' and adverse discrimination they said they experienced: 'All the kids from the Home were treated as kind of losers. . . . I cannot say it didn't bother me.'

Over a third of those adopted, but almost 60 per cent of those who grew up in Homes, said that their behaviour or handling of situations posed mostly moderate problems for them at school, though a minority referred to severe problems. Types of problems described included bad tempers, fights, petty thefts, insolence and running away. Whilst adoptees tended to attribute most problems to their parents', and less often to teachers', attitudes towards them, those who grew up in Homes attributed them mostly to the attitude of other children towards them and sometimes to those of teachers. More male than female adoptees reported problems, but this did not hold true of the residential people. Those who reported especially serious problems at school were also likely to express mixed or negative views about their adoption or residential experience.

The Newsom Report (Central Advisory Council for Education 1963) referring to older children at secondary modern schools, estimated that about 5 per cent of pupils presented serious behavioural problems. Stott (1966) asserts that some 8 per cent of girls and 11–15 per cent of boys show behavioural disturbances at school. School teachers responding to Holman's (1973) questionnaire reported that 51 per cent of the privately fostered children posed problems within the school setting. Wilson's study (1962), whose sample was drawn from families displaying social problems, showed that 36 per cent of the children were misbehaving at school.

Nineteen (44 per cent) adoptees said they thoroughly enjoyed school and had no problems or difficulties. Another 21 (48 per cent) were rather ambivalent, with a minority implying that enjoyment at school was spoilt for them because of prejudice on the part of some teachers and children towards them for being adopted. Four (9 per cent) said they 'hated' school mainly because of parental pressures to achieve. Somewhat more residential people (58 per cent) said they enjoyed school and another 37 per cent expressed mixed views. Only three expressed outright dislike. The National Children's Bureau cohort study of 16 year olds quotes a figure of 30 per cent of children saying that they did not like school and as many as 11 per cent of children saying that school was 'a waste of time'. A few respondents from each group in this study expressed retrospective regret for not making better use of their education and wished they had not left school early.

Whilst the majority of those who grew up in institutions enjoyed school they attributed difficulties and problems mostly to the prejudicial attitudes of other children and sometimes to teachers towards what they called the 'Homey' children. The label 'Homey kids' with all its associated connotations was to haunt many of them for a long time: 'Kids thought you were in trouble as they believed kids from Homes are in for something bad. Teachers thought we were uneducable and lazy.' 'the only problems was the jeering we got from other kids for being Home children.' Another typical comment was: 'I didn't like school . . . it was for being a "Home child" and being called the N. children.'

School for some was experienced as a hostile territory which reinforced existing negative images of themselves about being in care or in a Home and its meaning. A few linked school problems with their personal unhappiness and 'brooding' over the way they were growing up and the unhappiness surrounding it. Teachers and house-parents seemed unaware of the serious impact that such thoughts and preoccupations had on the children. The underachievement and behaviour of some of the children could not be separated from their preoccupation with their circumstances and with anxiety about the future.

Physical health
Pringle (1965) wrote: 'People working with young deprived children have noted that separation from the mother is often followed by indifferent physical health.' Whilst it is difficult to define what is 'indifferent' health, we decided to contrast the physical health of the two groups to establish possible differences for subjects who shared the common experience of being separated from their natural mothers, but experienced a different form of substitute care. The findings are based on the accounts of respondents themselves and cover the period during the adoptive and residential placements.

Adopted people reported an average of 2.4 illnesses each compared to 2.9 by those who grew up in Homes. When types of illnesses were compared a more interesting pattern emerged. Proportionally more adopted people reported measles and mumps and more residential subjects were treated for respiratory complaints (covering pneumonia, bronchitis, whooping cough) and for dysentery, and ear, nose and throat complaints. Taking the respiratory conditions alone, six residential people received treatment for pneumonia compared with only one adoptee. Respiratory complaints among residential people seemed to be of a chronic nature. Spence *et al.* (1954) and Douglas and Blomfield (1958) suggest from their work that there is a correlation between depriving home circumstances and respiratory illnesses. The deprivation relating to the Home children in this study could only be of an emotional nature as it is assumed that materially at least the children did not go short.

The main conclusion that can be drawn from these figures is that children growing up in residential establishments may be more likely than others to have a higher incidence of respiratory diseases and to suffer from dysentery and ear, nose and throat infections.

Emotional or behaviour difficulties before and during final placement
Social work records were used to abstract evidence indicating the presence or otherwise of emotional or behaviour problems before the

adoptive placement or the longer-term residential one. Typical comments that were classified under moderate or severe difficulties included:

> 'Very nervous and highly strung child.'
> 'Temper tantrums and craving for attention. Because of this adoption postponed.'
> 'Temper tantrums and becomes violent and aggressive towards other children.'
> 'A very nervous child.'
> 'Quiet, withdrawn.'
> 'Foster mother demands his removal because she could no longer cope. Attention seeking and difficult at school – very disruptive in class.'
> 'Bed-wets regularly. Behaviour problems.'
> 'Child nervous and very excitable.'
> 'Child seen at the psychiatric clinic.'
> 'Terrific temper and clinging with adults.'
> 'Quite a difficult child.'
> 'An emotionally disturbed child.'
> 'Quiet and withdrawn, violent tempers.'
> 'A shy nervous child given to sudden outbursts and temper tantrums, a disturbed child.'
> 'A very wild child – adoptive placement broke down.'

Two-fifths of those adopted, but only just over one-fifth of those who grew up in Homes, were reported to be displaying emotional or behaviour problems before their adoptive or final residential placement. On this evidence it would appear that the residential group started their long-term placement displaying significantly fewer emotional or behaviour problems compared to those joining their adoptive families. Adoptees who came into care when 1 year or under were not more likely than the rest to develop emotional problems before the adoptive placement. More emotional or behaviour problems among the residential group appeared to manifest themselves with the increase of the length of their stay in care.

Emotional or behaviour problems during childhood included stealing, being very troublesome to parents or house-parents, uncontrolled tempers sometimes followed by assault, difficult to control, being warned by the police, disruptive behaviour at school, being withdrawn or very timid, prolonged bed-wetting. Some of this behaviour resulted in children being referred to child guidance clinics, or to List 'D' schools (schools for delinquent or troublesome children) or to schools for the maladjusted. Among those displaying behaviour problems during childhood were 10 (23 per cent) adoptees and 20 (50 per cent) residential people who received police warnings for various misdemeanours, some of them trivial (four adoptees and three from the residential sample had appeared before a Children's Hearing).

Over one-third of those adopted and 70 per cent of those who grew up in residential care displayed emotional or behaviour disorders during their childhood, i.e. since they joined their adoptive families or started what was meant to be the long-term residential placement. Compared to the pre-placement period, the proportion of these problems remained about the same among adoptees, but more than trebled among those growing up in institutions (Table 4.6). Significantly more of those who grew up in Homes displayed problems compared with those who grew up adopted (p < 0.005). The residential persons' self-reporting of emotional, behaviour or psychiatric problems was very close to the reports of social workers, the difference between the two amounting to only 4 per cent.

Of sixteen adoptees who experienced emotional or behaviour problems during the adoptive placement ten had also experienced them before the adoptive placement. In effect, only six (14 per cent) developed emotional or behaviour problems during the adoptive placement (Table 4.6). On the other hand, of 28 (78 per cent) residential people who experienced emotional or behaviour problems during the long-term residential period, only nine had displayed such problems before. In effect, almost half developed emotional or behaviour problems with the increase of their period in residential care (Table 4.7). Overall the development of emotional or behaviour problems during childhood was much more a characteristic of the residential than of the adoption group.

The finding that over a third of adoptees displayed emotional or

Table 4.6 *Emotional or behaviour problems among adoptees before and during the adoptive placement*

		During adoptive placement			
		Problems present	No problem	Total	
		N	N	N	%
Before adoption placement	Problems present	10	7	17	39
	No problems	6	21	27	61
		16 (36%)	28 (64%)	44	100

Table 4.7 *Emotional or behaviour problems among residential people before and during the long-term residential placement*

		During the long-term residential placement			
		Problems present	No problems	Total	
		N	N	N	%
Before long-term residential placement	Problems present	9	—	9	22
	No problems	19	12	31	78
		28 (70%)	12 (30%)	40	100

behaviour problems whilst growing up in the adoptive home is not too dissimilar to the 50 per cent or so reported by Raynor (1980). The development of similar problems among 70 per cent of residential people is almost identical with Wolkind and Renton's (1979) findings of 71 per cent of 'neurotic and anti-social' disorders among children in long-term residential care. Pappenfort and Kilpatrick (1969) reporting from a survey of over 2000 residential institutions in the United States found that three-quarters of all children in institutions were believed to be emotionally disturbed.

The earlier adoptees and residential people came into care the more likely they would report emotional problems during childhood. Residential people who came into care under 4 years appeared more vulnerable to emotional (as well as psychiatric) difficulties compared with those received between the ages of 4 and 9. The indications were that the break with the natural family was more damaging to the younger child. The finding that the earlier a child was received into care the more likely he or she would report emotional or behaviour problems during childhood disappeared at interview. The explanation for this may lie on the impact of new experiences in the lives of both groups. Yule and Raynes (1972), however, found little evidence to support the argument that the age at which a child first leaves his family or the number of placement surrogates he experiences are related to later behaviour.

Age at final placement and the number of moves between placements appeared unrelated to the development of emotional problems during the growing-up period. Illegitimate residential people, however, were more likely than the rest to report such problems during childhood.

Psychiatric referrals
Three adoptees had been referred for psychiatric help before the

adoptive placement. None of the residential group had been referred before they started their long-term placement. During the adoptive placement and before leaving school, six (14 per cent) of those adopted and fourteen (35 per cent) of those who grew up in Homes were referred for psychiatric help. Significantly more of those who grew up in Homes were referred for psychiatric help compared with those who grew up adopted. Three of the six adoptees who had psychiatric help had been referred for similar help before they joined their adoptive families. It is very possible that residential staff resorted more readily to psychiatric referrals compared to adoptive families. Such a step by the latter might constitute a threat to their parenting. On the other hand, the literature on the subject tends to suggest that adoptive parents, because of their predominantly middle-class background, are more likely than other parents to seek psychiatric services.

The referral rate of adoptees to psychiatric services during childhood (14 per cent) is similar to that found by Raynor (1980) for early adoptions. These findings do not support the concern expressed in some clinical studies about the large proportion of adopted children being referred to child guidance services (see Humphrey and Ounsted 1963; Sweeny *et al.* 1963; Schecter *et al.* 1964; Borgatta and Fanshel 1965). Pappenfort and Kilpatrick (1969) report that between 1 and 13

Table 4.8 *Psychiatric referral before and during the adoptive and final residential placement*

	Adoption		Residential	
	N	%	N	%
Before final placement	3	7	—	—
During placement	6	14	14	35

per cent of children in institutions in the United States are being referred to psychiatrists depending on the type of institution. Wolkind and Rutter (1973) found from their study of children aged 10–11 that over one in six of the children diagnosed as having a psychiatric disorder had been in care, a rate which differed significantly from that of their control group. The rate of psychiatric referral for residential children featuring in this study was more than double the proportion suggested by either of these studies. Millham *et al.* (1975) reported that 42 per cent of approved schoolboys required psychiatric help – a figure nearer to this one which refers to children in Homes. Estimates of moderate 'maladjustments' amongst 12–16 year olds in the United

Kingdom tend to be around 15–18 per cent, with the prevalence of severe problems between 3 and 7 per cent (Pringle 1967; Gath *et al.* 1977).

Reasons for psychiatric referral during the adoptive and residential placements varied. The main ones quoted by the six adoptees involved had to do with being 'difficult' at home which they attributed to their parents' 'strictness' or 'high aspirations' to which they would not respond: 'I was referred because of problems at home – very strict parents. Forced to do school work, underachieving at school'; 'for being difficult at home. Very strict parents. Sent to Child Guidance and then to school for maladjusted'; 'troublesome at home and at school – high expectations by my parents – sent to residential Home at 13'; 'nervous breakdown whilst still at school'; 'withdrawn and unresponsive at home. Parents expecting too much – sent to see the psychiatrist.'

Residential subjects explained their referral to psychiatrists mostly in terms of their experiences and reactions to being in care or in a Home. They were referred to psychiatrists for being 'difficult', 'having bad tempers', 'confused and bewildered', 'running away', 'for running away repeatedly', 'for being troublesome and stealing', and 'for rebelling against the system'. One subject found life in the Home so strict and intolerable that the only thing he could do was run away. Another one associated his 'stealing and troublesome' behaviour to being brought up to believe that both his parents were alive and coming for him one day. He was shocked and became 'confused' when he was told that his father was in prison and his mother was dead. Another one who also kept running away found the transfer from one Home where he was settled to another 'bewildering and strange'. He added: 'I felt strange and didn't want to accept life as it was. I felt depressed and uncertain about what was ahead. I had the feeling I wanted to be on my own away from everyone.'

Like the display of emotional or behaviour problems, the possibility of psychiatric referral during childhood for those growing up in residential establishments was higher for those coming into care when under 4 years old. No such relationship was established in the adoption group.

The number of moves before the adoptive placement was unrelated to the development of psychiatric problems in adoptees. An increasing number of moves between institutions somewhat increased the possibility of psychiatric referral for residential people. It is also possible that the reverse was true, i.e. that 'disturbed' or 'troublesome' residential children were more likely to be moved around.

The presence of emotional and psychiatric problems during

placement was closely linked with 'mixed' or 'negative' views concerning the adoption and residential experience. Similarly, the display of emotional or psychiatric problems by adoptees was accompanied by decreased attachment and closeness to the adoptive mother or father.

Wolkind and Rutter (1973) suggest that children experiencing short- or long-term institutional care are at risk of anti-social disorder, not so much because of the care itself, but because of aspects related to the child's family. Wolkind (1974) goes on to argue that many children appear to be severely damaged by their experiences prior to their admission to care. Most residential people in this sample, however, displayed their emotional or behavioural or psychiatric problems at different stages well after their admission into care.

To test the suggestion that anti-social disorders are the result not so much because of the care itself but of aspects related to the child's 'disturbed' family background, the following correlations were carried out. First, all those who had psychiatric treatment in childhood or in adult life in each of the two samples were separately correlated with each of the following indices signifying 'disturbance' among the families of origin: criminal record, alcohol abuse, severe disruptive relationship problems, and 'psychological instability'. In the end no evidence was found to link the presence of psychiatric disorder among respondents in either sample with any of the indices of 'disturbance' described above. When, however, psychiatric disorders among respondents were correlated with having a 'disturbed' family background, there was significant evidence that residential people displaying psychiatric problems during childhood were likely to have a 'disturbed' family background ($p < 0.005$). This association, however, did not hold true of the adoption group.

Summary

Over 80 per cent of adoptees rated their growing-up experience as ranging from 'fairly positive' to 'very positive' compared with 55 per cent of those who grew up in residential care. A high proportion of those adopted experienced very close relationships and attachments to one or both adoptive parents.

Real enthusiasm for growing up in residential care, as opposed to growing up adopted, was very rare. Even where residential experiences were satisfactory, respondents said they missed family life. On the whole, both adoptees and residential people did not appear to rate their satisfactions based on reactions to individual issues (e.g. physical forms of control, rigid rules, timing of adoption revelation). Instead they appeared to record overall experiences balancing positives and negatives. Residential people were very preoccupied with their circumstances, their families and their future. This preoccupation seemed to be an emotionally draining experience which affected their social and academic functioning.

A significantly higher proportion of adoptees had been identified as displaying emotional, behavioural or psychiatric problems before they joined their adoptive families, compared with residential people before they started what was to be their long-term residential placement. The earlier into care groups were more likely than the rest to display emotional, behavioural or psychiatric problems during childhood, but this association did not continue into adult life. Significantly more residential people developed emotional or psychiatric problems during childhood compared with adoptees. Early reception into care (i.e. aged under 4 years) increased also the possibility of psychiatric referral for residential people. The residential experience appeared to be decisive in the development of the disorder. Adoptees from very similar 'disturbed' backgrounds did not develop psychiatric problems.

Age at reception into care or age at placement did not appear to affect the quality of relationships between respondents and their carers, or the degree of satisfaction with the 'substitute' care experience. The presence, however, of emotional, behavioural or psychiatric problems among respondents adversely affected the degree of closeness with surrogate parents, as well as the degree of satisfaction with the growing-up experience. An increasing number of moves between reception into care and adoptive placement was unrelated to the development of emotional or psychiatric problems or to the degree of satisfaction with the adoption experience. An increase in the number of moves and surrogate placements for residential people, however, somewhat increased the possibility of psychiatric referral.

5 Genealogical and Personal Information

The previous chapter examined, among other things, the quality of the respondents' relationships with their carers because this was seen as a critical factor in the formation of personality. This chapter will consider the second ingredient which is seen as contributing significantly to the building of self; this is the need for information to be passed on to the growing child about his background, genealogy and personal history. The child who grows up within his original family has fewer tasks to accomplish compared to the child who grows up with people of whom one or both are not his parents. The former child has to identify with only one set of parents compared to the child growing up outwith his family. The latter has to base his self-concept on two sets of parents or carers (a biological and psychological set) and, as we shall see in the next chapter, also find where he fits into society as a result of his unusual upbringing. He relies heavily on those around him to produce information and fill the gaps. Triseliotis (1973, 1974, 1980a) wrote elsewhere how the past contributes significantly to an understanding of the present for the formation of a complete self. He particularly stressed the need for adopted and fostered people to know about their adoption or fostering as early as possible; to be given information about the circumstances under which adoption or fostering took place; and, more importantly, to be given genealogical information and details about their parents of origin. The developing child also needs to have a clear picture about his personal history covering events in his life. (Some of these ideas have already been incorporated into everyday child care practice, particularly in the preparation of children before moving to new families. Scrap-books and personal history books, which include information and photographs from the child's past, are now becoming standard practice. The main consideration is how to help children, especially those in care, to maintain their identity in situations of transition.)

Erikson (1968) also viewed the development of a person's identity in a psycho-historical context which related to his sense of genealogy in the life-cycle through which everyone has to pass. Erikson was referring to the development of any person and not necessarily of those growing up outwith their original family. Triseliotis's (1973) study in Scotland was instrumental in legislative changes which made it possible for adopted people in England and Wales to have access to their original birth records. In this respect section 26 of the Children Act 1975 provides for the meeting of psychological needs, something unique in social legislation. Annual figures provided by the Registrar General for England and Wales between 1977 and 1982 suggest that approximately 15 per cent of adoptees will seek access to their original records over the whole of the life-scale. In 1982, for example, 1685 adoptees over the age of 18 applied to Register House for access to birth records under section 26 of the Children Act 1975. This represents an annual rate of approximately 0.3 per cent of the estimated adoptees in the population entitled to access. Almost two-thirds of those enquiring were women, and over two-fifths said they intended to use the information to trace a natural parent (private communication by the Registrar General for England and Wales). Issues concerning genealogy and personal history are explored here with the two samples.

Revelation of adoption
With very few exceptions almost all authorities in the field of adoption recommend that telling about adoption should come before the child starts school, and it should be part of an ongoing process. From the age of about 2 onwards, telling can be linked to sex and childbirth and be discussed in an easy and relaxed way. Though the child adopted when older will know that he is adopted, he still wishes not only for reference to be made to his adoption, but also to have background and personal history information. Because of the older age at which children were placed with their adoptive parents, some had memories of living elsewhere and revelation as such was not important. Background information and general discussion of circumstances though were important to all. Many of those placed between the ages of 3 and 4 claimed to have no memories of living elsewhere and that the revelation when it came was the first time they knew. Over 40 per cent either always knew or were told when aged 5 and under. Half of them were told or found out when aged 6–11 and the remaining three (6 per cent) when they were 12 or over.

Adoptees generally appreciated being told early by their parents, but were not specific about how early. Those told when under 5 seemed to grow up with the knowledge of adoption in a way that it blended in with their personality and whole system. Even when told in a positive way at a later stage, especially when under 10, it was accepted though sometimes it created some confusion. Overall, the reaction to telling, provided it was not left unusually late (e.g. after the age of about 8), was related much more to the way it was done and the quality of relationships prevailing between the child and his family, rather than to its actual timing. The timing of telling by itself was unrelated to feelings of satisfaction/dissatisfaction about the growing-up experience. However, for those who had strained relationships with their adoptive parents, or who found out from outside sources, the revelation of adoption was most distressing. Like some other studies (notably Jaffee and Fanshel 1970; Raynor 1980) the actual timing of telling by itself is not important provided good relationships exist. Undue secrecy, however, can be associated with other dysfunctional patterns in the family.

The feeling of having grown up always knowing about adoption appeared to be the most satisfactory experience: 'I always had known I was adopted but cannot remember when I was told. It is not anything to make a fuss or bother. I am no different from anyone else.' Similar feelings were summed up by others: 'I had always known I was adopted. Better to be told than find [out] from someone else. . . .I was always happy especially as a child. I had no reason to believe that I would have been better somewhere else.' One person who was placed when 42 months old had only very vague memories of living elsewhere with an elderly person (granny) but it meant nothing to him: 'My mother told me right from the start . . . it didn't bother me. I had a mother who did want me. There was a feeling of great security and I had a happy childhood.' Another adoptee who was placed at the age of 4 was told when about 5 or 6 but did not understand what this meant till he was about 9: 'I just took it that they were my mother and father . . . it was as simple as that. I have enjoyed myself since they adopted me.'

Some of those who were told or found out between the ages of 5 and 10 generally received it with less enthusiasm. One person placed when aged 48 months old had only vague memories of living 'somewhere else'. She was told when she was about 8 and felt shocked and hurt. She couldn't talk about it until she was 16. The first time that D. realised he was adopted, though he was placed at 47 months old, was when he was about 7 when following an argument with his mother he heard his father say that they adopted him 'because he was a bastard.' A more positive reaction was reported by one adoptee who was placed at 34 months old: 'At the age of 8 or 9 my mother just sat down and explained it to me. . . . I cried a bit at the time but then it didn't really worry me. My parents were just like anyone else's.' The parents of one adoptee who was placed at the age of 2 used the opportunity of a TV film on adoption to explain: 'I was 10 at the time. I can remember crying vaguely, I wouldn't like to say why. It is hard to know why you cry because I can't say it upset me.'

Varied reactions were also reported by those who found out from outside sources, or who were told when in their teens. One adoptee worked it out from relatives' comments who would say to the mother, 'When you got J.', not 'When you had J.'. She went on: 'I didn't feel any different towards my mother as she was the only person I ever regarded as a mother.' C. who was about 21 at interview claimed that his parents didn't know that he knew of his adoption and he was trying to protect them from the knowledge as it might upset them. He was always aware that his brother was adopted and only found out about his own adoption from his girlfriend. Though being adopted created no problems, nevertheless he was shocked to find out. Others were told by schoolfriends or found out through documents: 'I went off my head. I couldn't understand it and got muddled up. Eventually I had to go to a psychiatrist . . . I think if I had been told a lot earlier and had thought about it . . . but being told late I had a chip on my shoulder about it.'

Overall no relationship was found between the timing of the revelation of adoption and views about the total adoption experience.

Just under a third of adoptees claimed to have some memories of living elsewhere, mostly in residential Homes. The memories varied from unhappy to more mixed ones and in a couple of cases to rather pleasant ones. One adoptee placed at the age of 6 described his elation at the prospect of being adopted: 'The first day my parents came through to the Home they took myself and my sister out. Then I cried because they went away. . . . I think I reckoned then that it was marvellous to have parents or maybe it was their kindness.'

M., who was placed at about 6, could remember the last residential Home which had left pleasant impressions on him. One young woman who had been moved from elderly grandparents who could not manage any longer, described how upset she was when she first left them but eventually it did not bother her because she found 'good' parents. She also enjoyed continued visits to her grandparents. A young man who was placed when he was 5½ remembered living in a Home and added: 'Looking back, I didn't dislike it but once I came away from the Home I realised what I had been missing.' Another adoptee who was placed from a Home when about 6 was said to miss the other children as he saw them 'as part of my family', but he enjoyed being made a fuss of and being treated as an individual by his new parents. One adoptee, whose adoption unfortunately did not turn out very well, could remember his tremendous pleasure and satisfaction when at the age of about 8 she went to live with her new family. This turned sour when she found them expecting too much of her and always comparing her with others.

Knowledge about the circumstance of being adopted or of being in care and growng up in a Home

Almost all subjects in each group would have liked discussion about their background and the circumstances of their adoption or of being taken into care and being brought up in a Home. They saw such information as vital to help them to understand themselves and their situation better. It was not necessarily a reflection on how things were working out for them. The key question for adoptees was, 'Why was I adopted?' and for residential subjects, 'Why in care and why in a Home?' Not having answers to these questions seemed to add to 'confusion' and 'curiosity'. They would have liked discussion on these matters to have been initiated by their carers and to have felt free to raise questions with them concerning themselves and their circumstances.

Only one adopted person in every four and one person in every six of those who grew up in Homes felt their circumstances were discussed with them (Table 5.1). The rest said that these were either hardly ever or never discussed. A third of those who grew up in residential establishments maintained that when they tried to ask questions they were put off. Again, the frequency or otherwise of these discussions did not appear to have any relationship to the subjects' views concerning the total outcome of their experience, but adoptees who said there was no discussion about their adoption and their background were somewhat more likely than the rest to have psychiatric help during childhood and in adult life ($\tau C = 0.26$, $p < 0.05$). This was the only significant association to be found between the absence of personal and background information and psychiatric referral. However, as psychiatric referral was closely associated with poor relationships, it is hard to tell whether poor relationships came first, contributing also to secrecy and evasiveness or the other way round. As other adoptees who had satisfactory relationships with their adoptive parents but who claimed not to have had sufficient personal and background information did not display psychiatric problems, we tend to think that the quality of relationships was of greater importance than discussion surrounding the adoption circumstances. Among residential people the move was in the opposite direction, and it is possible that the hostile reference of some residential staff towards the families of origin may have produced anxiety and 'disturbance'.

About one-third of those adopted and double the number of those who grew up in institutions would have liked more discussions about their circumstances. About a third, however, of those adopted would have liked less. They felt that sometimes their adoption was over-stressed, which tended to make them feel different, or sometimes information was given in an aggressive and hostile way constituting a form of attack. Over-stressing the adoptive status was generally resented

Table 5.1 *Frequency of discussion of circumstances of adoption or of growing up in a Home*

	Adoption N	%	Residential N	%
Very frequently or frequently or when subject wished	12	28	6	16
Hardly ever	26	60	20	53
Never	5	12	12	31
	43	100	38	100
Missing	1		2	
	44		40	

and may explain many adoptees' anxiety to emphasise that they were no different from anyone else:

> When I was young my mother used to introduce me as her adopted daughter. . . . I hated being introduced as that, it used to screw me up. She was trying to bridge a gap and make it easy but I hated it.

Approaches to the sharing and discussion of information concerning circumstances

Adoption sample

As stated earlier, only about a quarter of adoptees said that their adoption was discussed frequently, or as frequently as they wished; the rest said that it was hardly ever, rarely or never discussed. Most adoptive parents offered explanations that appeared understanding of the natural mother's position: 'that my parents could not look after me and were very sad to give me up'; 'that my mother, who was dying, gave me up so that I could have a good home'; 'that my gran was too old to look after me'; 'that my original mum found it very difficult to give me up'; 'that my mother was dead'. Other explanations had to do with offering the adoptee a home from a residential establishment. Another not infrequent comment was that they were chosen from many kids, which respondents seemed to like.

Where the parents took the initiative for any reference or discussion about adoption it was appreciated, but mostly it was the adoptee who had to ask. There was rarely much anger expressed about the absence of discussion especially when other relationships were good:

> My adoption was discussed as much as I wanted. My mum would also tell me, 'If you ever feel the need that you want to go and see her [natural mother] and tell her things . . .' but I never had the need because I had a good home and parents . . . I have no regrets.

Another said: 'my adoption has been perfectly open. I have mainly gone to mum for information when I wanted . . it hasn't worried me at all.' For another adoptee the discussion was about right: 'If I had any questions my mum wouldn't try to hide anything. She would give me the answer. . . . there was nothing I felt would have been better.'

These and other adoptees felt they could bring the subject up without fear or embarrassment. Others had more hesitations: 'I got information only when I asked – a bit embarrassing. I was embarrassed to ask and I think my mum was embarrassed to tell me.' Another one added: 'My mother and father never brought it up. They never mentioned it . . . it was always me who had to bring it up. . . . that's when I thought I hated them, but I didn't hate them.' D. put into words the kind of information other adoptees would have liked too: 'I think it was more me asking "Who was my mother?", "Who was my father?", "What were their names?", "Could I find out where they were?" Though I couldn't honestly say my parents were the ones to come out with it. It was me asking. Eventually through time my father explained everything and as I got older my "curiosity" grew less.'

Adoptees accepted the fact that often their parents didn't have any additional information to pass on and this they regretted: 'My adoption was never really discussed very much. My mother said I was adopted and that she didn't know much about my own parents at all. I would have like more discussion but she couldn't tell me any more.' A small minority felt they could not discuss it at all: 'I cannot remember when my adoption was ever discussed with me and I never brought it up'; 'I couldn't talk to my parents about my adoption. It was one of those things you didn't talk about'; 'my adoption was not talked about. I wanted to, but I never felt it was the place.'

Residential sample
Evasiveness in discussing and sharing information or in answering

questions was not a characteristic of adoptive families only. Staff in residential establishments often appeared unconcerned and dismissive of the children's need to know more about their circumstances and their possible future. As stated earlier, 84 per cent of those who grew up in residential establishments maintained that their circumstances were never or hardly ever discussed with them. Residential staff seemed to be out of tune with the children's anxieties, fears and uncertainties over important aspects of their lives. The main questions that troubled most subjects were: Why were they in care? Why in a Home? Why could not the natural parents look after them? What was going to happen to them? What was happening with their natural family? For how long would they continue to be in the Home? Undoubtedly though, the big question that bothered them was: 'Why am I in a Home?' or 'Why am I in care?'. Like its adoption equivalent 'Why was I adopted?', both questions seemed to be underlaid with another question as to whether they were wanted by their original families before 'being given up'.

Information offered by residential staff on the child's situation was usually confined to the family's immediate circumstances: 'mother being ill', 'unable to care', 'parents split up', 'mother deserted and nobody to care for me'. Other subjects were told that 'father wouldn't bother', 'parents incapable of looking after children', 'that I would be worse-off if I was with my parents', 'parents not fit to look after me'. Respondents generally felt that this information was not enough and it was not given within the boundaries of continuing discussion with someone who was interested in them.

In a minority of cases (16 per cent) the subjects felt that they could ask questions of the staff or the staff would take the initiative which they greatly appreciated. Particular value was attached to being told the truth, even if unpalatable: 'A lot of things were said in a nice way but I would have preferred the truth. I would have liked to have known the truth about my whole life from the beginning to end . . . even when you are a child you still want to know.'

A very positive reaction to being given information was expressed by one person who said:

> I always felt when I was discussing it with the cottage mother I got the right answer. I knew I could trust her. She gave me an answer I could accept. . . . I always came back with another question and I got a decent answer. . . . I always was told the truth . . . it was hard to accept because I felt I shouldn't be left where I was.

Others expressed similar appreciation: 'I think they did really a good job when they did discuss it, when I asked them. They told me exactly what I wanted to know and that was fine. It took a period of about 4 years to accept.'

These comments, however, were the exception as 84 per cent maintained that their circumstances were hardly ever or never discussed. Approximately two-thirds of those would have liked more discussion. The following comments were typical of many others: 'Neither house-mother nor house-father nor social worker nor anyone else attempted to discuss my circumstances with me whilst in the Home;' 'I was only told that I entered the Home at the age of 3. That was all. They never gave me any idea of why I came to the Home. . . . I found out that I did have parents on my sixteenth birthday, until then I thought they were dead.' Another one remarked: 'the Home staff never really discussed our circumstances with us. . . . I would have liked to have discussed a lot of things with them but they didn't seem to have the time. They were there to do a job.' One subject drew similarities with sex: 'It's like a kid asking his father what is sex . . . they sort of brush you away – they cannot tell you now, come back later. This is the kind of answer I felt I got.'

Doubts and confusion about natural parents and siblings were not infrequent: 'I hadn't any clue about why I was in the Home. I thought I had a dad and a mother but I wasn't awfully sure. I didn't know until I was about 12 that my mother was dead.'

Another subject put more succinctly the views of others: 'I didn't know why I was in the Home. I couldn't understand why I was in that place. I asked a few people but they didn't really give me an answer . . . it was after I met my parents at 12 that I really did begin to think . . . before that I was being given different answers and I got muddled up.'

The absence of information or lack of clarity and consistency in what was told would at times lead to confusion: 'The first time my circumstances were discussed was when I was 12 or 13, when my real mother got in touch. I was upset because I didn't know I had a mother. . . . I became confused. . . . I didn't feel I could really approach them in the Home.'

Some subjects relied on siblings to provide information or on a visiting relative: 'I never discussed with staff why I was in a Home. I would talk to my elder sister. It was she who helped me to get things clear. . . . I didn't find it easy to accept'; 'it was my uncle and aunt who tried to explain to me why we were in the Home . . . the Home made no effort to explain. It was only used as something against you. So I didn't ask.'

Similar to the adoption sample, the frequency of such discussions and the amount of information made available did not seem to be associated with the subjects' overall view about their growing-up experiences.

The family of origin
As already pointed out, children growing up in substitute forms of care such as adoption, foster care, in step-parenting relationships or in residential care need to know about their biological forebears (see Triseliotis 1973; McWhinnie 1967). The psychological need to know about one's background is linked to issues concerned with personal identity and self-concept and it is claimed that there is a need to help adoptees understand themselves better and build their developing personality on the concept of two families – the biological and the psychological. In addition, information about the biological family enables the adopted person to come to some terms with the original loss. Whilst the findings of this and other studies suggest that the psychological parents are the ones that matter more, persons brought up in such relationships require to know about their biological and genealogical backgrounds. Most of them, as the studies mentioned above have shown, are satisfied with just having information. Others may not be content until they have the opportunity of a meeting or reunion with one or both of the biological parents or members of the biological family.

Because adoptees featuring in this study were older at final placement a number of them kept in contact or were put in touch with one or more members of the biological family at some stage. In all twelve (27 per cent) of all adoptees had established some form of frequent or infrequent contact with a member of the original family. This was no reflection on the adoptive relationship as some of the contacts developed or were maintained because of the older stage at which the subjects were adopted. A minority of these contacts (two with grandparents and one with a sibling) developed into meaningful relationships, but the rest did not go beyond the stage of satisfying natural curiosity. Four other adoptees had written to Register House asking for a copy of their original birth certificate; two of these were intending to meet their natural mother 'out of curiosity' rather than to form a relationship, but the other two were not interested in a meeting, they wanted the information to satisfy their curiosity. Excluding the three adoptees who had already met a biological parent, of the remaining 41, 26 (63 per cent) were not interested in either further information about the natural family or in a reunion. They explained this mainly on the 'happy' outcome of their adoption and their current contentment with life. Another 13 (33 per cent) were only interested to have further information, and the remaining two to meet one or both of the natural parent(s). Obviously attitudes to access and tracing can change depending on new circumstances. Similarly those who say that they are only interested in obtaining information may decide to go further after the initial stage. Though the number of those who traced or who were intending to meet a natural parent was too small to draw firm conclusions from, nevertheless a strong desire for such a step, possibly with reunion in mind, was usually related to the poor outcome of adoption or to some serious crisis in the adoptee's life. A more generalised curiosity in origins and a wish for further information was not necessarily a reflection on the quality of the adoptive relationship. Social processes rather than personal circumstances may sometimes stimulate curiosity or increase the motivation for access. For example, the emphasis on minority rights and on access issues which was a phenomenon of the 1970s more than doubled the number of adoptees seeking access at the Registrar General's Office in Scotland. Raynor (1980) found that out of a sample of 105, only four adoptees showed an interest in establishing a relationship with birth parents, whilst 70 per cent had no wish for contact. The rest were curious to see what the original parents looked like.

Because of the nature of residential care about half of those who grew up in Homes were in touch with one or both parents at some stage in their lives. Four out of five grew up with siblings in the same institution and about half had met relations of the family. Eight subjects (20 per cent) had frequent contacts with one or both parents and 16 (41 per cent) had frequent contacts with siblings.

Earlier it was pointed out how many respondents in both groups felt about the absence of meaningful discussions concerning the circumstances of being either adopted or growing up in a Home. Similarly, respondents found that usually there was little or no meaningful information about the family of origin. Neither was genealogical confusion something restricted to adoptees. Many of those who grew up in institutions were equally confused and muddled about their families of origin, often being unaware whether their parents were alive or dead, or whether they had siblings or not.

Though 60 per cent of those who grew up adopted and three-quarters of those who grew up in Homes were told or knew something about their families of origin, the knowledge was often considered to be insufficient. The remaining respondents maintained that they knew or were told nothing about their biological parents. About half the subjects were offered some kind of explanation of why their parents could not care for them.

Adopted persons and their families of origin

It was noted above that about 40 per cent of adoptees had no information whatsoever about their families of origin and that many of the rest found the information given by their parents rather inadequate. There was also the view among some adoptees that their parents in some instances concealed information. Though over half of those adopted were not currently interested in more information, others felt differently. Questions such as 'Who am I?', 'Who were my parents?', 'What did they look like?' 'What sort of people were they?' were still nagging them and generated the wish to know more, but not necessarily the wish to search. For a start, many of these did not want to do anything that might upset their adoptive parents. A not untypical attitude was expressed by E.:

> It is good for the child to have a background but then it all depends how they were brought up. If they didn't have a happy life with their parents they would wonder what their own parents were like. I was lucky. I had a very happy life, I was well looked after with plenty of love.

Some adoptees stressed that they only needed information and that they had 'no wish for another set of parents'. Faced with a crisis though, even adoptees who said they had no interest in contact or in further information might feel and act differently. One of those who was contemplating writing to the Registrar General had never recovered from the loss of the adoptive mother to whom he was very attached; another one had an unhappy adoption and had already met his biological mother. Though many were disappointed about the paucity of information, 60 per cent had no wish to set out in search of information. They found satisfaction in the good relationsips they had with their families.

D. considers his adoptive parents as his only parents, but he would have welcomed more information about his natural family: 'I wouldn't call my first "parents" parents', yet he wouldn't like to go ahead to find more because of fear of upsetting his parents. Another adoptee summarised the views of others about how little information he had:

> All I knew about my natural mother is that she was just a girl when I was born. I didn't know who my real father was. To be honest I am not particularly interested. I am quite happy where I am. If I attempted, my mother would be upset but she wouldn't stand in my way. But I don't have the inclination to do it.

A more definite acceptance was implied in the following typical comment: 'I just accepted the fact that my mother couldn't keep me and it didn't seem worth thinking about it. . . . I feel strange saying "my own mother" because I don't really think of anyone other than my adoptive mother as my mother.'

Some adoptees commented that they had no wish to seek out natural parents or siblings because they would be total strangers: 'The only mother and father we have are the adoptive parents.' Another one added that her (adoptive) mother told her everything she knew about her first mother when she was 6 or 7 and she had no desire to meet her.

Adolescence was certainly the period when some adoptees thought of possible meetings with the birth parents: 'The only time I even thought about my real parents was when I was between 12 and 16 when I was growing up. . . . I never went to extremes looking for my mum or dad'; 'there was always sort of curiosity; who was my mother? And who was my father?. . . . but my adoptive parents are mum and dad as far as I am concerned. . . . I didn't know anybody else.' Another one added: 'I was told that my first parents were dead . . . whether or not this is true I don't know. I don't care about finding out more. . . . I don't know what I would do if they were alive. . . . I just feel that this is the family I have grown up with.' T.'s comments supported those of others:

> At 14 I was very conscious of my adoption and very enquiring, but not now. I am quite content . . . in my schooldays it stuck in my throat but after school I was rather proud of the fact that I was adopted and got on in life.

Attitudes towards the parents of origin
The general attitude towards the parents of origin was one of ambivalence. Except for a couple who had strong feelings either way, the rest were uncertain about their feelings. The possible explanation was that they knew little or nothing about their first parents to enable them to form definite views one way or the other. A few were trying to be understanding, particularly towards mothers who it was thought had no choice and who wanted them to go into 'a good home'. Though to be given up for adoption involved an element of rejection, generally there was no bitterness towards natural parents: 'If they put me up for adoption there must have been a reason. . . . I have never felt resentful being given up'; 'personally I think she [natural mother] was quite right to give me up as she was left in the lurch.' In a similar vein N. added: 'I suppose I felt grateful so far as my [natural] mum was concerned because she couldn't look after me.' J. thought he went into a Home because his parents separated: 'I once thought bad of them and then I changed my mind and thought sorry for them. . . . I didn't bear them any grudge at all. It can happen to anyone.' The question coming back to some of them was why the parents did it: 'Even at the age of 5½

[when he was placed] you wondered why your original parents or mother didn't want you'; yet another added: 'How could she do it? . . . I just couldn't understand.'

The residential group
The comment was made earlier that concealment or the neglect to pass on information concerning the biological family is not a characteristic of adoption only. Though a number of residential people retained some memory of one or both parents, and in some cases a parent might still be visiting, they would have liked the kind of information from staff that would have helped clarify who their parents were, whether they were still together, whether they were alive, had any plans for them, and what their current circumstances were. Others who had no knowledge at all about their natural family were even more keen to know details about their genealogy, including siblings, aunts and uncles:

> When I was older I asked a couple of times but I never seemed to get much of an answer . . . they just said, 'You've got no parents', but they wouldn't tell me what happened to them. I knew I was in a Home because of my parents, but they wouldn't tell me what happened to them.

Another said: 'You did wonder what on earth was happening . . . why was I put in the Home, what am I doing here, have I got parents, where are they, what are they doing?'

Acceptance of having to live in a Home seemed to be dependent on their understanding of unavoidable parental circumstances that prevented the latter from caring for them. Generally, respondents were forgiving and understanding towards parents who had tried but could not cope: 'My mum was ill but I didn't know exactly what it was. I didn't ask. . . . I remember being taken away from her . . . she was in a helpless state'; 'my mum told us she couldn't afford to look after us. When she left us for a while I thought she deserted us . . . when she came back it was all right. We saw her every week. . . . I didn't like being in the Home but that was it. I knew enough to know that.' Another, whose mother had left them said: 'I felt sorry for my father for the way he had been left to cope with us without a wife and I realised why he had put us in a Home. I had an understanding feeling towards my father but my mother I felt had cheated my father.'

About a quarter of those who grew up in Homes entertained negative feelings towards their parents for having 'deserted' them or put them in a Home. Deserting parents and those failing to visit or keep in touch were held in low esteem: 'I resented my parents for actually having to put me there . . . in a sense it was their fault. All the time I was in the Home they never bothered contacting me at all until I was 14, before that they never bothered.' Another person could understand why his parents could not visit as he thought he was an orphan, until he discovered that this was not the case.

Visiting parents would evoke very positive feelings in their children as well as pleasant memories: 'When I was first taken into care I hated it. My mother used to visit and we would walk up to the bus stop and would really break my heart after. . . . I wanted to be with my mother because I had known a mother's love until the age of 7 and then it was taken away from me and I really, really missed it. Nobody could take her place because nobody ever tried'; 'I loved my father, he came to visit us most weekends'; 'my mum and dad used to come and visit [before the mother died].'

A few people who could remember what life with their parents was like had few regrets about the separation: 'I can remember living at home – that is a sad point in my life because I can remember fights between my mum and dad. There was a lot of rows and maybe I got a slap or belt – I always got it . . . usually it was me that came off worse. Even as a tot of 2 or 3 I got walloped which is probably natural to some folk but it is a thing I never forget'; 'my parents couldn't care for me because they were incapable of looking after children. I knew I wasn't getting enough to eat and my other sister was ill and so was my baby sister. I knew we were all under-fed and not properly cared for.'

Another person could remember her mother being drunk and when years later she met her at her sister's wedding it was the same story: 'I didn't like what I saw. Before I met her I sort of remembered the good things about her.' A young man added: 'After I found out what my mother and father were like I would think "If I wasn't brought up in a Home what would I be like now?"' Another one also spoke disappointingly: 'I met my mother when I was in Borstal. She was in prison. I didn't like her at all.'

The overall conclusion from the various comments is how hard many subjects found accepting being in care and particularly in Homes. The assumption is that more explanation and discussion surrounding their circumstances and the condition of the natural family could have helped reduce the stress and the 'confusion'. The lack of knowledge and understanding about themselves and their situation, while not the sole factor, contributed towards states of anxiety, confusion and restlessness. Many of the comments either highlighted the value of parental visits and contacts or the bitterness and unforgivingness felt towards those parents who deserted or who failed to keep in touch or keep promises. Particular hostility was reserved for non-visiting parents who stood in the way of a couple of respondents who might otherwise have been placed for adoption.

Summary

Not only adoptive parents, but residential staff too, were said to have great difficulty in talking about the children's natural families and their circumstances. Yet respondents in both groups were insistent that they wished to know the truth about their status and circumstances – why they were adopted, who their natural parents were, what kind of people they were and whether there were siblings, grandparents or other relatives. For those growing up in Homes especially, it mattered considerably to have up-to-date information about their family of origin. Yet in spite of these strongly held and expressed views, no direct association was found between the disclosure and timing of adoption and the sharing of background and genealogical information and a number of variables concerning satisfaction/dissatisfaction with the experience. Adoptees, however, who said that there was no discussion concerning their adoption and their background were more likely than the rest to receive psychiatric help in childhood and in adult life. Whilst both groups felt strongly about these matters, other factors and particularly the quality of relationships were ascribed even more importance by respondents in both groups. What the study suggests is that talking about backgrounds is a very difficult area for both adoptive parents and adoptees. If the blocks for this failure were emotional for adoptive parents, the dismissive approach of residential staff appeared to be related to a failure to recognise the psychological significance of this topic to residential children.

A reasonable criticism levied at Triseliotis's (1973) study was that it was based on a sample of adoptees who obtained access to their birth records, and not on a general sample based on adult adoptees. The present sample of adopted adults confirms that access to birth records and/or the search for a natural parent is still a minority response. More importantly, the study found that it is not inevitable for adoptees to have identity problems or identity crises. Far from it, the vast majority of adoptees in our sample had positive self-concepts and did not feel different. Negative self-concepts were a characteristic of very few, and this was closely associated with their perception of the adoption outcome. The adoptees' motives for access to their records, leading perhaps to the tracing of a natural parent, is not static. Besides personal factors, social attitudes and changes influence such decisions.

6 Current Social and Personal Circumstances

Having looked at the experience of growing up adopted or in residential care, the study now turns its attention to examine the personal and social circumstances of the respondents at the time of interview. The question asked was: 'How are respondents doing now?' It could be argued that irrespective of how people grow up, what matters more is the way they are coping with current life situations. At the same time an explanation of current circumstances and feelings affords an opportunity to examine the effect of childhood experiences on adult life. For example, to test again the extent to which discontinuities in care in early life, moves between institutions, and the presence of behaviour and emotional difficulties in childhood have their effect on adult life. It was also a chance to examine how far the opportunity to establish new relationships and attachments which the adopted had made any difference when compared to the residential people who continued to live in institutions. The main approach was to record facts as stated by the subjects and for the qualitative side to rely on the respondents' descriptive accounts and self-rating of conditions and experiences. A number of concrete life situations, such as occupation, employment pattern, adequacy of take-home pay, housing circumstances, delinquency and crime, alcohol consumption, emotional and psychiatric conditions, and a range of subjective experiences were identified, described and coded. Eventually, these facts and experiences were related to the growing-up experience to establish possible connections or correlations.

Occupation, employment pattern and income adequacy
It is generally accepted that educational qualifications determine, to a large extent, type of occupation, and this in turn can affect levels of income and job security. In the previous chapter it was noted that half of those who grew up in residential care, and about a third of those adopted, did not continue their formal education beyond the statutory school leaving age. On the other hand, about a fifth of adoptees and one in seven of those who grew up in Homes obtained a Certificate, Diploma or Degree. In both the adoptive and residential homes, there

appeared to be a fair amount of encouragement towards making use of educational opportunities, in fact more than that found within foster homes (Triseliotis 1980b).

Classification by occupation

Approximately half of the subjects in the adoption and residential samples had undergone some form of 'in service'-type of training (as separate from induction course connected with their jobs). Similarly, about a third of those in the adoption sample and a fifth of those in the residential sample attended a day release course or went to evening classes with the aim of acquiring some specific skill or qualification. Again, there appeared to be a fair amount of encouragement by adoptive parents and the staff of Homes to subjects to attend some sort of course that would enhance their opportunities in the employment market.

Table 6.1 Social class by occupation

Social class	Adoption		Residential		Foster care*		Gen. population 1971	
	N	%	N	%	N	%		%
I & II	14	32	7	18	—	—	I & II	16
IIINM	4	9	5	12	4	10	IIINM &	51
IIIM	14	32	5	13	4	10	M	
IV & V	10	23	18	45	24	60	IV & V	33
Army	2	4	5	12	8	20		
	44	100	40	100	40	100		100

* Data from Triseliotis 1980b

Almost a third of those adopted, and just under a fifth of those who grew up in institutions, were classified in social classes I and II (Table 6.1). At the other end, about a quarter of those adopted and over two-fifths of those who grew up in Homes held semi-skilled jobs. More adoptees were classified in social classes I and II compared with the general population, whilst those who grew up in residential care did as well as the general population for classes I and II (though no residential person was classified in social class I) but were less represented among the non-manual and manual skilled occupations. As will be shown later, both groups achieved considerable upward mobility compared to their families of origin. Some of the occupations held by adoptees and classified in social classes I and II included quantity surveyor, civil engineer, nurse, hotel manager, radiographer. Jobs classified in social class II and held by those in the residential group included nurse, houseparent at children's Homes, management and laboratory technician. Staying on at school beyond the statutory school leaving age correlated with non-manual occupations. The social class and occupation of each group broadly reflected the educational path they followed.

Residential people currently holding unskilled jobs were likely to report emotional and psychological problems during the period of residential care ($p < 0.004$), attend school less regularly, report below average school performance, ($p < 0.05$) and more likely to appear before an adult court ($p < 0.05$). In fact, residential people who had psychiatric treatment in childhood were mostly holding semi-skilled and unskilled jobs and none was classified in social class I or II. It is a matter of speculation how far the staff focused their encouragement and attention on those children who were problem-free – a point that will be discussed later in this chapter. Adoptees holding professional and managerial jobs were more likely to say that being adopted created moderate problems for them. As pointed out in the previous chapter, this feeling was related to views about the amount of pressure they experienced to fulfil parental expectations.

Table 6.2   *Social class of adoptees contrasted to that of their adoptive fathers**

	Adoptees' social class						
	I	II	IIINM	IIIM	IV	V	Total
							N
I	—	—	—	2	1	—	3
II	—	5	3	—	—	1	9
IIINM	1	3	—	1	1	—	6
IIIM	1	3	—	8	3	—	15
IV	—	1	1	2	1	1	6
V	—	—	—	2	3	—	5
	2	12	4	15	9	2	44

* For purposes of comparison those in the armed forces were classified on the basis of their rank and occupation.

The following provides a more explanatory comparison of social class:

Adopted person's occupation similar to that of adoptive father	14
One social class lower	8
Two social classes lower	1
Three social classes lower	2
Four social classes lower	2
One social class above	8
Two social classes above	7
Three social classes above	2
	44

There was no significant difference between the social class of adoptees and that of their adoptive parents (Table 6.2). Overall adoptees did as well as their adoptive parents. Another way of looking at social class is to match the social class of each adoptee with that of his adoptive family and observe how many experienced downward or upward mobility. Again no significant difference emerged between the two groups. It can be confidently said that adoptees in this sample did as well as their adoptive parents and better than the general population.

Job changes since termination of full-time education

Adopted people had a mean of 3 (s.d. 2.0) job changes since the termination of their full-time education compared with 4 (s.d. 2.6) jobs held by those who grew up in Homes. Among residential people those with some form of qualification and/or training tended to have fewer job changes compared to the rest ($\tau C = 0.18$, $p < 0.06$). Burgess (1981), who studied young people in care in transition to working life and adulthood, writes:

> Young people in care, more than most, need the stability, confidence and maturity which they will derive from work in their growth towards adulthood. Unemployment for any extensive period represents a wasted opportunity to gain such experience.

Half of those who grew up adopted had only one or two jobs since the termination of their full-time education compared with a quarter of those who grew up in Homes. Though adoptees were somewhat older at interview compared with residential people, only 10 per cent of the former had five or more jobs since the termination of their education whilst this accounted for over a third of those who grew up in Homes. In effect, therefore, adoptees changed their jobs much less frequently compared with those who grew up in Homes (τ C = 0.44, p < 0.004).

It is difficult to be precise about the amount of unemployment subjects experienced since the end of their full-time education, mainly because of necessary reasons for which people could be out of work, such reasons would include motherhood, illness or the absence of employment in a particular region. (The interviews took place in the years immediately before the recession of 1980/81 when unemployment soared to 2 500 000 by March 1981). These reasons for being out of work were taken into account when compiling the various tables. Overall, approximately 70 per cent of those adopted were mostly in regular employment compared with only half of those who grew up in residential establishments. The amount of unemployment experienced by those who grew up in residential establishments was unrelated to the amount of preparation and help they said they had received before or after leaving the institution. In the long run there was no connection between the amount of unemployment experienced and the acquisition of qualifications or training. Personal factors in some instances were more decisive than qualifications or training.

In the months preceding the interviews, only three (7 per cent) adopted people had been out of work for 32, 8 and 1 weeks respectively. In contrast, twelve (30 per cent) of those who grew up in Homes were out of work for periods ranging from 6 to 72 weeks. At the time of interview the proportion of those out of work in the residential sample was six times that of those who were adopted. A fifth of those formerly fostered were also unemployed at interview (Triseliotis 1980b). Put another way, adopted people were out of work for 2 per cent of the time in the 12 months before the interview, formerly fostered people for 17 per cent, and residential people for 23 per cent. A consistent relationship was found between increased unemployment among the residential group and the presence of moderate to severe emotional problems at interview, but not of psychiatric problems (emotional: τ C = 0.48, p < 0.003). A close association was also found between increased unemployment and 'mixed' views about growing up in residential care (τ C = 0.38, p < 0.01) but emotional 'closeness' or 'distance' from house-parents was unrelated to unemployment. Being out of work was unrelated to court appearances or alcohol abuse.

Satisfaction with present job
Leaving aside those out of work, 80 per cent of those adopted and over 40 per cent of those who grew up in Homes expressed great or a fair amount of satisfaction with their present job. The greatest difference

between the two groups was the significantly higher proportion of adoptees who expressed great satisfaction with their jobs compared with residential people. A decrease in job satisfaction among those adopted tended to be associated with a decrease in satisfaction with the outcome of their adoption ($\tau C = 0.39$, $p < 0.0008$) but this was not true of the residential group. Similarly, emotional distance from the adoptive mother or father was also likely to be associated with a decrease in job satisfaction (adoptive mother: $\tau C = 0.20$, $p < 0.04$; adoptive father: $\tau C = 0.24$, $p < 0.03$). Residential subjects who experienced dissatisfaction with their jobs were likely to have had police warnings when under 16 ($\tau C = 0.59$, $p < 0.003$) and to a lesser extent to have had conflicts with their house-parents and to have truanted from school.

Adequacy of take-home pay

Approximately 80 per cent of adoptees and three-quarters of residential people said that their take-home pay was adequate and a few added 'more than adequate'. The remainder said that their income was 'inadequate'. Being on social security did not necessarily indicate perceptions of inadequacy of income. When asked to comment about their standard of living, 70 per cent of respondents in each group found it satisfactory or fairly satisfactory. It is recognised that the personal perceptions about satisfaction with one's income or standard of living are relative to each person's economic situation. For example, adoptees who expressed some misgivings about their income and/or standard of living did not necessarily share similar economic and housing conditions with residential people. The fact is that adoptees who expressed such misgivings broadly did so from a more comfortable position compared to residential people. Brown and Madge (1982) comment from their survey of studies in deprivation and disadvantages that deprivation is, to a considerable extent, in the eyes of the beholder: 'it is not always the poorest and the worst off who complain most about their conditions.'

In the 12 months before the interviews, adoptees barely made any claim on the social security system compared with residential people (Table 6.3). Four of the eleven residential people on benefits were claimants for more than a year. Approximately a third of the married residential people were on benefits compared with 2 per cent of all married couples with children for the year 1977 (*Social Trends*, 10, HMSO 1980). Among single residential people 28 per cent were on benefits compared with a national average of 6 per cent for the year 1977 (*Social Trends*, 10, HMSO 1980). Female residential people were far more likely to be on benefits than males. There was also an overlap

Table 6.3 *Weeks on social security benefits[1] in the 12 months before the interview*

Number of weeks	Adoption		Residential		Foster care[2]	
	N	%	N	%	N	%
No benefit	42	96	29	72	33	82
Up to 12 weeks	1	2	1	3	2	5
13–25 weeks	—	—	4	10	2	5
26–40 weeks	1	2	—	—	3	8
41 weeks and over	—	—	6	15	—	—
	44	100	40	100	40	100

[1] Social security benefits cover all types of benefits.
[2] Triseliotis 1980b.

between married residential women on benefits and difficulties in the marriage. In effect, married females who grew up in residential institutions were more likely than married males to be on social security either because the marriage was in trouble or the spouse was out of work. Residential people on social security benefits were also likely to express mixed feelings or dissatisfaction with their residential experience ($\tau C = 0.38$, $p < 0.01$). The holding of qualifications and/or training did not affect dependence on social security. Personal and emotional factors appeared to complicate the economic circumstances even of those holding qualifications.

Housing circumstances and conditions

Respondents in both groups were asked a number of related questions concerning their current living circumstances, the type of housing occupied, and their level of satisfaction with housing. At the time of interview about a third of the adopted sample were still living with their adoptive parents (two of them married) and another two (5 per cent) who were single at the time were living with siblings. In contrast, only one residential subject was living with his parents but eight (21 per cent) were living with siblings or relatives, mostly because they had no other place to which to go.

Type of housing occupied was examined in relation to married subjects only because of the many problems involved in classifying single people living with parents or siblings. A quarter of married adoptees owned their own house. (Three single adoptees had also purchased their own dwelling by the time of the interview.) The percentage living in local authority housing was about the same as the general population (approximately 52 per cent of the Scottish population during the period of the study were living in council houses compared with just over 30 per cent in England and Wales), but 40 per cent of married residential subjects who were in tied accommodation were living in army-supplied housing.

Approximately 80 per cent of those adopted, and 70 per cent of those who grew up in Homes, expressed satisfaction or considerable satisfaction with their current housing situation. Only two adoptees and five residential people expressed outright dissatisfaction about the quality of their housing. Another four adoptees and seven residential people expressed mixed feelings. Two of those adopted and seven of the residential group had been in touch with housing departments for what were described as 'moderate' to 'severe housing problems'. The amount of satisfaction/dissatisfaction expressed refers, as always, to the respondents' subjective feelings. An objective observer might have drawn attention to the significant differences in the type of housing and localities where the two groups resided. Adoptees overall tended to live in better-off residential areas, whilst it was not unusual for residential people to be found in neglected tenements and in down-graded local authority property. This, however, did not appear to affect the amount of satisfaction/dissatisfaction felt by the respective groups. So when an adoptee or a residential person expressed mixed feelings or some dissatisfaction these were relative to their current conditions rather than to any general criteria. It was also to be expected that more dissatisfaction about housing was confined to those married or to those who had separated from their spouses. Residential people, for instance, who expressed 'mixed' feelings about their housing conditions were also likely to report spouse problems ($\tau C = 0.31$, $p < 0.03$) in later life and to say that residential care makes life difficult for you and that their income was inadequate. Mixed feelings or dissatisfaction about housing and 'inadequate income' overlapped among residential people but not among adoptees.

Summary

Four (9 per cent) adoptees and 13 (33 per cent) residential people were facing serious financial and/or housing problems at the time of the interviews (Figure 6.1). Another four (9 per cent) adoptees and seven (or 17 per cent) residential people were reporting less serious financial and/or housing problems. (One adoptee and seven residential people were experiencing both financial and housing problems of some severity). The fact that the social conditions of half of those who grew up in institutions appeared satisfactory may appear reassuring, but there must nevertheless be concern about the half who were experiencing problems.

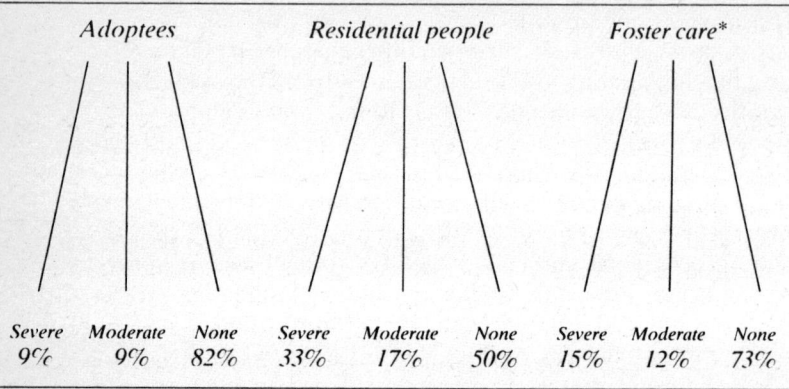

Figure 6.1 Proportion of respondents with severe, moderate and no financial and/or housing problems

* Triseliotis 1980b.

Marital status and family life

About half the people in each sample had married at least once by the time of the interview. In general, residential people tended to marry somewhat younger compared with adopted ones. Marriage for most of them represented independence and a 'home', something they say they never had because of their residential experience. Of the 21 adoptees who had married at least once, five (24 per cent) had already divorced or were living apart. Two of them had remarried and claimed to have 'very happy' second marriages. Of those currently married only three referred to relationship problems with their spouses which at some point had posed a threat to the marriage. All three maintained that the problems had cleared up and that they were now leading settled lives. The remaining couples referred to no unusual marital problems or difficulties.

Those adoptees who claimed to have no unusual marital difficulties talked of being 'very happy' or 'never been happier', 'no problems', 'we get along great'. A minority referred to early problems which cleared through time: 'At the start it was rough, but it is getting better. We've been through a lot of problems but we are still here, and very happy.' Unemployment created unusual strain in one marriage but, 'I got the job and everything cooled down.' Another adoptee spoke of problems with his in-laws but this, he claimed, did not affect spouse relationships. Two of the women divorcees claimed to have left their husbands on account of the latters' cruelty and added that their second marriages were working very well: 'Now I am really very happy. I couldn't have a better husband.' The second one remarked about the first husband: 'he was a terrible drinker and he started beating me up . . . eventually we got divorced and I married 2 years later. The children get on well with R. [second husband] and we are quite happy.' Adoptees were conscious of their adoptive parents' support, including some of those who got divorced and remarried: 'My mum and dad helped me over problems with separation and divorce'; 'my parents were upset but were very good about it.' In general, adoptees who experienced spouse problems did not think it had anything to do with their adoption.

Of the 22 married people who grew up in Homes, four (18 per cent) had already divorced or were permanently separated, and another five (24 per cent) referred to serious relationship difficulties, some of which led to separations and reunions. Overall, of those currently married seven (32 per cent) expressed some dissatisfaction with the marriage, but the remaining 15 (68 per cent) expressed from some to considerable satisfaction. In this respect twice as many residential people expressed some dissatisfaction with their marriage compared with those adopted.

Those residential people who claimed to have happy marriages also talked about being 'close' to their husbands, having 'a happy enough marriage', 'getting on well', 'fairly happy – money is the big problem', 'very happy, no problems' and 'mostly or fairly happy'. One woman attributed her considerable dependence on her husband as resulting from having no one before to be close to. Besides the four who divorced or separated, five others talked of what appeared to be severe problems in the marriage. One woman who described her marriage as having been 'on the rocks' for some time attributed this to the different ethnic origin of her husband and his 'strange' habits. Another one referred to herself as being 'absolutely disgusted with the marriage', and spoke of her husband trying to strangle her. One person blamed herself for continuing to exhibit within the marriage the same 'rebellion' she exhibited in the Home: 'I feel it wasn't all his fault because there was a lot of my rebellion still in me, still is . . .' Another one who left her husband talked about his drinking and violence: 'I just left, I was heading for a nervous breakdown.' Another one explained the problem as being due to her inability to let 'anyone near her'.

A number of residential people who divorced or separated blamed themselves for 'rushing' into marriage. They thought that this was one way of getting away from the unhappiness of the residential Home, or of creating a home of their own: 'If I had been happy [in the Home] I wouldn't have got married . . . getting married meant getting out of the Home. Sixteen years old and standing at the Registry Office! . . . now I have a broken home and my child is suffering a lot.' Another one: 'Maybe I rushed into marriage looking for a home of my own. . . . I think I knew it wasn't going to last.'

Partner problems among the residential group were associated with the presence of emotional/psychiatric problems at interview (emotional: $\tau C = 0.23$, $p < 0.04$; psychiatric: $\tau C = 0.25$, $p < 0.02$) and with a poor sense of well-being ($\tau C = 0.35$, $p < 0.009$). Partner problems were unrelated to the closeness or otherwise of respondents to their carers during childhood or to their overall satisfaction with the growing-up experience. However, those who said there was nothing satisfying about being brought up in a Home or put emphasis on material satisfactions were also likely to be experiencing partner problems ($p < 0.03$).

The subjects' children
Seventeen of the 21 married couples in the adopted group had one or more children, making a total of 23 children at the time of the interview. One woman in the adoption group had a child before she married which she had placed for adoption. She remarked that if her child had as good a home as she had then he would be very lucky: 'It hurts at times but no regrets.' Twenty of the 22 married couples in the residential group had one or more children making a total of 28. One woman had given birth to an out-of-wedlock child. These findings do not fully support Wolkind's (1977) claim that of women seen at an ante-natal clinic those who had been in care were more likely to be teenagers and unmarried. Teenagers they may have been, but not unmarried. Though all the respondents claimed to have close relationships with their children, nine (45 per cent) parents in the residential group referred to difficulties or uncertainties about relating to them. Compared with adoptees, parents in the residential group expressed more uncertainties and anxieties about their parental role. Rutter and Quinton (1980 and 1981) reported that mothers who had severely adverse childhood experiences were also likely to have parenting problems, but went on to add that having been in care during childhood did not inevitably lead to difficulties in early parenthood.

Residential people who said they were experiencing some difficulty in relating to their children were also likely to report emotional problems during childhood ($\tau C = 0.35$, $p < 0.02$) and at the time of the interview ($\tau C = 0.49$, $p < 0.0003$) and to have had psychiatric help in the 12 months before the interview ($\tau C = 0.46$, $p < 0.005$). The same group were also likely to report a 'poor sense of emotional well-being' at interview ($\tau C = 0.46$, $p < 0.006$). All adoptees referred to good and close relationships with their children. Typical comments were: 'Very close to him, no difficulties'; 'I have three, love them all, no difficulties'; 'no problems, very close'. Five children were in the families which experienced divorce or separation. One mother said that she tended to lose her temper with the child early on but she had learned to control herself and there were no difficulties about relating to the child now.

Whilst all parents in the residential group expressed closeness to their children, almost half referred to difficulties in relating, particularly in the early stages. Three mothers referred to feeling very depressed and unable to respond to the child after his birth in what sounded like a state of post partum depression. Some of them blamed the way they were brought up in the Home for experiencing some difficulties in relating to their children: 'I had an awful job accepting him when he was born. It took about a year and a half of help before I came close at all.' She blamed the Home for not giving her 'any love or care', and added: 'sometimes I used to hate him [child], really hate him . . . when you are in a Home you have a lot more difficulty in bringing up your own family.' Another one also commented:

> when he cried he got on my nerves. I have been shaking him, literally shaking him. . . . one time I shook him and then I dropped him . . . after that I really hated myself for it but at the time I couldn't help it. . . . I couldn't stand his screaming.

She blamed being strict with the child to the punishment she used to get in the Home: 'Folks say, "Look, this is not a concentration camp", but I don't mean it to be, I can't help it.' One mother who felt depressed on leaving hospital said that she couldn't understand why she had to take the child home and look after it. Another one commented in a similar vein: 'I couldn't love her [the child] as I wanted to love her at first, I didn't know how to give love back.' A young mother linked the difficulties in relating to her children to her growing up in a Home, and added:

> I didn't really know how to relate to children. . . . I didn't know how to treat my own children. I found I was treating K. like a house-mother in a children's Home. It bothers me. I sometimes think to myself that I am bringing her up to have the same emotional problems. . . . I am bringing her up too much like a child in a children's Home. I found I was sometimes too hard on her. . . . I revert back to how I was brought up sometimes.

A young man, commenting on his difficulties in trying to be a father, said: 'as a bairn I got nothing from the Home . . . if I see a child "giving cheek" it bugs me. . . . we never got off with it and I don't see how other folk should get off with it. I ken it's stupid.'

One mother who had some difficulties in relating to her children early on had fears of the child being taken away because she had grown up in a Home. The health visitor's visits made her feel very anxious. A couple of other mothers referred to early difficulties and rejection of the child, one of them saying: 'I found it hard to get close to her after she was born. I found it difficult to accept that someone actually did care for me and I rejected her'; the other: 'I rejected him a bit at first. . . . I felt he was a big responsibility. . . . I am coping with him now.' Another mother who was finding the child a bit of a 'handful' was getting help from a psychiatrist. One child was 'seeing a social worker to settle her down because she was hyperactive.'

Other parents because of their own experiences were determined to give as much love and attention to their children as possible to make sure they did not suffer.

> I look after my son in a way that he would never land up in a Home. . . . I try to give him as much love . . . it is easier for me to do this because I appreciate the difference between not having a parent and having one. . . . I know what it is not to have love and affection.

Other typical comments: 'I always said to myself, "If I ever do get married and have a kid I will always make sure he gets something better than I did." I feel dead close to him'; and 'I thought when my son was born that was the greatest thing in my life.' One of them referred to the child as 'the only thing I have got . . . I feel close to him.' None of the anxieties described above featured to any significant degree in the adoption group. In spite of the personal and social problems faced by a fair number of residential people, no child had yet been taken into care.

Wolkind *et al.* (1976) conclude from their study of primiparous women that certain childhood experiences such as separation are strongly related to psychological and social adjustment in adult life. They go on to add that a 'disrupted' childhood may produce an adult maladjustment for women in the form of social and family difficulties which in turn may be associated with difficulties for their children. From our experience a 'separation' in childhood is not enough to produce such conditions as evidenced by the fact that adopted mothers who experienced a disruption before adoption had no unusual difficulties in relating to their children. It is again our view based on these findings that a 'disruption' in early life will not lead to subsequent social or personal difficulties if a stable and caring environment is provided. The latter was lacking from the lives of many residential people. Oppel and Royston (1971) also link low maternal age (a factor present in the residential group) and less adequate care of the child.

Emotional behaviour and psychiatric problems at interview

Emotional problems
Whilst childhood emotional difficulties appeared mostly in the form of stealing, tempers, shyness, being withdrawn, fears and persistent bed-wetting, in late teens and later life they had more to to with generalised 'depression', 'unhappiness', 'shyness', 'being mixed-up', 'problems in relating' and 'getting into trouble'. One woman who grew up in residential care commented: 'I find it difficult to let people come near me . . . when I have a good relationship I break it . . . everybody thinks I am a bit crazy. . . . I fabricate a lot of stories.' It needs to be remembered that, along with other statements, the presence and extent of emotional problems at interview relies on the views of the respondents themselves, i.e. how they saw themselves in relation to this issue. Whether those who said they were 'introverted and shy' and rated themselves as having moderate emotional problems should be seen as such is a matter for debate. The alternative would have been for the researchers to ascribe a value which would have added to the complications. We have seen in the previous chapters, though, that the residential people's self-rating of their emotional problems during their childhood coincided very closely with the social workers' recorded views on the matter.

Ten (23 per cent) of those adopted linked what they described as their 'moderate' emotional problems to issues concerned with their identity and adoption. They talked of being 'mixed-up', and they would add: 'It is difficult for me not knowing who my real parents were . . . it makes me wonder and worry'; 'having a chip on my shoulder for being adopted'; 'feeling mixed-up because of unhappy experiences' and concern about behaviour such as drink or crime. Less frequently emotional states were linked to depressive feelings, to relationship problems, or to feeling 'agitated and nervous'.

Half of those who grew up in Homes linked feelings of 'unhappiness', 'depression', 'inferiority' or being 'mixed-up' mostly to having grown up in a Home: 'I feel I carry the inferiority complex of the Home'; 'being brought up in a Home makes me feel very self-conscious, mixed-up and unsettled'; 'the institutions made me feel I was a bad girl. . . . I can't get away from it now'; 'a lot of people think I am mental because of my upbringing. . . . I get depressed . . . very depressed.' Three others talked of feeling 'barmy' or 'crazy', or at least that others perceived them in that way. A few referred to their 'quick' or 'bad' temper: 'I get fed up easily, quick tempered, things building inside me and getting rather depressed . . . it comes and goes'; 'I blow up over the smallest problems.' One person who recently lost his father felt in a rather suicidal mood for a while but refused any help: 'I've felt like committing suicide but I'll have to get over it. Coming from a Home . . . makes me feel emotionally upset.' Another one remarked: 'Mentally I am not very healthy.' As stated in the previous chapter, possible genealogical confusion is not a characteristic of adoption only. Some residential subjects too spoke of their genealogical bewilderment: 'not knowing my identity, not knowing your parents . . . mixed-up . . . there are a lot of questions I want to ask and I just cannot get an answer.' Others were brooding over their feelings of rejection by their natural parents and how this still affected them: 'it meant that your mother and father didn't care about you and they just stuck you in a Home.' Others talked about feeling 'inferior' or 'having a chip' on their shoulders or still experiencing the 'stigma' of having been brought up in a Home. Strain, worry, feeling 'mixed-up' being 'quick tempered', having relationship problems, being 'introverted' and 'shy' were some other conditions to which they referred.

Table 6.4 shows that more than twice those who grew up in Homes reported emotional problems at interview compared with those who grew up adopted ($\tau C = 0.23$, $p < 0.02$). The presence of emotional problems at interview was closely associated with negative or mixed feelings about the adoptive experience ($\tau C = 0.40$, $p < 0.003$) and similarly of the residential experience ($\tau C = 0.27$, $p < 0.002$). In effect, those who reported emotional problems at interview were also likely to express mixed feelings or dissatisfaction with their growing-up experience as adopted or in residential care. Age at reception into care, number of moves between placements and age at placement, sex and status appeared unrelated to the presence or otherwise of emotional or behaviour problems at interview. Residential people, however, born out of wedlock continued to be more prone to emotional or behaviour problems.

Table 6.4 summarises the presence or absence of emotional/behaviour problems at different stages. The presence of emotional problems among adoptees decreased from 37 per cent during childhood to 25 per cent at interview and among residential subjects from 70 to 50 per cent. Of the 44 adoptees in the sample at least 27 (61 per cent) reported moderate emotional or behaviour problems at some stage in their lives. At interview only 11 (25 per cent) were still experiencing similar problems. Srole *et al.* (1962) found from a study in the United

Table 6.4 Summary of emotional problems before and during placement and at interview by group

	Adoption				Residential			
	None		Moderate/severe		None		Moderate/severe	
	N	%	N	%	N	%	N	%
Before placement	27	60	17	40	32	80	8	20
During placement	28	63	16	37	12	30	28	70
At interview	33	75	11	25	20	50	20	50

States that 23.4 per cent of adults in the general population were 'impaired'. Of 40 subjects who grew up in residential care 28 (70 per cent) reported moderate emotional/behaviour problems at some stage from birth to interview time and 20 (50 per cent) were still experiencing such problems at interview. Overall, residential people were far more likely than adopted people to report emotional or behaviour problems at interview (< 0.05). The presence, at interview, of emotional or behaviour problems in adoptees was unrelated to the presence of similar problems in childhood. Of 23 (52 per cent) adoptees who displayed emotional/behaviour problems in childhood (17 of them had displayed these difficulties before placement) only seven (16 per cent) were having similar problems at interview. Another four adoptees who had not shown such difficulties in childhood were displaying them for the first time now. The main conclusion is that difficulties present before the adoptive placement and some that developed during placement did not continue into adult life in any significant numbers. Of 28 (70 per cent) residential people who displayed emotional or behaviour problems during childhood 18 (64 per cent) were still displaying them at interview. Unlike adoptees, emotional or behaviour problems among residential people in childhood persisted into adult life in significant numbers (p < 0.05). The persistence of emotional/behaviour problems in residential people could be explained either as the result of their residential experience compounded by current problems in living or as due to some genetic transmission through their parents. Yet no such transmission seems to operate in the case of adopted people.

Psychiatric problems in adult life
It was noted in the previous chapter that six (14 per cent) adoptees and fourteen (35 per cent) of those who grew up in residential

establishments had been referred for psychiatric help during childhood; also that the adoptees' most common explanation for the referral was conflicts connected with their school performance or their general behaviour which they linked to parental 'strictness' or 'high expectations' of them. The residential people explained their 'disturbed' behaviour mostly as a reaction to growing up in residential care and the unhappiness surrounding it.

Five (11 per cent) adoptees and ten (or 25 per cent) who grew up in Homes were also referred for psychiatric help as adults (i.e. after leaving secondary school). Two of the adoptees had treatment for depression resulting from family and personal problems, and two for what they described as 'nervous breakdowns' or being 'mixed-up' and depressed. Two adoptees and six who grew up in Homes were referred to a psychiatrist in the 12 months prior to the interview. The rate of psychiatric problems among former foster children was broadly similar to that of adoptees (Triseliotis 1980b). Of the ten residential subjects who received psychiatric help in adult life, three were treated for 'overdose' and one for being a 'danger to himself': 'I took an overdose just after my child was born and was rushed to hospital. . . . I just went through a series of suicidal attempts, which I didn't really want to do.' One person had psychiatric help as a child, and after she gave birth to her child and in the 12 months prior to the interview: 'Everything I did was trying to fight the system . . . when I had a depression after my child was born everybody thought I was the same bitch as I was when I was young.'

Another person who grew up in residential care attributed her need for psychiatric help to her ruminations about the whereabouts of her parents. She spent 3 years in a psychiatric hospital between the ages of 15 and 18 following an overdose. She was currently under medication for 'nerves'. The rest were treated for what they described as 'emotional problems and varying states of depression'. Another one, who had seen an 'endless' number of psychiatrists since she was in care, could not be bothered any longer in spite of her doctor's insistence that she needed treatment.

Table 6.5 sets out psychiatric referral at four different stages in the subjects' lives: before placement, during placement, in adulthood and in the 12 months before the interview. The table shows a consistently higher rate of psychiatric referral among the residential than the adoption group following placement. Of the three adoptees on whose behalf psychiatric help was sought before the adoptive placement, all continued to display difficulties during childhood, but only one needed psychiatric help in adult life (Table 6.6). One of the three adoptees who developed a psychiatric condition after joining his adoptive family

CURRENT SOCIAL AND PERSONAL CIRCUMSTANCES

Table 6.5 *Psychiatric referral before, during placement and in adulthood by group*

	Adoption N	%	Residential N	%
Before placement	3	7	—	—
During placement or childhood	6	14	14	35
In adulthood	5	11	10	25
In the 12 months before interview	2	5	6	15

needed psychiatric help in adult life, but none had sought treatment in the 12 months leading up to the interview. In effect, of six adoptees who displayed psychiatric difficulties as children, only two needed psychiatric help in adult life. Three other adoptees required help in adult life for the first time. Two of these saw a psychiatrist in the 12 months before the interview. Looking at the picture as a whole nine (20 per cent) adoptees were referred or referred themselves at some stage for psychiatric help. The suggestion again is that among adoptees

Table 6.6 *Psychiatric help during childhood and in adult life in adoptees*

		Psychiatric help N	In adult life No psychiatric help N	Total N	%
In childhood	Psychiatric help	2	4	6	14
	No psychiatric help	3	35	38	86
		5 (11%)	39 (89%)	44	100

psychiatric problems tend to recede in adulthood, though some people who never experienced them before may do so for the first time. The five (11 per cent) who needed psychiatric help as adults is within the proportion of people in the community who are likely to require psychiatric help at some stage in their adult lives. Obviously the respondents here were comparatively young and it is difficult to predict how many more may seek help at a later stage.

Of the fourteen residential people who were referred for psychiatric help during the residential placement, eight were also referred for psychiatric help in adult life ($p < 0.005$). Another two who had never sought psychiatric help before did so for the first time (Table 6.7). In all, of the 40 residential subjects, 16 (40 per cent) were referred or referred themselves for psychiatric help at some stage in their lives, compared with nine (20 per cent) of those adopted. Overall, more residential than adopted people were referred for psychiatric help but the difference was not statistically significant. The proportion of residential people requiring psychiatric help in adult life was twice that found among the general population. Residential people referred for psychiatric help in adult life were also likely to have seen a psychiatrist in childhood ($p < 0.005$) (Table 6.7).

Table 6.7 Psychiatric referral during childhood and in adult life of residential people

		Adult life			
		Psychiatric referral	No referral	Total	
		N	N	N	%
During childhood	Psychiatric referral	8	6	14	35
	No referral	2	24	26	65
		10 (25%)	30 (75%)	40	100

Though the overall figures of psychiatric referral in adult life are rather small to draw conclusions from, it seemed that age at reception into care, number of moves between placement and age at final placement were unrelated to the presence of psychiatric problems in adoptees. Residential people who came into care when under 4 years were more likely than the rest to be referred for psychiatric help in adult life and were more likely than the rest to express mixed or negative feelings about their experiences in residential care ($p < 0.02$). An increasing number of moves between institutions also increased the possibility of psychiatric referral for the residential group ($\tau C = 0.21$, $p < 0.03$). There was no significant difference in the ratio of male to female being referred for psychiatric help but women were somewhat more likely than men to experience psychiatric difficulties in adult life (this is also true of the general population).

In final conclusion both emotional/behaviour and psychiatric problems among adoptees tend to decrease significantly in adult life but these tend to persist with those who grow up in residential care.

Physical health

Subjects in both groups were asked a number of related questions concerning their physical health as adults including number of hospitalisations, number of times they visited their general practitioners in the 12 months prior to the interview, and finally to record a subjective rating about their physical health.

Few differences emerged between the two groups. Seven out of ten rated their physical health as 'good', and the rest 'average'. Only one person who grew up in residential care rated it as 'poor'. Twelve (28 per cent) adoptees and eleven (28 per cent) residential subjects had been hospitalised at least once, but ten (25 per cent) of those who grew up in Homes and three (7 per cent) of those who grew up adopted were hospitalised more than once. (Maternity cases were excluded.)

When respondents were asked to record visits to their GPs in the previous 12 months, eight (20 per cent) residential people and three (7 per cent) adoptees visited their GPs five or more times. Overall, residential people made more demands on the health services compared with adoptees ($p < 0.05$). Adopted people visited their GPs or went into hospital for accidents, skin trouble, two with chest trouble, persistent nose bleeding and colds. Residential subjects visited their GPs or went into hospital for colic trouble, epilepsy, high blood pressure, accidents, headaches (attributed to strain and worry), kidney trouble, stomach and back trouble, nerves, ear trouble, psittacosis, and one person who saw about nine doctors to ensure that he was 'fit'. In the previous chapter the point was also made how residential people experienced a significantly higher proportion of childhood respiratory illnesses compared with adoptees.

Delinquency and crime

Delinquent and criminal acts were examined at three different stages: first, apprehension and warning by the police; second, appearance before a Hearing (equivalent to a Juvenile Court); and third, appearance before an adult court (Table 6.8). Residential people had double the rate of police warnings compared with adoptees. When it comes, however, to appearances before a Hearing or an adult court, the differences between the two groups were small. Twelve (27 per cent) adoptees and 16 (40 per cent) residential people had appeared one or more times before an adult court. Two adoptees and six (15 per cent) of those who grew up in residential care had appeared three or more times. Four of the residential group had been convicted 4–7 times each. Three subjects in each group were convicted for motoring offences only; and another three adoptees for 'breach of the peace' for what appeared to be youthful pranks. Former foster children had a lower crime rate compared to the other two groups. Drink as a source

Table 6.8 Delinquency and crime

	Adoption		Residential		Foster care*	
	N	%	N	%	N	%
Police warning	10	23	19	47	8	20
Hearing	4	9	3	8	4	10
Adult court	12	27	16	40	5	13

* Data from Triseliotis 1980b.

of crime featured particularly among residential people with such offences as 'drink and drive', 'breach of the peace whilst under the influence' or being 'drunk and disorderly'. Four (9 per cent) adoptees had been convicted for stealing compared with six (15 per cent) residential people. One adoptee had been to approved school and to Borstal and was later placed on probation; another was sent to prison, and three others experienced probation or supervision. Residential people spent varying periods of time in List 'D' schools (N = 1), Borstals (N = 2), prison (N = 1), training centres (N = 2), probation/supervision (N = 6). Those growing up in foster care had the lowest rate of court appearances in adult life (Table 6.8).

Overall, of 44 adoptees, 14 (32 per cent) appeared before a Hearing or adult court compared with 17 (43 per cent) of those who grew up in Homes. The main conclusion that can be drawn from these figures is that when it comes to court appearances differences between the two groups were small, but residential people were more likely to reappear in adult court. The 17 (43 per cent) residential people who were convicted by courts contrast with the 20 per cent quoted by Ferguson (1966) for all those who had been in care (i.e. including foster care) up to the age of 18. The proportion of adoptees convicted by an adult court (28 per cent) is about 40 per cent higher compared with figures quoted by Bohman and Sigvardsson (1980) from a comparable Swedish investigation. The difference however may be accounted for by the fact that Bohman's subjects were about 2 years younger at interview and his exclusion of all those convicted of an alcohol-related act if it carried less than 60 days' imprisonment. Bohman regarded the extent of criminality among his subjects to be of the same magnitude as in the general population. If a similar classification were to be followed in this study it would yield broadly similar results. West (1979), who examined the crimes of a sample of boys in a working-class area of London, found that approximately one-third had been found guilty of crime by age 24. McClintock and Avison (1968) calculated that about every third male and every twelfth female received a conviction for at least a trivial offence at some point over the life-cycle.

Court appearance seemed unrelated to the respondents' perception of their growing-up experience or to age at reception into care, to reported school truancy or to emotional or psychiatric problems. Adoptees and residential subjects who had police warnings were likely to report dissatisfaction or mixed feelings with their growing-up experience. Being warned by the police in childhood also increased the possibility of court appearance in adult life for the residential group.

Men in both the residential and adoption samples were more likely than women to appear before an adult court, but females growing up in residential care were more likely to become delinquent than those growing up adopted. Similarly, being an only adopted child appeared to increase the risk of appearing before an adult court. Respondents from both groups who at some stage had contact with a member of the natural family were likely to have or to acquire a criminal record, though very few adoptees had such a contact.

Alcohol consumption
Approximately 90 per cent of respondents in each group said they took alcohol in small or large quantities. The frequency with which people drank varied, but at least three of the residential people took alcohol more than once a day. Put another way 15 (34 per cent) adoptees and 13 (35 per cent) residential people said they drank at least twice a week. Those who drank less often than once a week said it could have been once every month or when there was a celebration such as Christmas, New Year's Day or a wedding. The percentage of non-drinkers in both samples (7–11 per cent) seems to be near the national average of 11 per cent (Ritson 1980). (The general population in Scotland drink more than in England and Wales.)

An important question that is often asked is what amount of alcohol constitutes excessive drinking or, to put it another way, how much drink it is safe to consume. Kenyon (1977) points out that this is a very difficult question to answer. Consideration, he argues, must be given to the variables of age, body weight, and most important of all, for how long the individual has been drinking and in what quantity. The effect of a given amount of alcohol will also vary according to how much food the drinker has ingested prior to starting to drink, how tired the person is, and how physically fit the person is. The Report of the Committee of the Royal College of Psychiatrists (1979) suggests that the intake of 4 pints of beer a day, 4 double spirits, or 1 standard-sized bottle of wine constitutes a reasonable guideline for the upper limit of drinking. Davies (1980) maintains that an intake twice daily of 5–6 pints is bound to cause harm in time. Only three residential subjects took alcohol more than once a day, and another three adoptees and two residential people consumed alcohol daily. Adopted people had an average of 6.6 pints each session (s.d. 5.2), compared with 8.5 pints (s.d. 5.6) consumed by residential people. Acknowledging the difficulties faced in reaching a decision as to what constitutes excessive alcohol consumption, Table 6.9 sets out the number of drinks people said they had each time they drank. If we were to take 11 pints or more as a sign of excessive drinking at any one time, then 13 (36 per cent) of those who grew up in Homes, and five (13 per cent) adopted people would come into this category. Though significantly more residential than adopted people were classified as heavy drinkers, if we were to take 8 pints or more as constituting heavy drinking then the differences between the two groups would be small. Heavy drinking among former foster children was insignificant (Triseliotis 1980b).

Table 6.9   Amount of alcohol consumed each time

Number of pints at each session (or equivalent)*	Adoption N	%	Residential N	%
No drinks	3	8	4	11
1–3 drinks	15	38	8	22
4–6 drinks	6	15	6	17
8–10 drinks	10	26	5	14
11 drinks or over	5	13	13	36
	39	100	36	100
Missing	5		4	
	44		40	

* In constructing the table, 2 spirits were equated with 1 pint.

Whilst the amount of drink did not appear to be related to the adoptees' view of the outcome of their adoption, increased amount of alcohol comsumption among the residential group was associated with negative or mixed feelings about the experience of growing up in a Home ($\tau C = 0.31$, $p < 0.05$). Similarly, increased amount of drinking was associated with increased emotional distance from the adoptive father and somewhat from the house-mother. Heavy drinkers among the residential group were also more likely to have contacts with natural parents. However, as there was no connection between heavy drinking among residential people and their families of origin, it cannot be assumed that the former were influenced in this direction by their families. In other words, those who had contact with their parents were likely to be heavy drinkers, but the parents were not. The contact may have been a search for relationships and support.

Timing of reception into care, age at placement and number of moves did not appear to be related to the amount of alcohol consumed. Females growing up in Homes were more likely than those growing up adopted to drink excessively.

Age started to drink
Eleven (26 per cent) of those who grew up adopted and 19 (38 per cent) of those who grew up in Homes started to drink when under 16. Respondents in both groups gave similar reasons for taking up drink. The most common one had to do with being a 'man', and being 'like the others'. Typical comments were: 'everyone else was doing it', 'others did it,' 'to be big and show off', 'it was the thing', 'it's the fashion', 'it seemed the big thing to do', 'I wanted to be a man'. Others referred to boredom, to having nothing else to do, and to liking it. One person who started drinking at 15 or 16 summarised many other similar comments by saying: 'Trying to be big, it was the thing to do.'

Almost all drinking was done in company with others and it was rarely a lone activity. The reasons for which people drank did not differ between the two groups. When respondents were asked whether there were certain times when they were likely to take alcoholic drinks, most replies were linked to being in a particular mood, such as anger, pressure, worries, after an argument, emotional upset, to relax, when things are on top of me, when bored. On the social side, subjects referred to taking alcohol at celebrations, special events and happenings and on other occasions to be 'sociable'. Whilst a couple mentioned depression as one of the likely times when they would drink, at least twice that number made the point that they avoided alcoholic drinks when feeling depressed.

Problems linked to drinking
Alcohol-related problems did not differ significantly between the two

groups. A fifth of those adopted and a quarter of those who grew up in Homes said that their drinking often led to moderate problems, with two of the residential people describing them as 'severe'. Both adoptees and residential people reported fewer alcohol-related problems compared with the general Scottish population, but this might be related to their young age at interview. Plant (1982) claims that when the overall level of consumption rises, so alcohol problems increase, but the precise relationships between alcohol and certain types of problem remains obscure.

Drinking and driving, breach of the peace whilst under the influence of drink, or assault following drinking were some of the common problems. More domestic-type problems included arguments with spouse and parents. Heavy drinking overlapped considerably with court appearances and adversely affected the respondents' feelings of well-being ($p < 0.002$). Residential subjects reporting alcohol-related problems were also very likely to report emotional problems at interview and to have recently had psychiatric help. Similarly, psychiatric problems in childhood among residential people were almost always indicative of alcohol abuse in later life.

Friendship

Seven (16 per cent) of adoptees and eleven (28 per cent) of those who grew up in Homes reported difficulties in making friends and in mixing. These ranged from moderate to severe difficulties. One residential person, for instance, spoke of how he was unable to relate to people of his own age and how he preferred to be on his own most of the time. Another one remarked that she was very 'frightened' to allow people to get close to her. Other residential people, particularly, talked about being 'lonely', 'isolated' or 'too shy to initiate friendships'. A young woman talked of her 'suspiciousness' towards people and so avoided social relationships. Another one talked of having 'acquaintances' but not friends. R. talked of a 'barrier' going up between her and other people which prevented her from making any friendships. Lack of 'trust' was mentioned by some for preferring their own company.

Those expressing some difficulty in the area of friendships and relationships were also likely to express dissatisfaction with their growing-up experience. Adoptees who reported friendship problems were also likely to have experienced psychiatric problems, to say that their adoption made life difficult for them, and in addition to feel distant from their adoptive mother. Residential people reporting friendship and relationship problems were also likely to report distance from the housemother. Residential people, but not adoptees, who reported friendship problems in childhood were also likely to report them in adult life.

'Disturbed' respondents

The next step was an attempt to identify the most 'disturbed' respondents in each group. Respondents who shared two or more of the following four indices signifying some form of psychological or social disturbance were classified as disturbed: (i) serious relationship problems with marital partners and friends; (ii) psychiatric referral in adult life; (iii) heavy drinking (including one person on drugs); and (iv) acquiring a criminal record (except for motoring offences). Based on this classification seven (16 per cent) adoptees and 15 (38 per cent) residential people were classified as disturbed. In effect, significantly more residential people than adoptees came under this classification (χ^2, $p < 0.05$). One adoptee and seven residential people had three or more indices signifying 'disturbance'.

Taking those who had serious material problems (i.e. income and/or housing) and those who were classified as 'disturbed', ten (23 per cent) adoptees and 23 (57 per cent) residential people were classified as either facing serious material problems or being 'disturbed'. Only one adoptee and five residential people were classified as being both 'disturbed' and as having serious financial and housing problems. This would suggest that poor material conditions and 'disturbed' behaviour do not necessarily overlap in any significant way. In other words, respondents who had serious money and housing problems were not necessarily also 'disturbed'. It is possible that in the long run their social conditions, if remained unchanged, might affect their psychological well-being or their 'disturbed' behaviour worsen their material conditions.

In an attempt to identify how far current material inadequacies among respondents were the result of possible personality factors, the following procedure was adopted. Based on the assumption that people with personality problems would have a history of psychiatric help in childhood, a number of correlations were attempted between certain conditions indicating material inadequacies and psychiatric help in childhood. In the first place no relationship could be established between housing and income inadequacies (including dependence on social security) and psychiatric referral in childhood. There was equally no evidence that those facing the worst financial and housing conditions were likely to have had psychiatric help as children. There was some evidence, though not statistically significant, showing that residential people drawing social security were likely to have had a psychiatric referral in the 12 months leading up to the interview. Similarly, dependence on social security among residential people was linked to the presence of moderate to severe emotional problems both in childhood and in adult life. However, when it comes to psychiatric conditions, and a large number of residential people had psychiatric help, no significant relationship could be established between dependence on social security, income or housing inadequacies and psychiatric referral in childhood or in adult life. These findings suggest that financial and housing inadequacies in the sample groups existed independently of personality problems.

Current sense of emotional well-being
Respondents in both groups were asked to describe and rate feelings of contentment and well-being relating to themselves and about life in general at the time of the interview. Nine out of ten of those adopted, but only six out of ten of those who grew up in Homes rated their feelings from 'good' to 'very good', with the remaining ones recording them as 'uncertain' or 'poor'. Overall, adoptees reported much greater contentment and satisfaction within themselves compared to those who grew up in Homes. Those who felt contented and positive about themselves used expressions such as: 'very satisfied', 'very happy', 'I wouldn't change my life', 'I have a good life', 'I couldn't ask for a better life', 'I have very good feelings' and 'good generally'.

Significantly more of those who grew up in Homes expressed uncertainty and a poor sense of well-being at interview. Though only four adopted people expressed uncertainty about their emotional life, all four also expressed somewhat less satisfaction or outright dissatisfaction with their adoption. This also held true of those who grew up in Homes, who also tended to view the influence of institutions on their lives as of 'mixed value' or as downright 'harmful' ($\tau C = 0.46$, $p < 0.0008$).

There was no significant relationship between feelings of well-being and age at reception into care or age at final placement, but an increasing number of moves between different institutions increased the possibility of poor feelings of well-being expressed by the residential group. Those who experienced no change or a single change were more likely to say they felt 'good', 'happy' or 'content' ($\tau C = 0.22$, $p < 0.05$).

Capacity to cope with life
Almost 90 per cent of those adopted and two-thirds of those who grew up in residential care expressed confidence in themselves to cope with life's demands. The rest expressed different states of uncertainty. In effect, significantly more of those adopted saw themselves as coping 'adequately' compared with those who grew up in Homes ($p < 0.025$). The majority of respondents in both groups showed remarkable

confidence and optimism in their capacity to cope in spite sometimes of fairly adverse social conditions among a number of residential people. Those who felt they were coping adequately sometimes would also qualify that statement: 'I think I am coping quite "adequately" taking everything into account'; 'no great worries'; 'I reckon I'm not doing bad'; 'I am coping adequately, I feed my kids, I clothe them, I bring them up'; 'I feel I cope as well as can be expected'; 'I think I have done rather well, I cope pretty well'; and 'I think I have accomplished something'. Residential people were especially pleased when they were doing well: 'I am coping splendidly'; 'I can cope with life very well'; 'I can cope very well with living on my own.' They generally seemed to connect adequate coping as a challenge to the way they grew up and to their parents' failure to cope.

Residential people who were less certain used expressions such as 'on my own I am uncertain', 'I have got some reservations', and 'I am feeling like running away from things sometimes.' One residential person who was being helped by a social worker over problems connected with rent arrears and electricity commented: 'I suppose I am O.K. Just that at times I don't feel like living anywhere . . . things get on top of your shoulders.' Adoptees and residential subjects who expressed uncertainties about their coping abilities were also likely to report emotional problems at interview. In addition, residential subjects were also likely to have had psychiatric help in the 12 months preceding the interview.

Level of satisfaction with their present life
When subjects were asked about the level and kind of satisfaction they had with their present life, all but three adoptees reported themselves to be very happy or fairly happy (Table 6.10). In contrast, only two-thirds of those who grew up in Homes expressed similar feelings, with one-third reporting mixed feelings. Perhaps the biggest difference between the two groups was the proportion of outright satisfaction (61 per cent) expressed by adopted persons compared with only 20 per cent by those who grew up in Homes. Even when the levels of satisfaction are combined into two groups, i.e. very happy and fairly happy, and contrasted with mixed views and fairly unhappy, significantly more residential subjects said they were less happy compared with those adopted ($p < 0.01$). Considering the background of the adopted group and the discontinuities of care they experienced in early life, the high level of satisfaction expressed about themselves, their positive sense of well-being and their capacity to cope with life could be seen as considerable. It is a reminder of Clarke and Clarke's (1976) conclusion that the whole of development is

important, not merely the early years. There is as yet no indication that a given stage is clearly more formative than others; in the long term all may be important. Though our samples were small, the indications are that deficiencies and 'deprivations' can be modified through subsequent positive and compensating experiences. This does not, of course, mean that children should be exposed to psychological hazards because of the possibility of reversibility of the condition later on. It could equally be claimed that residential people, in spite of a life of institutional living, discontinuities in care and moves, whilst doing significantly less well than adoptees, nevertheless were showing a remarkably resilience to continual adversities. The difference between those doing 'well' and the rest cannot be explained by simple experiences in the past but by a complexity of past and current circumstances. Past deficiencies, though, were a determinant factor when not ameliorated.

Table 6.10 Life satisfactions by groups

	Adoption		Residential	
	N	%	N	%
Very happy	27	61	8	20
Fairly happy	14	32	19	47
Mixed views	2	5	12	30
Fairly unhappy	1	2	1	3
	44	100	40	100

The most frequently quoted satisfactions expressed by residential subjects were connected with having a family: 'having a wife and son', 'house, marriage and present way of life', 'having a baby', 'marriage', 'husband, family life', 'son and family'; work was another area of satisfaction. Most adoptees expressed feelings of general 'happiness', and typical comments included: 'everything very satisfactory', 'couldn't have asked for a better life', 'just happy in general', 'very satisfied with most things', 'very satisfied with personal and social circumstances', 'generally happy'. Family life featured too but it was subordinate to wider feelings of satisfaction and 'happiness' with the way things were. In effect, family life seemed to matter much more to residential people who felt they missed it in their own childhood than to adopted people who took it for granted.

Grey areas of dissatisfaction among adoptees included comments about work: 'Not settled enough in job'; 'getting fed up with job sometimes'; and about being 'lonely', or 'boredom' and with aspects connected with being adopted such as 'unhappy with my adoption at times'; 'wish I was somebody else'; 'regret not having met natural parents'; one expressed fear of losing her adoptive family. Whilst two said there was nothing to feel satisfied about, some others quoted more individual areas of dissatisfaction, such as: 'Would like to know more about my history'; 'lack of mum and dad to baby sit'; 'loneliness'; 'job' or 'arguments'.

The influence of the past on the present
Respondents in both groups were asked a number of interrelated questions aimed at eliciting information about the possible influence of the past on their current personal and social functioning. They were asked to comment upon and rate: the overall influence of adoption or residential experience on their present life; to say how far the experiences made life difficult for them and in what way; and indicate whether they missed anything by having grown up adopted or in residential care.

The influence of the past on the subjects' present life
Seven out of every ten of those adopted and four out of every ten of those who grew up in Homes said that the form of care they experienced was beneficial to their current lives, but 13 (30 per cent) of those adopted and 24 (60 per cent) of those who grew up in Homes expressed mixed views or said it was 'harmful' (Table 6.11). Overall, adoptees were far more likely than residential people to say that the past had a beneficial effect on their current life. Many residential people were particularly critical and bitter about their experience. The lack of individuality, care, understanding and of 'normal' life was still affecting them, they claimed, in many areas of their lives. Bitter comments such as 'erase' institutions, or 'abolish' or 'close' them were made. As stated before, only a minority said that institutions were 'beneficial'. One of the memories from the past that still affected some adoptees but even more so residential people was the feeling of rejection by their own families: 'I felt unwanted and rejected by my parents . . . they didn't care about me, that's why they put me in a Home.' For a minority of adopted people the element of rejection still mattered, but for most it seemed to have no meaning because, as many put it, they were wanted by their adoptive parents.

Table 6.11 The influence of the past on the present

	Adoption N	%	Residential N	%
Beneficial	30	70	16	40
Mixed	11	25	16	40
Harmful	2	5	8	20
	43	100	40	100
Missing	1			
	44			

Does being adopted or having grown up in an institution ever make life difficult for you?

The point was made earlier that an important ingredient in personality development is the experience of being perceived by others as a worthwhile person. The work of Goffman (1963) has alerted us to the fact that the images we develop about ourselves are considerably influenced by the way others see us. In effect, that our self-concept is partly based on the perceptions of others about us, which in turn affects where we think we fit in society. Goffman developed the concept of 'spoiled identity' to signify the impact of stigma and labelling on individuals and minority groups who are seen to be different or to defy the norm. Children brought up outwith their natural families may be seen as 'different' or as having no place, either because they are being reared by people other than their own kin, or because of the behaviour of their parents of origin. In effect societal attitudes can affect personal identity. Goffman (1961) pointed out how 'failure or success at manipulating such norms has a very direct effect on the psychological integrity of the individual.'

When respondents were asked whether being adopted or having grown up in a Home created any problems for them, significantly more of those who grew up in Homes referred to problems compared to adoptees ($p < 0.001$). About a third of adoptees expressed concerns which had to do with issues about self-concept and identity. In other words, they related their comments to genealogical factors and very few to feeling discriminated against or being perceived as 'different'. On the other hand, most of the 71 per cent who grew up in residential

Homes and who said that such an experience 'makes life difficult' connected their difficulties primarily with lack of individual care, regimentation and community labelling. Genealogical factors were important but somewhat secondary compared to the quality of caring they had and the community's perception of them. Respondents from both groups who felt that their growing-up experience made life difficult for them were also likely to report emotional/psychiatric problems at the interview. Among adoptees this view correlated with an increase in the number of all children in the family (τ C=0.30, p < 0.04) or with being the youngest child.

Adoption group. As stated above, 68 per cent of those adopted said confidently that being adopted did not create any problems or make life difficult for them. The most typical responses were: 'My adoption causes me no problems'; 'I have no trouble over being adopted'; 'being adopted never bothered me'; 'it never worries me'; 'my adoption never made me feel mixed-up or led me into any trouble whatsoever'; 'I quite like it, no trouble at all'; and 'I think personally I was better off.' One adoptee remarked: 'I never think of myself as being adopted. . . . I am glad that I was adopted'; others, 'I am not treated any differently by other people'; 'it has never bothered me being adopted. . . . I regard my mum and dad as a real mum and dad'; 'it never bothered me that I was adopted. It never made me feel any different. . . . I don't foresee any difficulties from being adopted.'

Others too added that their adoption never stood in their way and it never made them feel different. Some adoptees connected this with their readiness to share the fact of their adoption. Most of them were clear that they did not mind telling other people that they were adopted, but as this was a personal matter they wanted to be selective about the people with whom they shared this important bit of information:

> I don't go round telling people I was adopted. If it comes out in conversation I don't mind telling them . . . it is a private business. . . . I don't mind telling friends. . . . I found it easy to accept my adoption.

Similarly, they didn't like their parents telling everybody that they were adopted. They perceived this either as a form of attack or as a way of stressing the differences: 'What bugged me when I was young was that my mother introduced me as her "adopted daughter" – I hated being introduced as that. It used to screw me up.' E.'s hatred of the idea of being seen as different made her unable to talk about her adoption for some time: 'I thought it was a real sin to be adopted.'

Most adoptees did not feel that they were treated differently by other members of the community because they were adopted: 'I assume people round about had known I was adopted . . . but I don't think it made any difference to how I was treated'; 'Everyone who spoke to me about my adoption accepted me as one of the gang – I was always made to feel much the same as others.' Only a tiny minority referred to some discrimination and to possible prejudice. Though they did not necessarily feel that their adoption created problems for them, nevertheless, they were sensitive to comments that made them feel somewhat different. J., who experienced his adoption as most beneficial and who said that there was nothing about adoption that made him unhappy, felt 'stigmatised at school for being adopted' and that because of his adoption he was not fully accepted by the extended family. One adoptee said that he had it thrown at him by other boys at school that he was 'only adopted' and another felt that a lot of young people tried to make him 'feel different': 'Their appreciation was that you were different – that originally someone didn't want you – secondhand – that kind of attitude.' Other adoptees and residential people linked rejection by the original family as something that would always nag them. One person who was often teased at school for being adopted remarked: 'At school there were a few of us adopted. I got teased about it and got called all sorts of names but it never really bothered me.' The stress some adoptees put on 'not being different from anyone else' could be interpreted as an indication of some concern about their place in society.

Quite a number of adoptees who did not necessarily connect the fact of being adopted with any personal 'crisis' or 'unhappiness' nevertheless made comments which indicated their wish to know more about their genealogy and background 'to complete' themselves. This was the only connection they could think linking adoption with personal situations: 'The only question is that of identity – families can go back to their family tree, but I can't. I always question myself on this but there is no answer.' Others too said that their adoption didn't bother them, but that they wished they knew more about their original parents and their background and why they were given up. There was no suggestion that such thoughts were unduly bothering them but information around these areas would have added to their contentment: 'It is difficult for me not knowing who my real parents were, you know. . . . I am not unhappy for having grown up adopted at all, but sometimes I wonder and worry about them.'

Not surprisingly the few adoptees who were decisive about the fact that their adoption created problems for them were also likely to express mixed feelings about the outcome of their substitute care: 'I feel as though I am a lesser person up to a point, though I know I am not. . . . I suppose I feel awkward about it, although I cannot actually say in what ways. I don't know myself'; 'it took me a while to accept my adoption . . . chip on my shoulder . . . maybe I thought I was different from everyone else. Maybe that is why I am really fighting authority.' P., who never thought of her adoptive parents as real parents, attributed her difficulties in relating and expressing feelings to her adoption. Similarly, H. attributed his personal problems, including being sent to approved school, Borstal and prison to the failure of his adoption and the way he was brought up. E., who had mixed feelings about his adoption, claimed that being adopted made it difficult for him to make friends easily and since breaking off with his mother and father he had no one to turn to. A., though feeling satisfied with the way her adoption turned out, was terribly saddened by the death of both adoptive parents and felt 'out on a limb'. She went on: 'I often wish I was someone else, I don't know why. Maybe it is the fact that I was adopted. I don't know.'

The views of residential people. It was stated earlier that 71 per cent of residential people said that being brought up in a Home created moderate to severe problems for them. Apart from the lack of individual care, etc. discussed in Chapter 4, the main problems here were that being brought up in a Home 'makes you feel different from others'. The sense of being different was especially experienced at school and to a lesser extent when looking for their first job. Subjects tended to compare themselves with others and to see themselves as different because of having no parents and having to live in an institution. They were aware that not all of these feelings were the result of outside prejudice and discrimination but the combination of how other people saw them and how they came to see themselves. This seemed to have left its mark on their self-concept and identity. The feeling of being different, 'stigmatised' or 'labelled' because of growing up in institutions cut across perceptions of satisfaction/dissatisfaction with the care experience. More important, such feelings were seen to influence their perception of themselves in adult life. Meacher (1972) and Szasz (1973) maintain that perceived stigma can shape both the behaviour of the residents and staff and community responses to them.

The experience of being different in the school environment. Residential subjects generally felt that there was prejudice towards them and that they were looked down upon by other children and seen as 'inferior' or 'bad'. The term 'Homey' or 'convent' kids which was applied to them came to have a derogatory and stigmatising effect:

'Just being in a Home made me feel different and inferior to others . . . everyone else has their own parents. . . . I wanted parents like everybody else.' One person remarked that she felt different from other school children and from her friends because she never had a mother and father and for the fact that she was always called a Home kid. Another one added:

> When you said you lived in E. Home there was an instant dislike by other kids because you were different. . . . I knew I was different from them. I couldn't go round and pick my own clothes – I was wearing regulation drainpipe trousers. I went to secondary school in shorts and there was nothing more humiliating than that.

S., like others, also commented on how she was classed as a 'Home child' at school: 'At school it was the "Home children" this and the 'Home children" that. That is when it started coming [sinking] in. . . . People saying that if you are in a Home you are bad.'

J. spoke for others when he said: 'Other children used to make up names for us because we were from D.B.'s – trying to get at us because we had no parents or something. . . . the majority of the kids at school didn't want to know us so we never really got to know any adults outside.' In a similar vein, I. added:

> You had a certain amount of trouble because you were always recognised as being a child from the Home. We used to go to school on a special bus, we all dressed very similarly so you were very recognisable . . . you were different . . . you always stood out – you were classed as a child from the Home.

Residential people felt resentment for practices and regulations concerning clothing, outings and visits that made them stand out from the rest of the children: 'They knew you were in a Home basically because when you do go out you are always in groups with an adult.' Rigid rules discouraging frequent outings with non-Home children seemed to add to the feeling of being different and separate. Some people not only felt different from other school children but experienced real feelings of envy in relation to them because they had families: 'Fellow pupils knew you were in a Home and you yourself felt real bad because they were going home to their parents, warm homes, etc. When you went to visit your pals' house it was then that it [the difference] began to dawn on you.'

G. put it more simply: 'I felt different from others . . . they were staying with their parents and I was staying in a Home.' Another one: 'I hated others knowing that I was in a Home . . . they all had family lives and we didn't. . . . I would have liked to have been a normal kid, like everyone else – have a mother and a father.' A third person added:

'At school I was afraid to tell anyone that I lived in a Home.' E. was very graphic when describing why children from the Home came to see themselves as not being 'normal':

> I always felt I was different. We always said 'normal children' when referring to others, as though we were different. They [other children] thought that they must keep away from us because we were bad. How could you make them understand that you are not bad?

Only a small number of subjects experienced teachers as being prejudiced against Home children: 'Teachers thought we were uneducable and lazy kids and that you were a trouble being from the Home.'

Perceptions of the wider community. The most often repeated comment was the feeling that the wider community equated being in a Home with being 'bad'. One person expressed the views of others by saying: 'The attitude most people had was that if you were in care you must have done something wrong'; 'People feeling that if you are in a Home it's because you have been bad. . . . in the back of my mind was "what had I done so bad and terrible to get in a Home?"'; and 'If anything happened in the village the police would come to the Home.' Residential people generally didn't like outside people knowing that they were living in an institution because they were afraid of the 'stigma': 'You knew you were different from the way people looked at you and spoke to you. You did feel different.' Another one added: 'Outside the Home I seemed to think there was something different about me. . . . I don't know what it was. . . . I don't think anyone ever really treated me different, but I always thought they did. . . . I didn't get along well with people because I had a stigma. . . . I didn't like people knowing I was in a Home. I hated them knowing it at school.'

Residential people were aware that some people were well-meaning but possibly went about it in a way that made them feel awkward: 'People often say, "Oh, what a shame – no family."'; 'The more people try to make you feel the same the more different you feel'; 'The feeling that this is a poor little girl from the Home and we must make the kid feel welcome is hopeless, it never works . . . they make everybody notice you.' Another subject commented: 'People who knew you came from a Home tended to pity you . . . what a shame living in a Home . . . the pity made you feel different.' Whilst a few didn't mind telling others about growing up in a Home, others tried to conceal it or were unhappy when faced with questions concerning the issue: 'I wouldn't tell people I grew up in a Home – only if I were close to them.'

M. remarked that this started to strike her when she was asked, or is still asked, awkward questions such as 'What does your daddy do?': 'What on earth can you say? You can't say very much because you don't know yourself.' Another one: 'When they ask you where you are from you find yourself trying to explain about it and getting into difficulties'; 'I used to be called "Home kid" – now I never speak about it unless somebody asks . . . sometimes you wished you didn't have to say you came from a Home.' 'If', another remarked, 'you tell people you grew up in a Home you also have to explain why and it is not easy.'

Problems. The feeling of being different, the fear of being discriminated against because of having grown up in a Home, or of being unable to be like one's peers was experienced particularly by subjects who continued to live in Homes after the age of 16 and who were looking for jobs or attending establishments of higher education. Living in a Home and trying to get a job or filling in forms presented problems because they had to give the Home as an address. Sometimes they didn't even know the names of their parents or where they were born. Similarly, they resented staff or co-residents answering the 'phone to would-be employers and announcing 'This is ___ Children's Home'. Another one added: 'When you start work and people ask you where you live, it is difficult to say in such and such a Home.' Compared to those growing up adopted or in long-term foster care, those growing up in residential establishments were the most stigmatised.

Whilst most subjects made comments which indicated a sense of being made to feel different at some stage and how this might have a continuing effect on their self-perception, a minority did not perceive any difference and didn't mind telling others that they grew up in a Home: 'It never bothered me'; 'no difference, just the same as everybody else'; 'I don't mind telling people I grew up in a Home.' A couple of them stressed the fact that more people accepted than rejected them.

What respondents said they missed by growing up adopted or in residential care

Asked to say what they missed by growing up adopted or in residential care 31 (73 per cent) adopted people and six (15 per cent) residential subjects said 'nothing'. The rest were either uncertain or very specific about what they thought they missed. Those who said they missed something described it in terms of lack of roots or of family life, or of not being loved enough. The lack of roots or of family life was stressed by almost all residential people. Their comments contrasted sharply with those of adoptees, most of whom felt they experienced a secure family life. Typical comments made by about 70 per cent of adopted people included: 'I have never felt I missed anything'; 'nothing I can think of'; 'nothing missed'; 'nothing missed . . . you don't know if it would have been better not being adopted. I think my parents have done as much for me as they could.'

An equally realistic view was expressed by another adopted person:

> I wouldn't say I have missed anything growing up adopted, but I feel as though I have missed things with the parents I have but I couldn't put it down to the fact that I was adopted. . . . I suppose other people have missed out on other things . . . but not because of adoption.'

Another simply said: 'I had a nice home and a happy childhood, missed nothing.' Adoptees who felt they missed 'something' by growing up adopted were also likely to have reported school problems, emotional problems and psychiatric referral in childhood. Having a negative view or mixed feelings about the adoption experience was also associated with the feeling of having missed something by the experience but this association was less significant among the residential group. Those who felt they missed something were also likely to say that the community or relatives treated them differently.

What adopted people said they missed. 'Not knowing where my roots lie'; 'not quite the same as everyone else'; 'missed feeling of belonging'; 'I had not really been loved for myself'; 'missed real love from my adoptive father'; 'not close enough to adoptive mother when I was growing up'; 'could not bring kids home because of the age of my mother'. One person said that being the first and only child, his parents hadn't got 'past knowledge' of bringing up children, but he didn't think that he had really missed out.

What residential people said they missed. The most frequent statement made by residential people was connected with missing parents and family life: 'general family life'; 'mum and dad'; 'normal childhood'; 'one set of parents' love'; 'family love'; 'a home with parents'; 'parents'; 'a real home'; 'love'; 'a father-figure'; 'freedom to determine own life'; 'having my own things'. But one person missed 'the end of care'. Some other comments had to do with opportunities to mix with 'ordinary' children and people outside the Home. The theme of missing having one's own family was expressed in a variety of ways: 'I missed growing up with my mum and dad . . . being split from my sisters I thought – as bad'; 'I was fairly happy with the Home life but I would still like to know what it is like to have parents and to live in a family . . . you can never get as close to people as to a family.' Another one added: 'you missed your parents, their attitudes towards you, what they wanted for you'; 'missed the general family life, your mother and their coming to see you at night. . . . I always wanted to be part of a family.' Another person simply missed 'love' or 'a parent's love and care'. J. said he 'lost a lot of love' by being brought up in a Home; and G., by not having 'a real family life', felt she could not 'fit' and felt 'just a nobody'. Another person said that he 'missed a lot of his childhood'.

A few subjects linked this theme with their wish to have been adopted or fostered: 'I missed family life and would have liked to be adopted or fostered.' Another one spoke for others who felt they missed having a family when he said he wished he had been given the choice of being adopted 'having somebody that properly cared. I missed a family relationship. Love in a family.' Another one: 'I wish I had been brought up by good parents.' H. also remarked: 'I would have liked to have been adopted . . . now you are kind of left to fend for yourself and I think it is difficult though I am grown up.' A sadder comment made by one young woman was how it was only the 'younger ones who got adopted. It wasn't the in-betweens.'

Some respondents referred to the need for those living in Homes to be in touch with the wider community and mix with children from outside: 'Children in care should get into the world and see more people outside the Home; to discuss life with them, to socialise, to see the outside world. I got a shock when I first came out of residential care.' Another commented on the same theme: 'In the Convent we didn't have a chance to mix with any outside sort of children, so I didn't know any different'; 'You were not allowed out like other kids.'

Subjects also blamed the rigid rules and and outlook of the staff for not being able to mix, invite other children and be invited to people's homes. On the few occasions when some had the opportunity of visiting either their own families or other families or friends interested in them they appreciated it considerably and looked forward to the next opportunity. The occasional contact with children from outside the Home also generated considerable envy towards the children who had families to go back to. This was also accompanied by a fair amount of interest in the way 'normal' people lived and there was a wish to know more about it.

There were regrets about the uniformity of activities and particularly the lack of opportunity to play an active part in the daily life of the Home and equally participate in decisions about themselves. Life in general seemed to them to extend dependency through the lack of opportunities for sharing in the life of the Home and the community and from the absence of choices in their daily living. Miller and

Gwynne (1972) comment that 'the lack of any actual and potential role that confers a positive status in the wider society is tantamount to being socially dead.'

Only six (15 per cent) of those who grew up in Homes said they missed nothing by growing up in a residential establishment. A typical remark from this group was: 'the influence was not harmful but it could have been better . . . the only thing I missed was not having a father-figure around'; or simply: 'I didn't miss anything.' Among these were some who knew that if left with their parents they 'wouldn't have gone anywhere' in life.

Current feelings of closeness to adoptive parents or house-parents
Eight out of ten of those adopted and three out of ten of those who grew up in Homes said they felt close or very close to their adoptive parents or house-parents respectively. Most of the others described their relationships as mostly distant or very distant or having no contact at all at present.

Adoptees generally talked with warmth about their closeness to parental figures and with considerable sadness in the case of those who lost one or both parents through death: 'I appreciated more what they had done for me'; 'We get on exceptionally well'; and 'never been closer to each other'.

The respondents' view about the outcome of their substitute care experience was unrelated to their current closeness to adoptive mothers or residential house-mothers. However, distance from 'parent' figures experienced in childhood was likely to be reported also in adult life.

About a third of those adopted were still living at home with their parents, and another 20 (47 per cent) visited frequently, with eight visiting occasionally or rarely, and one not visiting at all. About a fifth of residential subjects visited the Home frequently and about a quarter occasionally. The rest either never visited or had no contact at all. (About a fifth of residential subjects claimed to be writing frequently or occasionally to house-parents.)

The next question was to ask adoptees living at home or those visiting to describe current home atmosphere. Two-thirds described the atmosphere as warm, friendly, welcoming, pleasant, relaxed, etc. Another four (9 per cent) described it as rather formal, and the remaining five (12 per cent) of those visiting found it edgy, tense or distant. The two-thirds who found the atmosphere welcoming and relaxed talked about it in enthusiastic and warm terms: 'Magic, it feels great'; 'very welcoming atmosphere'; 'I find it pleasant to visit my parents'; 'perhaps closer relationships now than before'; 'friendly atmosphere'; 'a very tolerant home'; 'my parents are very fond of me and glad to see me and my children'; 'they can't do enough for me when I go home'; 'the atmosphere is the same as ever with good relationships'; 'I feel a bit closer to my mother now'; 'better than ever before'; 'I am always glad to see my parents'; 'perhaps I see dad more than mum . . . I feel she [mum] can't let herself go though I feel she wants to'; 'I love them more than ever'; 'it is great going back home . . . fairly close to my mother'. One person who had mixed feelings about his childhood experience, now seemed to be looking forward to going home every weekend: 'I go home whenever I can . . . every weekend if I am not on duty. The atmosphere now is much better than when I was a child. I am very close to my mother now. . . . I speak to her easily and she is not so heavy and demanding.' The feelings of those who thought they had a secure base were expressed by one adoptee who said: 'my room is there, always tidy for me. . . . I look forward to going home. There are no conflicts.' And another: 'I always go down on a Monday and go and see gran on Thursday or Friday . . . as far as I am concerned I go and make myself at home.'

Those who found the atmosphere formal included one adoptee who felt she had to make an appointment before she visited her mother: 'An entry in my mother's diary – just someone else whom she has to see – an appointment, nothing else. The atmosphere at home is very formal.'

Some of those who found the atmosphere tense or edgy remarked: 'When I go home the arguments with my mother about my behaviour and my attitude towards them continue'; 'there is a tense feeling – not as good an atmosphere as before'; 'comfortable with my mother but not very comfortable with my father'. One adoptee said he was resentful about the obligation he felt towards his ageing parents. Another one, who went through a lot of difficulties, said that he was not allowed to visit.

Finally, respondents were asked to say whether they would have liked any aspects of their past experience to have been different. Six out of ten of those adopted and nine out of ten of those who grew up in Homes said 'Yes'. Not all of those who answered 'Yes' to this question found the experience dissatisfying, they simply wanted to stress how increased satisfaction would have been achieved if some of their wishes had been fulfilled. Adoptees put most of the emphasis on relationships and on more background information about the original family, whilst residential people stressed the lack of family life, poor relationships, absence of genealogical information and the absence of contacts with the community.

When adoptees were asked to say what they would have liked to be different, some of them linked it to feelings about their adoption: 'Wished I got on better with my adoptive father'; 'to have been loved for myself'; 'had less arguments with my mother'; 'were closer to my mother when I was growing up'; 'had not been adopted to replace someone else who had died'; 'had younger parents'; and 'that my adoption had worked out better'. Another group of four linked it with the need to have known more about their background: 'Would like to have known more about my adoption and my parents'; 'to have known more about my "first" mother and father'.

Most of the 36 (90 per cent) of those who grew up in Homes and who wished things were different linked it with their dissatisfaction of growing up in a Home: 'I wish the Home had been investigated'; 'I wish I hadn't been in the Home'; 'missed being a normal kid'; 'hadn't been so many people involved with my life'; 'had known about the outside world'; 'I wish I hadn't been in a Home'; 'I regret being in the Home'; 'I wish I hadn't had a bully of a house-parent.' A few others added that they wished they were adopted or fostered: 'I would rather have been adopted'; 'rather have been adopted or fostered'; 'rather have had a mother'; 'had parents all the time'.

Regrets about having grown up in a Home were also linked to feelings about the natural family: 'I wished my own mother and father had not died'; 'I wish my family had not separated'; 'that my own mother had not died'; 'that I had known my mum and dad'; 'to have known more about my parents'; 'that I had been with my own folks'. Whilst some adoptees regretted aspects of their adoption and others would have liked to have been closer to their adoptive parents, most residential people regretted most aspects of their residential life and the lack of family life in their formative years.

Preparation for leaving residential care

Recent literature on residential care has put emphasis on the preparation of young people for living in the community. Those living in residential institutions have distinct problems when trying to establish themselves both in adulthood and in the community. Apart from the handicap of being in an institution and all that is associated with this form of growing up, there is also the lack of support that most young people normally expect and get from their families. In contrast, the residential people featuring in this study had experienced disruptions, rejections and frustrations, not qualities to facilitate the transition from childhood to adult life. Because of this there is increasing recognition that young people leaving care require considerable preparation and help in a range of life-space areas. This kind of preparation and help, it is argued, should enable the young people to settle down and begin to make a life for themselves. The young people featuring in this study left care in the early and mid-1970s when awareness of the importance of preparation for leaving care was being given increased publicity. It could be rightly argued that preparation for leaving care should start on the day of reception into care rather than a few months before discharge.

Those who grew up in residential Homes were asked to say how much preparation and help they had before leaving the Homes in the following life-space areas: employment, accommodation, home management and money management. They were also asked to comment on how much general support they had from the Home after leaving care. Part of the aim was to establish whether such preparation in the end makes any difference to the overall social functioning of young people leaving care. The findings, however, need to be treated with caution because preparation for leaving care was mostly a haphazard and spasmodic effort rather than a well-thought-out and planned activity with close coordination between residential and field services. More important, any help given before leaving care was rarely sustained and continued by follow-up support. There was only a single example of one Home running a nearby hostel to which Home residents would move a few months before leaving care, and where they were given considerable responsibility in budgeting and running the place. The overall aim was to enable the young people to become more independent and be able to manage on their own after leaving the Home. In contrast one other Home 'pushed' the boys towards a career in the armed forces, thus avoiding any responsibility for preparatory or follow-up work. It is possible that these house-parents may have felt that children who grew up in residential care need the protection of another institution during their early adult lives.

The view of most respondents was that they received little or no preparation to face 'the outside world' and that they felt cut off from the surrounding community during their stay in the Home. (The 'cutting off' seemed to be a mutual process, i.e. Homes cut themselves off from the community and the community appeared to cut itself off from the Homes.) Residential people in the sample were generally appreciative of efforts to prepare them for outside living but in the absence of a definite policy and a planned programme, preparation depended on the initiative and goodwill of individual house-parents and more frequently of the fieldworkers. Perhaps as a result of the division of functions between field and residential services, most of the immediate help on discharge, according to respondents, came from fieldworkers. Whilst this was valued, subjects would have liked the Home staff to have played a much bigger part, particularly by acting as anchors or fall-backs for possible set-backs. The 'ever-changing' staff appeared to mitigate against this approach, along with the fact that no single person was usually delegated to plan leaving care and sustain continuity of support. In view of the often considerable conflict between staff and inmates, and the 'them' and 'us' feeling that was often expressed by the latter, the linking of any help with fieldworkers seemed to make its offer perhaps more acceptable. Surprisingly enough, Millham *et al.* (1975) did not find the 'them' and 'us' atmosphere prevailing in their study of boys in approved schools. Perhaps the short stay in approved schools does not give rise to the intensity of feeling and reactions that long residential living generates. Yet in spite of the 'them' and 'us' climate, the inmates were also considerably dependent on the institution and the staff. Whilst the prospect of leaving care was intensely desired, at the same time they were very anxious and fearful about living in the outside world. In fact, the staff did not always appreciate the extent of the youngsters' anxieties about first jobs, accommodation and above all coping.

Approximately a third of all subjects said they did not need help on a range of items either because they could rely on friends and family or because of a determined effort to prove that they could manage, and 'stand' on their own feet unaided.

Preparation and help with employment
Only a quarter of those who left residential care said they received a lot of help in finding employment, with almost 60 per cent saying they received none. Those who were helped were appreciative: 'The Home organised my joining the Merchant Navy'; 'they encouraged me getting a job and they also helped me'; 'they helped me to get into hairdressing.' Whilst those who maintained that they received no help said: 'I wouldn't say there was much help given'; 'no help from the Home'; 'they were prepared to help you be what they wanted, not what you wanted. It was all right if you wanted to join the army or become a nanny'; 'I didn't get any help from the Home staff.' A few who received help from fieldworkers valued it considerably: 'My social worker planned everything'; 'the social worker helped'; 'my social worker did her best'; 'the . . . department was great. They gave me help all the way.'

As stated earlier, a minority of young people were determined to show the staff that they could stand on their own feet: 'I said I preferred to find a job for myself. I didn't want any help'; 'I found my own job'; 'I wanted to do it myself'; 'a friend helped me'. Those who said they didn't need help with employment on leaving care were less likely to appear before a court or need psychiatric help. Burgess (1981) comments that the youth labour market may not be as well geared to the requirements of the less-qualified school leaver and the less-skilled young worker as it is to those of other categories of young people: 'In the case of school leavers in care', he goes on, 'it is a question of those who need the most help getting least.' He concludes that the gap between provision and need must be filled, in the first instance, by the residential worker. Whilst he does not expect residential staff to take on the role of job advisors or placement agencies, he sees staff as ideally placed to fulfil the vital role of helping young people in care establish their occupational identity.

Help with accommodation
Six out of every ten respondents said they received no help to secure accommodation on leaving care, but one in every six said they received a lot of help. The wish for help and support to secure accommodation on leaving care was linked to being able to return to the Home if things did not work out: 'I was always under the belief that when you left the Home that was it . . . you were no longer under their care'; 'I felt I was finished with the Home and couldn't return except to visit.' Others valued help they had from fieldworkers: 'My social worker found me a place to stay'; 'I was on my own. The social worker did her best. She was the only one who thought about anything for me.' Help and support with accommodation on leaving care or its absence had no bearing on whether subjects subsequently faced housing problems or contacted housing authorities. Similarly, satisfaction or otherwise with their present housing had no relationship to the type of help they obtained before leaving care.

Money management
Almost the sole preparation concerning the management of money was based on giving children pocket money and opening a bank or Post Office account for them either before they started a job or afterwards. Well over half of the respondents said they received no help or preparation in managing and using money. Only 5 per cent said they received a 'lot of help' with a quarter of the sample saying 'some' help.

Respondents claimed that whilst bank and Post Office accounts encouraged the concept of 'saving', they were rarely given the opportunity to handle any money or involve themselves in monetary transactions besides spending their pocket money. The general view was that the staff were organising and taking charge of everything, with the subject playing a passive role, even in situations where they were earning the money: 'Money was put in the bank and you were seldom allowed to touch it'; 'you got your pay and they divided it into the ways it was meant to go. It could have been better if you could have done it yourself. They just took it from you and they did it.'

Most of the subjects simply said that they received no help in managing money in the form of shopping, change of money and comparing prices. One person commenting on how difficult she finds it to shop added:

> Even if they [Home staff] had taken a few of us one week and done the shopping they would get us to know how to shop. . . . I go into the supermarket and say 'that is too dear', and maybe it isn't. I didn't have a clue how to shop.

J. and others similarly remarked: 'I didn't know how to manage money. I didn't know anything about money . . . they didn't attempt to help me'; 'you had no real training in dealing with money or coping with house problems'; 'I was working for £6 a week and I had to give all that for board. I never even got a bus to the end of town'; 'they saved money for you. They just gave you so much and the rest they kept.' This was not viewed as consisting of help. Other typical comments: 'You had no real contact with money . . . they tried to encourage you to save money and look after money . . . but you didn't come into contact with much money'; 'I didn't even know what money was. I would get some as pocket money if I was good, but not if I was bad.'

Help with employment or in the management of money was unrelated to the respondents' current financial situation.

Home management

Like other life-space areas, half of those interviewed said they had no preparation in domestic and home management. The rest said they had some or a lot of preparation within the Home. Preparation in home and domestic management was mostly pursued through the performance of different tasks in the Home. It was also hoped that in helping around children would develop skills and experience in home management. The majority of subjects, however, found such tasks as too routinised and unaccompanied by any discussion or explanation that could help as preparation for later living and home management.

Tasks such as laying tables, washing-up, cleaning floors and making beds were not carried out as part of explicit preparation for life but because they had to be done. Most of them recognised some value in the activities but there was the feeling that they could have been better organised and explained: 'You had to do it . . . but nobody explained this was preparation for your marriage'; 'no help at all in this way. Just cleaning, that was all.'

Others were more positive, and valued the experience of doing things around the Home: 'They have taught me how to look after my clothes and all that'; 'I used to help with the kids, set tea or dinner which helped me a lot'; 'we did get preparation with washing dishes, making our own beds, tidying or cleaning our own rooms, hoovering, dusting, etc.'; 'they always allowed you if you wanted to make scones, or improve anything which was good'; 'I got a lot of help looking after homes in general and that has been an advantage to me at present.'

Preparation for home management or its absence was unrelated to current economic and housing problems or marital difficulties.

Support after leaving the Home
When respondents were asked whether they had general support after leaving the Home, again almost half of them said they had little or none, with a third saying they received a lot of help.

When respondents were asked whether they felt they could go back to the Home for help and support if needed, most of them either did not want to have anything more to do with the Home or the impression they were left with on leaving was that they would not be welcome. With few exceptions, subjects did not view the Home as a place where they could go back to talk possible problems over or obtain any emotional support or nourishment: 'I would never go back'; 'I would not fall back on them'; 'I wouldn't fall back on them for anything'; 'you couldn't just go to them . . . you had to crawl to them, beg them'; 'they felt disappointed in you if you failed in anything you were doing so you didn't like going back'.

The need for such help was put across by one woman summarising the views of most others: 'When I needed help was when I had my baby. . . . I didn't have a clue. I was 17 then. I had nobody to turn to . . . now I would never go back and ask for any help. Never.' Another one added: 'I felt that when I left the Home they didn't want to know you.' One who felt 'completely cut off' once she left the Home remarked: 'I could have been doing with some support, somebody's help. Somebody to go and talk to, to help me . . . everyone needs somebody and I didn't really think they cared for me.'

Others who might have liked to go back to the Home found that the house-parents they knew had moved on and new staff were not always welcoming. Some visited once and when they did not find the staff they knew they never returned. The absence of a sort of 'home' to return to left quite a number who had not created their own base expressing a certain amount of bitterness. Berry (1975) found from her study of 44 residential units in England that one-third of staff stayed for less than a year in their job. Current turnover is estimated at 30 per cent annually. Worse than not finding a familiar face in the Home was to be told, 'You don't live here any longer.'

Some subjects, though, had no hesitation about going back to the Home and valued the idea of continued support: 'I felt they were just behind me . . . it was not as if I was on my own'; 'I had the support of the matron when I left and when we got married. We used to go up there and visit regularly'; 'the last thing I was told when I left the Home was, "You know where we are and you are always most welcome to come back", and I have asked on a few occasions for help and advice. The first night I was away I was a bit scared.'

Overall, no significant connection was found between the amount of preparation for 'outside' living that respondents said they had and their present social conditions.

The next step was to examine the amount of preparation respondents had in relation to the presence or absence of problems for which they had received psychiatric treatment. In this respect those who had psychiatric help were less likely to say that they had help with 'employment' ($p < 0.05$), 'home management' ($p < 0.02$) or 'support on leaving the Home' ($p < 0.005$). One conclusion that could be drawn is that the most 'disturbed' and needy were most likely to receive the least help. These were the same people who also had doubts about their coping abilities and who expressed mostly 'mixed' or negative feelings about their residential experience. The suggestion is that either because of their difficulties respondents were unable to use the help offered, or the staff paid less attention and offered less encouragement to the more difficult children. Whichever explanation is accepted, the fact is that residential staff, whilst able to establish contact and relationships with the more settled and trouble-free children, were least successful in doing so with those facing personal and social difficulties. Berry (1975) also observed from her study that 'it was the child's personality and behaviour which largely determined his popularity with the staff, rather than the child's basic and special needs determining the workers' attitudes.' Berry goes on to add that children who were on 'poorer' terms with the staff, 'were almost always said to be perceived by the staff as sly, or deceitful, manipulative, attention-seeking, conceited, superficial, disruptive or troublesome in some way.'

Taking the experience of the adoption group as a guide, what seems to contribute to a somewhat trouble-free adult life or 'success', barring major upsets, is a positive growing-up experience and a support group, such as family in the background to rely on. Residential people holding educational qualifications and training had less need for help in employment and housing on leaving the institution. In the long run, however, the stability of even this group was affected by personal problems.

The children of 'travelling' and 'tinker' families

Seven out of the 40 residential people in the sample were the children of what are called 'travelling' or 'tinker' families. The children came into care for similar reasons to the rest, i.e the personal and social circumstances of their parents, including alcohol abuse, illness, homelessness and serious relationship problems. The seven in the study fared less well compared to the rest of the residential sample. Six of the seven had left school without any qualifications; they were more likely to display emotional and psychiatric difficulties; to have no friends or to have relationship problems; to have no leisure activities; be heavy drinkers; be dissatisfied with their housing and with their overall residential experience. If residential care can have some beneficial effect on some of the children, it seems to have had no positive impact at all on the children of 'travelling' families. They have come off worst from the system than any other child.

Summary

Compared to those who grew up in institutions the material circumstances of adoptees were significantly 'better' in that the latter shared fewer material 'handicaps' by rarely being out of work or on social security benefits. Their housing circumstances were again more satisfactory and in many cases 'superior' to those of residential people. Overall, almost one-fifth of adoptees and half of residential people were facing moderate to serious financial and/or housing problems at the time of the interviews. But the social conditions of over 80 per cent of adoptees and of half the residential people appeared 'fairly good' or 'good' – those of adoptees falling mostly in the latter category.

On matters of social and personal adjustment, significantly fewer adoptees (16 per cent) were classified as 'disturbed' compared with residential people (38 per cent). In matters of material and psychological circumstances, adoptees tended to approximate the proportions among the general population, but residential people appeared significantly more disadvantaged on a range of indices. The overall picture to emerge was of a confident and well-settled adoption group expressing considerable satisfaction with their adoption and with their current material, social and personal circumstances. The residential group were less well-settled and more troubled. Overall, less than a quarter of adoptees and almost three-fifths of residential people were facing either serious material, social or personal problems. Adoptees who were facing such problems would also express 'mixed' or 'negative' feelings about their adoption blaming their current situation on the outcome of their adoption. The single factor that appeared to point to some relative social and personal stability in the current lives of some residential people was the extent to which they felt they experienced caring and good relationships with the staff. It is, of course, possible that these respondents were more benevolent towards their carers because they were not currently facing undue social and personal difficulties. Emotional/psychiatric problems among adoptees, but not as much in residential people, tended to decrease in adult life.

Though the two groups of respondents shared a common background of disadvantage (albeit this was much more pronounced in the residential group), they were now functioning significantly differently in many important life-space areas. Even when we looked at the adoptees with the worst possible backgrounds they did not differ from the rest of the adoption sample, and they were functioning significantly better than residential people. The main explanation that can be offered for the important differences between the two groups of respondents is the contrasting ways in which they grew up. Possible influences or genetic transmissions from the natural family and discontinuity in care seem to find their expression more often as a result of growing up in residential care than when adopted. The opportunity afforded to the adopted group to establish new attachments and relationships appeared not only to reverse early experiences of deprivation, but also to equip them with social and personal qualities enabling them to cope well with life. In contrast, the residential experience transmitted handicaps to the residential group, and as an experience had more to do with continuities of multiple difficulties than any transmissions from the original family. Paterson and Inglis (1975), who drew up pedigree charts of families in contact with social agencies, found that difficulties in one generation were not necessarily followed by difficulties in the next. (There will be further discussion on this issue in the next chapter.)

Table 6.12 was constructed in an attempt to present an overall picture of the 'quality of life' of respondents at the time of interview. The table is based on how many handicaps out of nine were shared by members of each group. The presence of a handicap is seen as affecting the 'quality of life' of each member. The table is again based on self-reporting and covers both tangible and intangible life-space areas. The nine handicaps considered and which have already been discussed separately are: dependence on social security; some or considerable dissatisfaction with current housing conditions; a criminal conviction in adult life; severe alcohol abuse; psychiatric referral; relationship problems; the expression of some or considerable doubt about the capacity to cope with life; uncertainty about emotional well-being at interview; and mixed feelings about levels of happiness.

Table 6.12 *The cumulative effect on respondents of nine social and personal handicaps*

	Adoption N	Residential N
No handicap present	17	4
1 handicap	10	7
2 handicaps	6	5
3 handicaps	6	9
4 handicaps	3	6
5 handicaps	1	3
6 handicaps	1	3
7 or more handicaps	0	3
	44	40

Table 6.12 shows that almost 40 per cent of adoptees were free of any of the nine handicaps outlined above. This compares with only 10 per cent of residential people ($p < 0.001$). At the other end, eleven (25 per cent) adoptees had three or more handicaps each, compared with 24 (60 per cent) residential people ($p < 0.005$). It should be stressed again that the number of handicaps is not necessarily an accurate indication of the seriousness or otherwise of a condition. For example, one handicap may be more incapacitating than, say, four. The table simply aims to show the possible cumulative effect of handicaps. What is also shown is that residential people were significantly more handicapped compared to adoptees. (Our assumption that the four residential people with no handicaps would mostly be the offspring of otherwise well-coping and caring parents faced with a sudden crisis, such as long-term illness or death, was not substantiated.)

7 The Respondents' Circumstances Contrasted with Those of Their Biological Families

It was stated at the beginning of this book that a basic aim of the study was to contrast the 'personal and social circumstances' of the respondents with those of their families of origin at the time of reception into care, the ultimate objective being to test how far attitudes, behaviour and social characteristics are transmitted from one generation to the next in situations where the children have been separated from the family of origin in early childhood. In effect, do mechanisms of transmission operate through the family, or are they mostly related to a range of other factors including the lack of material resources? Does life in an institution transmit its own handicaps irrespective of the circumstances of the family of origin? Reflecting on the lives of two of their sample, Coffield *et al.* (1981) concluded that 'the cumulative effects of years of poverty and unstable circumstances have become ingrained in their personalities, in their physical and mental health and in their modes of functioning.'

It is recognised that the two generations are not strictly comparable because of the different stages at which they are being contrasted. In some cases, such as history of crime, our data on the natural family may not be complete; a reminder also that in Chapter 3 it was pointed out that the various handicaps faced by the parents of residential people were generally more severe and chronic compared to those of the natural parents of adoptees. On the other hand, more questions were raised about the adoptees' physical and emotional health before they went to their adoptive families compared to residential people at reception into care. It is worth noting, too, that the adoption group were nearest to the biological mothers in terms of age, marital status and number of children. The residential group were rather younger compared to their natural families and were not yet burdened with the responsibilities of a large family. On the other hand, unlike most of their families, the residential group had to make their start in life without the support of a family and without an existing family base.

Chapter 3 identified a number of characteristics or attributes that were present in various degrees among the biological families and the same ones were also identified in respondents in Chapter 6. These were: social class by occupation; financial situation; housing circumstances; quality of relationships; a history of crime; heavy drinking or alcohol abuse; and 'psychiatric instability' (including psychiatric help) or a degree of 'mental handicap'. Throughout the present chapter each characteristic, or a combination of characteristics, prevalent among respondents will be contrasted with similar ones or with any other relevant attributes that were present in the family of origin at time of reception. A basic question to be asked each time is how far the same characteristics which appear in the natural family are also present in the respective offspring. (The word 'distributed' will signify the presence of two or more handicaps indicating disturbance as identified in Chapter 3.)

Social class by occupation
The point was made in the previous chapter that both adoptees and residential people featuring in the study experienced upward social mobility compared to their families of origin. In addition, the adoptees' social class was broadly similar to that of their adoptive parents, whilst that of the residential people was somewhat lower than that of the general population. Here the social class of respondents is contrasted with that of their biological parents and social mobility is accordingly monitored.

The adoption group
Table 7.1, which contrasts the social class of adoptees with that of their natural mother, shows that significantly more adoptees were classified in social classes I and II (29 per cent) compared with the natural parent (9 per cent). At the other end, only about 20 per cent of adoptees were classified in semi-skilled and unskilled occupations compared with 60 per cent of natural parents. If the comparison, however, was to be made between manual and non-manual occupations, i.e. non-manual = social classes I and II, and IIINM; and for manual = social classes IIIM, IV and V, then the differences are not significant (difference index = 6 per cent). Of eleven adoptees born to parents in non-manual occupations, eight were holding manual occupations. On the other hand, of fourteen adoptees holding non-manual occupations, eleven were born to parents holding manual occupations. In other words, the offspring of non-manual parents were mostly holding manual occupations and those of manual occupations were holding non-manual occupations. Hardly any generational transmissions can be claimed as far as social class is concerned.

From a direct matching of adoptees and their natural mother, the following pattern of downward and upward mobility emerges:

Table 7.1 *Social class of adoptees contrasted to that of their natural mothers*

		\multicolumn{6}{c}{Adoptees' social class*}	
		I	II	IIINM	IIIM	IV	V	Total
Natural mother	I	—	—	—	—	—	—	
	II	—	1	1	—	—	1	3
	IIINM	1	—	—	6	1	—	8
	IIIM	—	1	—	1	1	—	3
	IV	—	5	2	5	2	—	14
	V	1	1	1	2	2	—	7
	Total	2	8	4	14	6	1	35

* Nine adoptees could not be contrasted because the mother was either a minor and not at work at the time, or she had no occupation because of a mental handicap. Those in the armed forces were classified on the basis of their rank.

Adopted person's social class similar to that of the natural mother	4
Adoptee one social class below	8
Adoptee two social classes below	1
Adoptee three social classes below	—
Adoptee four social classes below	1
Adoptee one social class above	7
Adoptee two social classes above	6
Adoptee three social classes above	6
Adoptee four social classes above	1
Adoptee five social classes above	1
	35
Missing	9
	44

Whilst four adoptees attained the same social class as their natural families and another eight (23 per cent) were classified one or more social classes below, another 21 (60 per cent) were classified as one or more social classes above that of their natural mother. There was no difference between the social mobility of those adoptees who came from the most disturbed or disadvantaged backgrounds and the rest. In no way could it be construed that adoptees were holding jobs similar to those of their families of origin. On the contrary, a significant number experienced upward social mobility. In other words, background occupational variables were unimportant as far as social class was concerned.

The residential group

Problems emerged when trying to contrast the social class of residential people with that of their natural families because of the number of natural parents whose occupation was not recorded. As already stated, the main reason that no occupation was given for some natural parents was the fact that they had been out of work for some time. It is most unlikely that these parents held other than semi-skilled and unskilled occupations, but they could not obviously be included here. Overall, all eleven residential people holding non-manual occupations were born to parents holding manual jobs (Table 7.2). A more detailed analysis of social class revealed the pattern of social mobility outlined below.

Nine (28 per cent) residential people were classified in the same social class as their natural father, whilst five (16 per cent) were

Table 7.2 The social class of residential people contrasted to that of their natural father

		\multicolumn{6}{c}{Residential people's social class}
		I	II	IIINM	IIIM	IV	V	Total
Natural father	I							
	II							
	IIINM							
	IIIM	—	—	2	1	—	2	5
	IV	—	2	2	4	7	3	18
	V	—	3	2	1	2	1	9
	Total	—	5	6	6	9	6	32

Residential people's social class similar to their father	9
One social class below	3
Two social classes below	2
One social class above	8
Two social classes above	3
Three social classes above	4

Four social classes above	3
	32
Could not be matched*	8
	40

* Eight residential people could not be contrasted because the fathers were mostly out of work for long periods and no occupation was given.

classified one or more social classes below. At the same time 18 (46 per cent) were classified one or more social classes above that of their natural father. On the basis of these findings again no obvious similarity can be claimed between the two generations, but compared to the biological family residential people experienced significant upward social mobility. The five residential people classified in social class II (18 per cent) as against none of the natural fathers possibly demonstrates the influence of the institution in orienting the children towards different goals or aspirations from those of the parents. These findings contrast with those concerning long-term fostering which show that former foster children hardly experienced any upward mobility compared to their natural families (Triseliotis 1980b). Residential people who as children displayed psychiatric difficulties or those who came from families classified as 'disturbed' did not experience similar upward mobility to the rest.

Housing circumstances
In this section the present housing circumstances of the offspring are contrasted with those of the natural families at the time of reception into care.

The adoption group
Four adoptees expressed mixed feelings about the quality of their housing and two outright dissatisfaction. Among the parents of origin the housing conditions of sixteen (48 per cent) were judged to be unsatisfactory or very unsatisfactory. When the two generations were contrasted there was no evidence to show that adoptees expressing an element of dissatisfaction with their housing would mostly be the offspring of natural parents who faced serious housing problems at reception into care. Even the two adoptees who sought the help of housing authorities came from families with no housing problems at reception into care. As stated in the previous chapter, the housing circumstances of adoptees were beginning to approximate those of their adoptive parents rather than that of their families of origin.

The residential group

Five of the residential people expressed outright dissatisfaction with the quality of their housing, and another seven had mixed feelings about it. In all, twelve (31 per cent) of residential people expressed an element of dissatisfaction with their housing conditions. This group was contrasted with the 17 families of origin whose housing conditions at reception into care was assessed to be very precarious, some of them with a history of evictions or vagrancy, etc. (Table 7.3). Though on the

Table 7.3 *The housing satisfaction of residential people contrasted to the housing conditions of the families of origin*

		Residential people*		Total	
		Satisfactory to very satisfactory	Mixed views or unsatisfactory		
		N	N	N	%
Natural families	Fairly stable to stable	14	1	15	48
	Very precarious	7	9	16	52
		21 (68%)	10 (32%)	31	100

* Nine respondents could not be matched because they were either living in barracks (N=5), or their parents' housing conditions could not be accurately assessed.

face of it the housing circumstances of the residential people appear to be more stable than those of the families of origin, at the same time, of the ten people who expressed mixed feelings or dissatisfaction with their housing conditions and who could be matched with their families, nine came from families whose housing circumstances at reception had been judged as very precarious or unsatisfactory. This seems to indicate that offspring expressing some dissatisfaction with their housing conditions are likely to have families where serious housing conditions existed at reception into care ($\tau B = 0.56$, $p < 0.01$). This is the first direct association to be established as far as conditions are concerned between the circumstances of the two generations. Equally, of the nine residential people who had been in contact with housing authorities because of unsatisfactory housing circumstances in the 12 months prior to the interview, seven came from families whose housing conditions were very unsatisfactory at reception into care. McDowell (1982) has also shown the intergenerational persistence of housing problems.

The link found between dissatisfaction or mixed feelings concerning housing among residential people and very precarious housing conditions in the families of origin does not necessarily support a direct intergenerational transmission. It could simply be explained by the absence of sufficient 'good' quality housing in the community and the lack of resources for access to better housing. Another explanation is that this group of residential people may have been exposed to the influence of their parents through visiting or contacts, or through reference to them by staff and other relatives.

Residential people who expressed mixed feelings or dissatisfaction with their housing conditions were also likely to say that their income was 'inadequate' or that they had relationship problems with partners or spouses. Similarly, the same group were also likely to rate themselves as having emotional problems in adult life.

Economic situation

The aim here was to contrast the present economic circumstances of the respondents with those of their natural families at the time of the formers' reception into care. To do this three variables were selected, all referring to the economic conditions of the respondents. These were: dependence on social security; perception of the adequacy of their income; and perception of their standard of living as rated by the respondents. Each one of these variables was initially correlated with the economic condition of the biological family. Secondly, those respondents who shared two or more of the variables outlined above were seen as 'materially handicapped' and were again contrasted with the economic conditions of their natural families.

Dependence on social security benefits at the time of the interview
Knight and West (1977) concluded that the habit of making unusually frequent social security claims was transmitted from one generation to the next, and was a characteristic feature of the delinquent minority. Taking respondents in both samples with convictions such as theft, breaking and entering, assaults and causing malicious damage, there was no evidence that these were also beneficiaries of the social security system at the time of interview. It is difficult to predict what is likely to happen in the long run. Turning to the relationship between respondents and their natural parents, only two adoptees were receiving social security benefits (one for 32 and the other for 8 weeks) and these were not the offspring of parents who were experiencing unusual financial problems at the time of reception into care.

In the residential group, eleven (31 per cent) respondents had been receiving social security benefits for varying periods, six of them for 41 weeks or more in the 12 months preceding the interview. No significant association was found to indicate that those who were dependent on social security were more likely than the rest to have families who were experiencing serious financial problems at reception into care (Table 7.4). When the six (16 per cent) residential people who were on

Table 7.4   The residential people's dependence on social security benefits contrasted to the economic situation of their families of origin

		Residential people			
		On social security benefits	No benefits	Total	
		N	N	N	%
Natural family	Economic situation precarious or very precarious	6	15	21	57
	Economic situation fairly stable	5	11	16	43
		11 (30%)	26 (70%)	37	100
	Missing			3	
				40	

benefits for more than 41 weeks were matched with the natural families that were facing economic problems again no relationship emerged between the two. In fact, not a single offspring matched with a biological parent. The assumption therefore that residential people who are long-term beneficiaries of the social security system would be the offspring of parents experiencing similar conditions at reception into care was not substantiated. However the moderate to serious economic difficulties faced by many residential people is an indication that these can start independently as a result of current social and personal circumstances and are not necessarily dependent on intergenerational transmissions.

Income adequacy
Here the respondents' perception of the adequacy or otherwise of their income was again correlated with the economic situation of the families of origin to establish possible intergenerational connections.

Adoption group. There was no evidence to support the view that the eight adoptees who expressed a degree of dissatisfaction about their financial situation were likely to have families who were facing economic hardships at the time of reception into care.

The residential group. Like the adoption sample, no evidence was found to suggest that residential people who perceived their income as very inadequate were likely to come from families whose economic situation was precarious or very precarious at the time the children were taken into care (Table 7.5).

Table 7.5 *The residential people's perception of the adequacy of their income matched to the economic situation of their natural families*

		Residential people		Total	
		Income adequate or more so N	Income very inadequate N	N	%
Natural family	Economic situation fairly stable	14	2	16	43
	Precarious or very precarious	14	7	21	57
		28 (76%)	9 (24%)	37	100
	Missing			3	
				40	

Standard of living

Respondents in both groups were asked to describe and rate their perception of the adequacy of their standard of living. The degree of satisfaction or otherwise expressed was again correlated with the economic circumstances of the biological families at the time of the respondents' reception into care. Like adequacy of income, those expressing dissatisfaction with their standard of living were not likely to come from families who were experiencing fairly serious or serious economic problems at reception into care.

Summary

Adoptees or residential people who were on social security benefits, or who perceived their income as inadequate, or who were dissatisfied with their standard of living, or who had mixed feelings about it, were not likely to have biological families who were experiencing moderate to serious economic problems at reception into care.

Finally, the study identified one adoptee and eight residential people who shared three indices signifying income inadequacy, i.e. being in receipt of social security; some dissatisfaction with the adequacy of income; mixed feelings or dissatisfaction with standard of living. Again no evidence emerged to show that those sharing two or three indices indicating income inadequacy were likely to be the offspring of parents facing economic hardships at the time of reception into care. In other words, in matters of financial difficulties, no significant relationship could be established between parents and offspring growing up adopted or in residential care. When adoptees who were facing either serious income or housing problems (N = 4) were compared with natural families who were equally facing similar problems (N = 12), no offspring matched with a natural parent. When the thirteen residential people who were facing serious income or housing difficulties were compared with their natural families, only seven offspring matched with similar circumstances among the equivalent parents. This finding, however, was not statistically significant. It can be concluded that in matters of serious material disadvantage close intergenerational continuities could not be established, but many residential people were experiencing economic difficulties independently of their families. (It may seem strange that in these contrasts not all the families of origin were classified as experiencing precarious or very precarious economic conditions. The fact is that approximately 40 per cent of the parents had a very modest income at the time which, though, was not sufficient to purchase private care for their children.)

The quality of relationships

In Chapter 3 on the families of origin the comment was made that disruptive relationships between spouses or partners, often of a chronic nature, were characteristic of many families. The eventual collapse of most families came about as a result of relationships breaking down, though other social factors were often prominent. Here the respondents' relationships with spouses, members of the opposite sex, and friends are contrasted with relationship problems among the families of origin.

The adoption group

Spouse relationship. Of the 20 married adoptees, three referred to current problems in the marriage but none of these came from natural families experiencing disruptive relationships at reception into care. The next step was to add another five adoptees who experienced divorce, separation or marital problems at some stage. Again, no intergenerational connections could be established. In other words, no supportive evidence emerged that adoptees who experienced, or who were experiencing, marital problems were likely to have natural families facing relationship problems at the time of the child's reception into care. Only two of the eight adoptees were linked to natural parents with disruptive relationship problems. Similarly, adoptees who faced marital problems were not more likely than the rest to have a 'disturbed' natural family background.

Relationship problems with members of the opposite sex. When single and married adoptees were asked to say how well or otherwise they got on with members of the opposite sex, and whether they thought there were difficulties in this area, 15 (34 per cent) referred to some problems arising from such relationships which they attributed mostly to aspects of their behaviour or personality. However, no significant association could be established between them and natural parents who were experiencing disruptive relationships at reception into care. In other words, adoptees who reported partner problems were not more likely than others to have natural families who were also experiencing partner problems at reception into care. Neither was there any link between adoptees reporting some relationship problems and a 'disturbed' family background.

Friendship problems. Seven (16 per cent) of those adopted reported a range of difficulties in developing or maintaining friendships. Again, those expressing such difficulties were unrelated to natural parents facing relationship problems at relinquishment or to those parents identified as 'disturbed'.

In summary, no evidence was found to support the contention that adoptees facing relationship problems in a range of life situations would mostly come from biological families facing similar problems at reception into care. Neither were these adoptees likely to have a 'disturbed' natural family background.

The residential group
As with the adoption group, a range of relationship difficulties reported by residential people were correlated with similar problems in the families of origin and to a 'disturbed' family background.

Spouse relationship. At least nine of the 22 married people experienced or were experiencing marital problems. Some of these problems had led to separation or divorce. When all married residential people were contrasted with their respective natural families, no significant association emerged to link marital problems among residential people with severe relationship problems in their respective families (Table 7.6).

Table 7.6 *Marital problems among residential people and severe relationship problems in the families of origin*

		Residential people Problems present N	No problems N	Total N	%
Families of origin	Problems present	6	11	17	77
	No problems	3	2	5	23
		9 (41%)	13 (59%)	22	100

Relationship problems with members of the opposite sex. Eighteen (45 per cent) residential people reported some problem in relationships with members of the opposite sex. Seven of them attributed the problem to their type of personality, and the rest to aspects connected with their behaviour such as drink, crime or unemployment. When these 18 were contrasted with their respective families of origin, no association could be established between the two generations. In effect, no evidence was found to support the suggestion that those experiencing moderate or severe relationship problems with members of the opposite sex were likely to be the offspring of parents who were experiencing disruptive relationships at reception. When those reporting relationship difficulties were connected with 'disturbed' biological families, again no significant relationship could be established between the two, though there was some evidence pointing to this direction.

Friendship problems. Ten (25 per cent) residential people reported some or serious difficulties in relating to friends or to people of their own age, but no relationship was found between them and families of origin facing disruptive relationship problems at reception into care.

The next step was to take all respondents who reported relationship problems in two or more of the three areas identified earlier (i.e. problems with spouses, or members of the opposite sex, or friends) and contrast them with 'disturbed' biological families. The four adoptees who were identified in this way had no connection at all with a 'disturbed' family background. Nine residential people were also identified as having relationship problems in two or more areas of living, seven of them came from the 17 families who had been identified as 'disturbed', indicating a significant association between relationship problems among residential people and a 'disturbed' family background ($p < 0.05$).

Alcohol abuse
Heavy alcohol consumption followed by alcohol-related problems featured among respondents in both groups and among the families of origin. Here alcohol consumption among residents is contrasted with similar behaviour in the families of origin and also with a 'disturbed' family background.

The adoption group
Five (12 per cent) adoptees were classified as heavy drinkers and in eight (18 per cent) of the parents of origin there were reports of heavy alcohol consumption which was often responsible for the family's eventual breakdown. (As pointed out before, it is possible that alcohol abuse in the natural parents could be an underestimate because a large part of the data referred only to the natural mothers of adoptees.) When the two groups were contrasted no association emerged to support the view that adoptees who were heavy drinkers would predominantly be the offspring of parents who were themselves heavy drinkers. When all adoptees who drank in excess of 8 pints at any one point were included ($N = 16$), again no significant relationship could be established to link the two generations. Of these 16 adoptees, only two came from a biological family where there was heavy drinking. Neither could any link be established between alcohol abuse among adoptees and a 'disturbed' family background.

The next step was to contrast those adoptees who said that their drinking led to some problems with alcohol abuse in the families of origin. Again no connection could be established between the two generations and the findings in fact point to a significant relationship in the opposite direction. In effect, adoptees who reported alcohol-related problems were likely to come from families amongst whom there was no report of alcohol abuse (Table 7.7).

Goodwin *et al.* (1973, 1974) found from their Danish study a significantly higher rate of alcoholism among the adopted sons of alcoholic biological fathers than among control adoptees. On the other hand, adopted daughters of alcoholic biological fathers did not have a

Table 7.7 Alcohol-related problems among adoptees related to alcohol abuse in the families of origin

		Problems N	Adoptees No problems N	Total N	%
Family of origin	Alcohol abuse	—	8	8	18
	No alcohol abuse	8	28	36	82
		8 (18%)	36 (82%)	44	100

higher rate of alcohol abuse than control adoptees (Goodwin *et al.* 1977). Bohman (1978) also found links between alcohol abuse among adoptees and similar behaviour in the families of origin. Cadoret and Gath (1978) found that among 84 adoptees 18 years of age and older separated at birth from their biological parents and without further contact with them, alcoholism was found more frequently in those whose relatives included an individual with alcoholism or in whom heavy drinking had been noted. Not unexpectedly all the studies mentioned go on to suggest genetic factors behind alcoholism.

The residential group
Table 7.8, which contrasts alcohol abuse among residential people and their families of origin, again fails to establish any significant relationship between the two generations. Even after adding those who drank in excess of 8 pints of beer at any one time and one person who took drugs (N = 19), no evidence emerged to support significant links between offspring and parents. Neither was any meaningful relationship found between alcohol abuse among residential people and a 'disturbed' family background. The failure of this study, in contrast to those mentioned above, to establish intergenerational links may well be related to cultural factors or to definitions as to what constitutes alcohol abuse. However, even the most conservative interpretation of alcohol abuse here would still fail to support intergenerational continuities for separated children at least.

When psychiatric problems among respondents were correlated with alcohol abuse in the family of origin, no links were found between the adoption sample and their natural parents. A different picture though emerged with residential people with a psychiatric referral suggesting they were likely to have parents where one or both drank heavily ($p < 0.01$) (Table 7.9).

Table 7.8 Alcohol abuse among residential people and in the natural family

	Residential people		Total	
	Alcohol abuse N	No abuse N	N	%
Alcohol abuse	7	10	17	42
No abuse	6	17	23	58
	13 (33%)	27 (67%)	40	100

Table 7.9 Psychiatric referrals among residential people and alcohol abuse in biological parents

	Residential people		Total	
	Psychiatric referral N	No referral N	N	%
Alcohol abuse	12	5	17	44
No alcohol abuse	5	17	22	56
	17 (44%)	22 (56%)	39	100
Missing			1	
			40	

In overall summary, the only significant association to emerge in connection with alcohol abuse is that residential, but not adopted, people displaying psychiatric difficulties are likely to have had parents who were heavy drinkers or alcoholics.

Crime and delinquency

Like alcohol abuse, crime and delinquency featured among respondents in both the adoption and residential samples. Similarly, crime featured among the biological families. Though we are confident that respondents revealed to us their history of indictable offences without it being necessary to obtain their permission to refer to official statistics, doubts exist about the accuracy of the parents' criminal history. In the first place, in the case of the adoptees' natural families, the records referred mostly to the mother and not to both parents. In the case of both samples the records may have failed to obtain information about petty crime. The tendency was to record situations where crime played an important part in the break-up of the family. No recourse was made to official statistics first, because the dates and place of birth of the natural parents were unavailable; and secondly, because questions were raised about the ethical implications of seeking such information without the parents' consent. Whilst recognising these limitations it is unlikely that a significant margin of error exists.

Crowe (1972) found from a study involving adopted children that those with criminal natural mothers were more likely to commit crime in later years. Hutchings and Mednick (1974) also claim to have found a significant correlation between criminality among adoptees and their biological parents thus indicating a 'genetic transmission'; Bohman (1978) though found no such correlation, and adds that adoptees born to biological parents registered for criminality were not recorded more often for criminality than adopted controls with a non-criminal heritage.

The adoption group
Fourteen (32 per cent) adoptees had a criminal history, three for driving offences, three for 'breach of the peace' and eight for other offences. Eleven of the fourteen had been before an adult court. This contrasted with seven (16 per cent) of the natural parents (mostly mothers) with a history of crime. Though crime seemed to occur more frequently among adoptees than in their natural families, there was no evidence to indicate that those committing offences were likely to be the offspring of parents with a criminal record. Similarly, only two of the fourteen adoptees with a criminal record had a 'disturbed' family background. In other words, anti-social behaviour among adoptees was unrelated to similar behaviour in their natural families or to having a 'disturbed' natural family background.

The residential group
Seventeen (42 per cent) residential people had a criminal conviction, three of them for driving offences; whilst 20 (50 per cent) natural parents had a criminal conviction. Table 7.10, which contrasts criminal behaviour between the two generations, shows no evidence that the children of parents with a criminal record will acquire a criminal record

themselves, even though 10 of the 17 had parents with a criminal conviction. Rutter and Madge (1977) comment on the same issue that 'even when both parents are criminal, about half of the sons do not become delinquent.' Residential people with a criminal record, though, were more likely than the rest to have contacts with the natural family. However, the parents whom the respondents contacted did not predominantly have a criminal record. Like respondents who were heavy drinkers and who also were likely to have contacts with the natural family, the contact may have been a search for relationships and support.

Table 7.10 Criminal history among residential people and in the families of origin

		Residential people		Total	
		Criminal behaviour N	No criminal behaviour N	N	%
Family of origin	Criminal history	10	10	20	50
	No criminal history	7	13	20	50
		17 (43%)	23 (57%)	40	100

Psychiatric record

A history of psychiatric referral in childhood or in adult life featured among respondents in both samples. As only one of the natural parents of adoptees had a history of psychiatric treatment, direct comparisons between the two generations were not possible. Because of this, contrasts were first made between those adoptees with a psychiatric record and natural mothers described as having some degree of 'mental handicap'. There was no evidence to suggest that the children of women described by social workers as having a degree of mental handicap were likely to develop psychiatric problems. The second stage was to contrast adoptees with a psychiatric referral with those natural parents who were described as 'psychologically unstable' by the social workers. Again, no relationship emerged to link adoptees displaying psychiatric difficulties with natural parents who were described as 'psychologically unstable'. Neither were adoptees with a psychiatric history likely to have a 'disturbed' family background. Of the nine adoptees who had psychiatric treatment only two were connected with twelve natural parents (mostly mothers) who were classified as 'disturbed'.

Among the residential group 16 (40 per cent) respondents had been referred or referred themselves for psychiatric help compared with seven natural families who had psychiatric treatment. No evidence was found to indicate that residential people referred for psychiatric help were likely to have parents with a psychiatric history. However, residential people with a psychiatric record were very likely to have a 'disturbed' family background (i.e. families sharing two or more indices signifying personal or social 'disturbance': namely crime, alcohol abuse, severe relationship problems and 'psychological instability' ($p < 0.001$)) (Table 7.11).

Table 7.11 Residential people with a psychiatric history and 'disturbed' families

		Residential people		Total	
		Psychiatric problems	No problems		
		N	N	N	%
Natural families	'Disturbed' family	13	5	18	45
	No disturbance	3	19	22	55
		16 (40%)	24 (60%)	40	100

'Disturbed' respondents contrasted to 'disturbed' natural families

The next step was to contrast the seven adoptees and 15 residential people who were classified as 'disturbed' with the natural parents who were equally classified as 'disturbed'. The first correlation between 'disturbed' adoptees and 'disturbed' natural parents produced no evidence at all of any intergenerational links. In fact, the evidence pointed in the opposite direction, i.e. that adoptees classified as 'disturbed' came predominantly from non-disturbed families. A different picture though emerged when 'disturbed' residential people were contrasted with their families (Table 7.12). In effect, residential people classified as 'disturbed' were more likely to have a 'disturbed' family background ($p < 0.01$). Not only were residential people with a psychiatric history very likely to have a 'disturbed' family background, but equally residential people identified as 'disturbed' were very likely

Table 7.12 *'Disturbed' residential people and 'disturbed' families*

		Residential people		Total	
		'Disturbed' N	'Non-disturbed' N	N	%
Natural families	'Disturbed' families	11	7	18	45
	'Non-disturbed' families	4	18	22	55
		15 (38%)	25 (62%)	40	100

to have a 'disturbed' family background. Though both these findings point towards strong intergenerational links, possibly of a genetic nature, the fact that no such connections were found in the adoption sample may point to the potential the adoptive home may have in preventing certain vulnerabilities from finding expression. The residential environment, on the other hand, appears to contribute both to their development and expression.

Summary

This chapter has attempted to contrast the social and personal characteristics and circumstances of respondents in each sample with those of their families of origin at the time of reception into care. The main objective was to test the possibility of intergenerational transmissions operating in the case of children separated from their families in childhood. Some limitations and biases in the records were pointed out. The characteristics contrasted fall broadly into two categories. First, those that refer to material conditions, i.e. employment, income, standard of living and housing. Second, those that refer to aspects of social behaviour and psychological attributes, i.e. criminal record, alcohol abuse, relationship problems and psychiatric referral.

In terms of mobility, respondents in both groups experienced upward social mobility compared to their families of origin. Adoptees from very 'disturbed' backgrounds achieved similar upward mobility to the rest, but residential people from very 'disturbed' backgrounds did less well compared to the rest. The main explanation for the differences between the two groups may lie not in any intergenerational influences but in the interactions between residential people and residential staff. In other words, the same residential people who failed to achieve upward social mobility were also likely to have psychiatric difficulties and, because of their behaviour, they received less support and encouragement from staff.

The social conditions, particularly those of adoptees, were infinitely better than those of their biological families. No intergenerational transmissions were established as far as the economic situation was concerned. The material circumstances of those who grew up in residential establishments were more complex. Though the disadvantages of some were beginning to approximate those of the natural parents, those of others were operating independently of the families of origin. Whilst the adoption sample demonstrated that the past need not control the present, the residential group has shown that disadvantage can set in at any time. A long residence experience, lack of family support, continual lack of opportunities, and the command of very few resources all contributed to a developing picture of deprivation and disadvantage among a fair number of former residential children with the prospects for some others looking very uncertain.

When indices signifying behavioural or psychological 'disturbance' were directly contrasted no evidence emerged to link in significant numbers respondents with a history of crime, alcohol abuse, relationship problems or psychiatric difficulties with similar problems in their families of origin. In fact, in the case of adopted people, the evidence in some cases pointed in the opposite direction. In other words, when correlating individual aspects of behaviour present in respondents and in the families of origin, no significant association emerged. In certain instances in the residential group, the figures were moving somewhat in the direction of demonstrating such a relationship, but the association was weak.

However, a number of significant relationships were established between residential people and their parents when aspects of similar types of behaviour were grouped together. First, residential people facing serious relationship problems or psychiatric difficulties were likely to have a 'disturbed' family background (i.e. families sharing two or more indices signifying 'disturbance'). Second, the most 'disturbed' residential people (i.e. those sharing two or more indices signifying 'disturbance') were likely to have a 'disturbed' family background. These findings do not necessarily establish the case for genetic transmissions, especially as similar transmissions were not found operating in the adoption sample, many of whom had an equally 'disturbed' family background. Though such vulnerability may exist it never develops in the case of adoptees, but it finds its expression in residential people possibly because of their residential experiences and of continuing adversities.

8 Summary and Discussion

The study set out to answer a number of related questions concerning different patterns of substitute care for children, including the possible influence of the family of origin on the second generation. The main question asked was the extent to which aspects of behaviour, social handicaps and other characteristics or difficulties are transmitted from one generation to the next in situations where the children are separated and remain apart from their families in early life. A further question was whether there are quantitative and qualitative differences between late adoptions and institutional rearing, contrasting those who could be traced and agreed to be interviewed. This is an important qualification because it is well known that sample loss can have potentially distorting effects upon the results if these are held to reflect the outcome of all similar late adoptions at the particular point in time, and all similar residential rearing of disadvantaged children. We have already indicated some of the problems in this connection. Moreover, there are clear differences in the backgrounds of adopted and residentially-reared children which makes any simple comparison of differing outcomes unwarranted. We have here two samples with some similarities and some important differences in their backgrounds, which latter do not permit us to assume that the only variables in outcome are adoption/non-adoption–institutional rearing. What is nevertheless important is the bearing of the results of both samples on the question of transmission intergenerationally of background characteristics. Here we can give a much less equivocal answer.

Of the two samples being studied and contrasted, the adoption group was made up of 44 adoptees in their mid-twenties at interview, and who were placed with their adoptive families when aged between 2 and 8 years. The residential group was made up of 40 people aged around 23 who spent an average of 11 years of their childhood in residential establishments. All respondents had initially been received or committed into the care of a local authority or voluntary society. Adoptees featuring in the study were taken into care considerably earlier than residential people and experienced their natural families for an average of 12 months compared with 53 months by the residential group. The mean age of the adoption group when they went to their adoptive families was 41 months, having spent an average of about 30 months in care, mostly in institutions. The delay in their placement was mostly due to questions connected with the natural parents' social or emotional condition or with the child's physical or psychological state. In effect, there were many doubts at the time as to whether these 'high risk' children should be adopted at all.

Information and data for the study were collected from the records of social agencies. Detailed interviews were also conducted with the respondents and a large part of the study relies on their descriptions and on the rating of their experiences. The study falls into three identifiable parts: first, it examines and evaluates the growing-up period in the adoptive home or in the institution; second, it focuses on the respondents' current material, social and personal circumstances; finally, it contrasts the subjects' current conditions and circumstances with those of their natural families at the time of reception into care.

The growing-up period in the adoptive home or in the residential establishment

A significantly higher proportion of adoptees compared with residential people felt very positive and least negative about their overall growing-up experience. Well over 80 per cent of those adopted expressed from a fair to a considerable amount of satisfaction with their adoption experience compared with 55 per cent of residential people. A major difference between residential people and those who grew up adopted, as well as fostered (see Triseliotis 1980b), was the high proportion of people in the latter two groups who expressed 'very positive' views about their substitute care, which they attributed to the family-type rearing they had. The expression of satisfaction by over 80 per cent of adoptees is in line with the outcome of early adoptions found in recent studies. Their late adoption and 'high risk' status did not adversely affect the adoption outcome.

Adopted people enjoyed the feeling of belonging to a family, of being accepted for themselves and made to feel as one of the family. They generally enjoyed close and warm relationships with parental figures, with siblings and with members of the extended family. The closeness of the relationships continued into adult life and was a great source of support and satisfaction to the adoptees. The latter saw themselves as the children of their adoptive parents whom they looked upon as their 'real' parents. At no stage did they perceive themselves as parentless or as orphans because of the loss of the original family. Some element of 'rejection' by the original parent(s) was present, but less noticeably so than in the case of residential people. When adoptees thought or spoke of parents it was the adoptive family they had in mind, and not an imagined set of biological parents. In matters of feelings, the natural family occupied an insignificant place in the adoptees' preoccupations and concerns. Some of the adoptees had memories of living in institutions, and they were quick to express their preference for the opportunity to grow up with people who wanted them. The descriptive accounts given by the great majority of adoptees indicated a mutual attachment and bonding with their adoptive parents. As no relationship was found between adoption outcome and the presence of own children, it can be assumed that parenting qualities are more important than the status of the child.

The less than one-fifth who expressed mixed feelings or dissatisfaction with their adoption linked it mostly to pressures to fulfil parental ambitions, or to the absence of closeness and emotional warmth on the part of the parents, which was experienced as rejection. Most dissatisfactions were expressed by adoptees who grew up in what could be described as middle-class-type families. The inability of some adoptees to respond to parental aspirations created stress and guilt, and sometimes resentment. What was valued by both groups was encouragement and support to pursue their own ideas, wishes and ambitions. The qualities in the parents which were perceived as having contributed to the success of adoption were love, closeness, warmth, stability, confidence in parenting, openness and honesty about adoption, and encouragement and support. For the adoption workers there still remains the question of how to recognise these qualities in would-be adopters. The recent practice of considering almost anyone prepared to offer a home to a 'hard-to-place' child, though a move in the right direction, should not disregard some of the qualities outlined above which appear to contribute towards successful outcome. After all, not every biological parent can become a psychological one too.

The age at which a child came into care, the number of moves experienced before the final placement, past behaviour, parental background, health risks and age at placement did not affect the outcomes of adoption. An element of risk, though, was associated with the placement of children with adoptive parents aged 45 and over, and those described as financially 'very comfortable' as opposed to 'average'. The good adjustment achieved by the vast majority of adoptees indicates that given a new caring and enabling environment, children can form fresh attachments and overcome past deprivations and deficits. Adoptees with 'inferior' background histories, including those born to women described as suffering from a degree of mental handicap, did not function any differently from the rest.

The few residential people who were very positive about their experience valued continuity of care, individual attention, the caring attitude of some staff, the opportunity to get close to them, flexible rules and a relaxed atmosphere. They also felt that the institution offered them the opportunity to make something of themselves compared to what might have become of them if they had stayed with their own families. Residential people generally appreciated and could remember with affection individual members of staff who showed them kindness and understanding, and who tried to care or explain, or who were patient with them. Even if at the time they were difficult, which some of them acknowledged, they still seemed to carry positive feelings towards staff who persisted in being understanding and caring. The respondents' comments and descriptions, however, indicated that staff were more responsive to the well-behaved child than to the troublesome one. This suggests that residential staff appear more successful with those children who are able to establish relationships and least so with the more troublesome child who has difficulties in forming and maintaining attachments.

Residential people generally valued being kept with their siblings, and they had some very harsh and bitter words to say in cases where they were unnecessarily split, sometimes for sheer administrative convenience. What hurt most was the fact that the other sibling often provided the main nurturing in an establishment that otherwise had little or none to offer. Sibling relationships continued to provide one of the main sources of comfort and support to former residential people in their current lives. They relied on each other when faced with difficulties such as marital upsets, evictions or money problems. Whilst adoptees (and from our other studies former foster children) could count on the support of their adoptive or foster families, residential people relied heavily on siblings, in-laws or the social services. Parents were rarely in evidence. A major challenge that emerged was how to provide supportive networks for many of the residential people who had none. If siblings have be be separated on account of their very different needs, ways should be found to keep them in touch.

Though most residential people had very few good words to say about their experience in residential care, they also avoided being extravagant in their criticisms or of appearing vindictive. Many felt, however, that the experience spoiled their whole childhood and was affecting them in their current lives. They generally saw it as a 'waste' of their childhood. Most of the criticism had to do with the lack of individualised care, the absence of opportunities for close relationships, with being treated as a group, the absence of privacy, the lack of explanation and discussion about their circumstances of being in care or in the establishment, the rigidity of rules, the harshness of punishments and the endless routine. The feelings of being isolated from the 'real world' came in for particular criticism, as well as their perception of being 'stigmatised' by the wider community. It was their firm belief that the community equated being 'in care' with the being 'bad'. In fact, some came to refer to themselves as 'not normal'. The frequent staff changes also instilled in them feelings of mistrust towards adults and particularly towards new staff trying to get close to them. Interaction between staff and children on a personal level seemed at a premium and was mostly confined to situations when orders were being given or discipline enforced. A situation of 'them' and 'us' would fit many of the descriptions made by respondents and would explain some of the tensions found in residential establishments. Residential respondents generally tried to be understanding of staff trying to do a difficult job, often without training and without adequate assistance. A change of house-mother or of institution would herald a better or worse period depending on who was in charge. Subjects generally associated positive changes with the arrival of trained staff who tried to introduce reforms, such as doing away with unnecessary rules and with the worst types of physical punishment. Staff who took time to listen and talk to residents were particularly liked, even if at the time the subjects were not very responsive themselves. In the eyes of respondents, staff would give up too quickly when no immediate response was elicited, failing to recognise the underlying suspicion and mistrust. Ancillary staff, such as cooks and gardeners, who took the trouble to listen were remembered with considerable affection.

Running away from the Home was one way for some of them to escape from what appeared to them an 'intolerable' situation. Some women used early marriage as their way of 'escaping' from care and the institution. Like adopted people, residential ones expressed the need to have information about their families, who they were and where they were. They wanted answers to such basic questions as 'Why am I in care?' and 'Why am I here?'. A number of them maintained that they were unaware, whilst in care, whether one or both parents were alive or dead. Others were suddenly faced with the news that a parent was about to visit, when they thought all along that he or she was dead. At other times, they were told of the existence of siblings in other Homes about whom they had previously known nothing.

Our findings lead us to the conclusion that the identity of children growing up in residential establishments is negatively affected by three factors we investigated: the absence of significant closeness with carers; ignorance about their personal history and the circumstances of their families; and the feeling that they are perceived by the outside world as 'bad' or 'worthless'. In contrast, adoptees only missed out by sometimes not having sufficient genealogical information. In their view, the love of most adoptive parents went a long way to make up for this drawback. The core of the adoptees' identity was mostly built around their adoptive families. The natural family played a very small but crucial part in their concept of themselves. The vast majority were uninterested in, though in a quest for, the original family. Access to original birth records or the search for a natural parent remained a very minority response. Overall, most adoptees displayed a firm sense of self and it would be wrong to equate adoption with identity confusion. Such a confusion can occur only under certain circumstances. Many residential people having 'failed' to identify with what they experienced as an 'uncaring' institution, were left with no sense of belonging and not much sense of security. Outside society was also perceived as prejudiced towards them and making them feel different from the rest.

Both adoptees and residential people displayed a range of emotional, behaviour or psychiatric problems at different stages of their lives. Significantly, more adoptees were described as having emotional problems before joining their adoptive parents than residential people on coming into care and for the immediate period afterwards. In spite of a background of disadvantage and apparent 'disturbance' residential children did not begin to display emotional/behaviour or psychiatric difficulties to any appreciable extent until some time after entering care. As the period in care continued residential children were then more likely than adoptees to display emotional/behaviour or psychiatric difficulties. The higher rate of such problems among residential people compared to adoptees continued into adult life. Psychiatric referral of adopted children was found to be much lower than a number of clinical studies have suggested. Neither was the presence of emotional/behaviour or psychiatric problems among adoptees in childhood predictive of similar behaviours in adult life.

Residential people who came into care when aged 4 and under were more likely to be referred for psychiatric help during childhood. An increasing number of placement changes for residential people equally increased the possibility of psychiatric referral. Some caution, however, is needed here because there was evidence to suggest that children who were already identified as 'difficult' were most likely to be moved around. Overall, those reporting emotional or psychiatric difficulties were also likely to express less satisfaction with the adoption or residential experience. Adoptees who had psychiatric help were more likely than the rest to say that there was no discussion of their adoption and their background. Psychiatric and emotional problems in residential people in childhood were predictive of similar difficulties in adult life. Equally, psychiatric problems in residential children were almost always predictive of heavy alcohol consumption in adult life. Being warned by the police in childhood increased the possibility of court appearances in adult life for the residential group. Cass and Thomas (1979), in a study designed to test the assumption that social and personal adjustment in adulthood can be predicted from behaviour symptoms, social adjustment, personality variables and family characteristics in childhood, reported that except in extreme cases of personality deviation, including the threat of psychosis and extreme anti-social behaviour, 'there seems to be little continuity between disturbance in childhood and adulthood.' Their study was designed to study children in residential establishments.

In terms of physical health, those growing up in institutions were more likely than adoptees to report a higher incidence of respiratory disease (particularly pneumonia), dysentry, and ear, nose and throat infections. Measles and mumps were reported more frequently by adoptees. The poorer health of the residential children may come as a surprise in view of the regular medical attention they are meant to receive. It is possible that their general unhappiness about being in the institution made them more prone to respiratory diseases. Adopted children with physical disabilities before placement did as well as the rest.

The respondents' current material, social and personal circumstances
Overall the current material, social and personal circumstances of residential people compared unfavourably with those of adoptees. The former were more likely to be unemployed and draw social security benefits, express mixed feelings or dissatisfaction with their income or housing, and be rather dissatisfied with their jobs and with life in general. The material circumstances of at least one-third of the residential respondents were very inadequate. There was no statistical evidence to link respondents currently experiencing financial and housing problems with psychiatric referral in childhood or adult life. Mattinson (1970), who followed up ex-patients of a subnormality hospital who were known to have married each other, and whose average length of stay in hospital was 13–15 years, found that most of these families were 'successful' in spite of their low income. Depending also on how the figures are viewed, in spite of all the adversities, half of the residential people were coping in matters of income and housing adequately. Unlike the parents, income and housing deficiencies among the offspring did not correlate with 'disturbance' as defined by the study. In other words, income and housing insufficiencies only

occasionally linked with serious personal and relationship problems. However, in view of the precarious circumstances and coping of a fair number of them, and of the increasing environmental stresses, the possibility of material and personal circumstances overlapping in future cannot be excluded.

Divorce and separation, and general relationship problems featured among respondents in both samples, but again these were more pronounced among those who had a residential rearing. In addition, almost half of the residential people who were parents expressed some difficulty about relating to their own children; most of them blamed their institutional experience for their predicament. The absence of a planned approach to prepare them for community life also came in for a fair amount of criticism. Many felt that they were left to cope unaided and unprepared and with no opportunities to make mistakes without losing the support of the institution. Shame arising from failure prevented some from returning to the establishment to visit or to ask for help. Residential people seemed to want to demonstrate that they could make a go of things and stand on their own feet. No such anxiety was found among adoptees (i.e. to prove to their parents that they could manage on their own). Some others who wanted to return to the institutions were deterred by the turnover of staff or the absence of a place for them to stay overnight or for the weekend.

The proportion of adoptees and residential people appearing before a criminal court did not differ much, but residential people were more likely to reappear. The latter were also more likely to be heavy drinkers, to be referred for psychiatric help in adult life, and to report emotional problems at interview. Men in both the residential and adoption samples were more likely than women to appear before a court, but women growing up in residential care were more likely than those growing up adopted to become delinquent or heavy drinkers. Heavy drinking among residential people was often accompanied by the presence of emotional or psychiatric problems at interview and, as already stated, psychiatric referral in childhood was predictive of alcohol abuse in later life.

Not only were the adoptees' social conditions and material circumstances significantly more stable than those of residential people, but this was also true in matters indicating personal contentment, well-being and personal satisfactions. Residential people were more likely to report uncertainty about themselves, their 'sense of well-being' and their capacity to cope with life. They were also infinitely more likely than adoptees to say that they had few satisfactions in their lives, and that the past and the way they grew up still created problems for them. A major factor contributing to successful coping seemed to be the amount of support respondents obtained in their current lives, particularly in exercising their parenting roles. In the case of most adoptees, significant support was almost always available from their adoptive families. A residential upbringing of the type we studied seems to produce adults who are less certain about themselves and who are generally more vulnerable to adversities. In summary, the former residential persons' 'quality of life' compared unfavourably with that of those who were adopted.

Contrasting respondents with their natural families
Both groups of respondents shared a common background of disadvantage and social deprivation. At the time they came into care their families were facing a range of material, social and personal problems of varying degrees and severity. Though the proportion of natural parents in the two groups facing moderate to severe material difficulties was not significantly different, the handicaps faced by the parents of residential people were more severe and chronic. The older age of the residential parents also meant that some of their problems acquired a chronicity that was not the case with the younger natural parents of the adoption group. Overall, 40 per cent of the families of adoptees and about two-thirds of those of residential people were facing three or more indices signifying material deprivations and personal difficulties. The following characteristics in the natural parents and the respondents were examined in an attempt to establish possible transmissions from parents to children.

Social class by occupation
Both adoptees and residential people experienced upward social mobility compared to their biological families. The adoptees' social class was nearer to that of their adoptive parents and they were over-represented in social classes I and II compared with the general population. There was no evidence of any continuities with their families of origin in this area, and if anything the evidence was of definite discontinuities. Whilst many residential people continued to hold semi-skilled and unskilled jobs like their parents, an appreciable proportion were in non-manual occupations. It appears that in the case of separated children the type of socialising influences experienced after separation is a more important determinant of occupational status than the influence of the family of origin.

Financial and housing circumstances
In matters of income adequacy, no continuities of any kind could be established linking adoptees with their families of origin. A more

complex picture emerged with regard to residential people. Whilst half of the residential people were more comfortable financially compared to their parents, a more complex picture emerged for the remaining half. The material circumstances of some had similarities with those of the parents, reaching statistical significance in matters of housing, thus suggesting certain continuities. The material disadvantages of others, however, were unrelated to the conditions of the parents. There was no doubt from our findings that the children of the poor mostly continue to be poor, but answers to the problem must be sought much more in the economic structure rather than ascribed to background influences. Rutter and Madge (1977) suggest that even with forms of disadvantage where they are strong, discontinuities are striking. They found that at least half of the children born into a disadvantaged home do not repeat the pattern of disadvantage in the next generation. Wright and Lunn (1971), who followed up the children of administratively-defined 'problem families', claim to have found evidence of considerable intergenerational continuities, though the new generation as a whole showed improved functioning on a number of indices such as work records, debts and contact with welfare agencies compared to their parents. Handler and Hollingsworth (1971) found, from a study of low income American families, that of a sample dependent upon welfare benefits only a third had parents who had been similarly placed. The researchers concluded that the stereotype of 'second generation' claimants was inaccurate.

Social and personal behaviour

No significant association could be established between individual forms of deviant social and personal behaviour such as crime, drink, psychiatric referral, relationship problems and similar behaviour or attributes in the biological family. Unlike some other studies, when single forms of behaviour in the offspring was correlated with similar behaviour in the parents, no significant association could be established. In the case of adoptees the evidence usually pointed in the opposite direction. We can confidently say that the social and personal attributes of the family of origin were irrelevant to the current social and personal behaviour of adoptees. This point is confirmed by Bohman and Sigvardsson (1980) who concluded from their studies that the 'social heritage' seems to have been by and large neutralised by the secure placement which a well-prepared adoption offers. A very significant association, however, was established suggesting that residential people, but not adoptees, referred for psychiatric help or who experience serious relationship problems are likely to have a 'disturbed' parental background. Similarly, residential people classified as 'disturbed' (i.e. facing more than one handicap signifying 'disturbance') were likely to have a 'disturbed' family background. Our failure to establish significant connections between psychiatric disturbance in offspring and individual types of behaviour in parents is stressed by Rutter (1978), who observed that 'even with chronic family stresses the children were not particularly at psychiatric risk. However, when any two stresses occurred together the risk went up no less than fourfold.' Our findings suggest that when two or more types of dysfunctional behaviour occur simultaneously in the parents, dysfunctional behaviour is also likely to appear in the offspring. Again, this form of possible transmisson did not hold true of those adopted when contrasted with their original parents.

Discussion

The adoption sample demonstrated definite discontinuities with the material, social and personal circumstances of the natural family. Overall, adoptees were much more likely to resemble in circumstances their adoptive than their natural families. In the case of residential people, there was only limited evidence of intergenerational transmissions in material circumstances. Similarly, though no direct links were found in matters of behaviour, there was evidence to support the view that residential people exhibiting more than one form of 'disturbance' were likely to have an equally 'disturbed' family background. As already mentioned, similar correlations were not found in the adoption sample. On the basis of the findings from the adoption sample, it could be claimed that the transmissions found in the residential sample need not have happened. A more plausible explanation for the persistence of these conditions among residential people is the residential experience and their continuing exposure to conditions of acute disadvantage and of very limited opportunities. Atkinson *et al*. (1983) have concluded from their study that the fate of individuals can be described in terms of chances not continuities, probabilities not predestination.

This view is further supported by the fact that, in contrast to the families of origin, no significant correlations were yet found linking residential people experiencing material adversities with those exhibiting 'disturbed' behaviour. One explanation for this was the relative youth of residential people at interview, suggesting that it is the chronicity of adverse conditions and of long-term marginal coping that contribute to the compounding of a family's handicaps. Besides chronic adversity and marginality, a further factor that seems to add to the problem is the quality of interactions between the disadvantaged and resource agencies. Many of the social services have yet to reach the most needy and vulnerable in ways that are acceptable to them, and free of unnecessary bureaucratic rules and sometimes stigma. Campbell (1979), for example, demonstrated the protracted administrative negotiations that usually take place before even paltry sums of money are made available by social workers to clients to see the latter through crises. Jordan (1981) also criticised the paternalistic principles, conditions and attitudes of housing departments and the Supplementary Benefits Commission towards unsupported mothers. These and other similar attitudes can give rise to mistrust, resulting often in the avoidance of a service until a very late stage and when conditions may be irreversible.

It goes perhaps without saying that it is in the best interests of all children to grow up in their own families where biological and psychological bonding can occur simultaneously. Any disruption in the life of a child can set in motion a series of events that could lead to problems from which he may never recover. As a rule, the separation of children from their families should be undertaken only in situations of unforeseen crises; when the child is at serious physical or emotional risk; or when his behaviour causes very serious concern. Adverse environmental factors alone should not constitute reason for reception into care. Though it is not the purpose of this study to discuss the kind of broader socio-economic policies required to tackle material and social disadvantages at the structural level, nevertheless it is important to stress that focusing attention solely on identifiable families is not enough. In the absence of fundamental structural changes, generational scars of deprivation will be borne by new families exposed to continued conditions of disadvantage.

We would like to paraphrase Wilson and Herbert's (1978) conclusion from their study of parents and children in inner-cities, and add that the solution to 'family failure' may ultimately lie not as much in individual and family approaches but 'in drastic fiscal measures to bring about a reduction of extreme inequality'. Interventions at the individual and family level should be supplementary to broader economic measures. Approaches at the former level should preferably be reserved for those families whose material needs are complicated by non-material factors.

Our findings suggest that successful adaptation in adult life is strongly associated with the presence of a stable and supportive network such as a family. This calls for considerable investment in strengthening both one- and two-parent families and in preventive work well before conditions necessitating reception into care or other forms of separation set in. Yet in Britain there is no identifiable social policy about the family. Similarly, at the local level the personal social services have no explicit policies, planning and programmes specifically designed to promote the welfare of one- and two-parent families. Those familiar with the scene will dispute that any appreciable effort has been made in the direction of preventive work with families in the last 30 or so years. Parker (1980) comments that we still don't know which preventive policies are successful and what types of prevention work best. Faced with heavy demands, rising expectations and limited resources, the personal social services, with some exceptions, have traditionally concentrated on temporary remedies. For the same reasons the recently established social service departments have been limiting themselves to mostly emergency, crisis and short-term responses, with less attention being paid to long-term planning and social rehabilitation. The increasing financial cuts imposed on these and other social services are unlikely to benefit those requiring a range of resources and services over a long period of time. Goldberg (1978), in a review of social work since 'Seebohm', calls for the investment of resources in preventive activities. She refers particularly to the early identification of families with relationship and personality problems and the offer of counselling and support services. Until 1970 the Children's Departments (the nearest equivalent to the present day Social Service Departments) were the main statutory agencies concerned with families and children requiring social work services. Their main function was to assess the need for the reception of children into care and to make suitable arrangements for their reception, including rehabilitation. The 1963 Children's Act, under section 1, placed a duty on local authorities to make available 'advice, guidance and assistance' to families in order to promote the welfare of children by diminishing the need to receive them into, or keep them in, care. The Act also gave powers to local authorities to extend assistance in kind, and in exceptional circumstances in cash, if they saw fit.

The main problem with this Act is that its provisions are so broad and vague that local authorities can do much or little and still be within the spirit of the law. Heywood and Allen (1971) found wide variations in the use of expenditure under section 1. The Act, as it stands, does not give powers to local authorities to provide assistance well before the conditions that give rise to child care need set in. A Home Office Memorandum on the 1963 Children's Act (Home Office circular no. 204/1963) stated that section 1 'does not give powers to intervene in family difficulties or domestic problems unless there is some reason to suppose that this may create the risk of children having to be received into the care of the local authority.' This circular has not been revised.

Working on the assumption postulated by a number of writers that both remedial and preventive work with some families may have to be on a long-term basis, Goldberg (1978) claims that 80 per cent of incoming cases in a social services department were closed within three months of referral. Similarly, 75 per cent of the cases in which marital strife and violence, desertion, separation, divorce, child neglect, delinquency or adolescent rebellion were common occurrences were equally closed within three months of referral. In 30 per cent of these cases the social workers decided to withdraw their services mainly because they had not got the resources in personnel or the community facilities to enter more closely into these precarious family situations. If social services departments are starved of resources to tackle such cases, it is hard to see how they can be expected to carry out any meaningful forms of preventive work. Goldberg also makes the point that some young families who referred themselves for mostly financial, material and housing problems, and were dealt with on a short-term basis, were experiencing other stresses, and a substantial proportion reappeared with other requests within a short time of closure. Whilst emergency, crisis and short-term work are the order of the day in social services departments, the possibility that some families may require longer-term support should not be ignored. Mattinson and Sinclair (1979) found that social workers gave priority to a small group of clients who were severely deprived and whose problems were chronic. The dilemma for these clients was that they felt helpless, but distrusted any help offered. The authors concluded that what such clients needed was a long-term, reliable relationship through which the stresses of living might be better understood and managed. Instead, efforts were directed towards making short-term responses which, while alleviating current crises (for social workers and their management as much as for their clients), often failed to provide help which might modify future crises. Goldberg and Warburton's study (1979) and Parsloe and Stevenson's reports (1978) present a similar picture. Kahan (1979), a former Assistant Director, Social Work Service in the Department of Health and Social Security, laments what she sees as the lack of opportunity to work in depth, which has led to greater emphasis by social workers on crisis and short-term work with a consequent reduction of attention on the needs of children in long-term care. Specht and Vickery (1977) argue that interpersonal problems such as alcoholism, gross emotional deprivation and gross lack of social skills are often linked to severe material deprivation, and such clients require a 'more comprehensive (even long-term) service than a circumscribed one which helps them over one or two areas in their lives.' Heywood and Allen (1971) add that 'perhaps it must be faced that, in the majority of cases, realistic goals are skilled support and help – including financial help – through the continuing crisis of family life until the children are independent.' Jordan (1981b) also adds on this point, 'In the present situation, we are simply not going to come across families who are candidates for long-term or intensive work unless there is also a fairly immediate risk of their children coming into care. Substitute care will not just be a vague possibility – it will increasingly be the first issue on the agenda.' In effect, what the various studies suggest is that not only is preventive work a distant dream, but the social work approaches currently used to help families already in serious trouble may not be the appropriate ones. Mattinson and others in evidence to the NISW inquiry on the role and tasks of social workers, conclude on this issue: 'In short, the evidence suggests that a small group of very deprived clients monopolise an unduly large share of social worker resources, and the secure professional identity and skill necessary to respond to these clients in a way which increases their self-reliance is often missing' (see *Social Work Today* 15 December 1982).

We are not saying that disadvantaged families require the therapeutic attention of social workers, but that along with other necessary structural and organisational changes, social workers have an important role to play in some cases. The use of money by social workers to aid families usually raises objections in the community on the basis that 'neglectful or mismanaging parents are rewarded with additional assistance'. Social workers are themselves unhappy about using money for fear that they will become income maintenance agencies. Their fears seem justifiable in view of the findings of studies by Jackson and Valencia (1979) and Hill and Laing (1979), showing that up to 80 per cent of assisted clients had no need of social work help. The separation of income maintenance from the provision of personal social services has been a characteristic of British social policy for many decades. British social workers are generally in favour of this separation as it relieves them from means-tested relief services which are seen as 'demeaning' and 'degrading'. An integrated framework of income maintenance and social work service delivery, it is argued, confuses clients and makes it appear that people who are simply poor have personal problems and need counselling services. The opponents of separation could argue that an integrated service offers greater opportunities for preventive work through early identification and through combining where necessary help in cash or in kind with support and counselling. Maybe the biggest obstacle to the possible integration of the services in Britain is the historical context within which supplementary benefits have developed, particularly the stigma and the 'Poor Law' image with which they are associated. In countries where the services are new and therefore free of historical connotations, the integration of income and social welfare services has not raised the same objections as it has here. A 'welfare stereotype' with connotations of failure has developed here over centuries and continues to taint all welfare services.

The success of any preventive programme may depend on its flexibility and quick response to need, on the way inter-agency and inter-professional links are developed, as well as on the range of resources made available such as day care provision, supported accommodation, home-help services, peripatetic foster parents, even the payment of the parent(s) to stay at home and look after their children where this could prevent their reception into care. We have not yet fully explored the variety of ways which could be employed to keep children out of care. Particular emphasis may have to be placed on the kind of resources that can be made available to couples whose relationships break up to enable them to set up again jointly or separately with the children. After all, when the relationships of the better-off in the community break up their children do not come into care. Long-term child care as shown by this study usually has as its immediate cause the irretrievable breakdown of relationships between couples, married or unmarried. Considering the heavy financial cost incurred, apart from the human suffering, when children are taken into care and kept in residential institutions planned preventive work is preferable. Clough (1982) argues that 'there are probably sound economic arguments to suggest that more practical supplement care would lead to less long-term care.' No amount of preventive work will altogether stop the reception of some children into care. When a situation like this develops, it is important that a whole range of fostering and residential services are made available for use according to individual need. Already a large percentage of children coming into care return to their families within six months of reception. Though the idea still requires testing in this country, it is our view that the investment of substantial additional supportive resources in the form of material help and counselling during the first few weeks following reception into care, is likely to result in an even higher percentage of children returning to their families than now. Jones *et al*. (1976) have shown that if intensive intervention directed towards rehabilitation of children with their families is undertaken, even at the stage of reception into care, a considerable proportion of children can return to their families. Studies by Sherman *et al*. (1973), Jones *et al*. (1976) and Aldgate (1977) have also identified a number of conditions which can be predictive of a child's length of stay in care. In theory this should enable social workers not only to plan with greater confidence, but also to concentrate their efforts in promoting those conditions which can result in quicker restoration. Yet studies by George (1970), Aldgate (1977) and Thorpe (1980) suggest that the amount of support extended to parents of separated children to enable them to resume parenting is frequently far from adequate. Obviously more knowledge is needed to identify those situations where restoration work is more likely to succeed compared to the rest.

The temptation to use adoption as an outlet for the children of the most disadvantaged must be resisted. This should only be contemplated when it can be shown to be in the long-term interests of the child and provided certain conditions have been met. It is in this respect that aspects of current adoption policy and practice give rise to a number of concerns. The reduction almost to a trickle of the number of illegitimate children being released for adoption, and with inter-country adoptions having come to a halt, it is not surprising that the search for children has turned to those coming into care. The move to extend the traditional boundaries of adoption to children in care started in the early 1970s with the publication of Rowe and Lambert's (1973) study, *Children who wait*. This was followed by a concerted effort to place for adoption some of the children identified in the study. Social workers, anxious perhaps to avoid the build-up of a new group of 'waiting' children, have been keen to find new and permanent homes for those whose families were unable or unwilling to make a home for them. What was seen as the need for quick action, though, has meant that the interval between reception into care and permanency plans, mostly adoption, has been getting increasingly shorter. In some cases time-limits of six months are operating between reception into care and permanency plans. Not surprisingly these developments have brought social workers into a much sharper conflict with natural parents than ever before. Unlike the parents of 'children who wait' identified by Rowe and Lambert (1973), many of the parents of the present children are still around, some of them retaining some bonds with the children.

It is the absence of explicit preventive and restoration policies with accompanying programmes that raises serious questions about the legitimacy of adoption placements for children coming into care for reasons unconnected with adoption. The impression that is conveyed is that the state is more anxious to support adoption as a means for resolving issues and dilemmas in child care than to support natural families. The use of public expenditure to pay allowances to adopters or to professional foster parents is usually given as an example. Hill (1983) makes the point that the shift 'raises issues of general significance, which relate to the boundaries of responsibility between the family and the state and to considerations of equity between the need of differing categories of people.' Whilst we support the idea of adoption allowances and the child's right for continuity and permanency of care, nevertheless such ends cannot be pursued without a clear family and child care policy. In other words, adoption cannot be practised as a 'child care service' without at the same time consideration being given to the forces which generate child care need. A policy of non-family intervention, favoured by some, is likely to divert more children from disadvantaged backgrounds towards adoption.

A reaction to the practices described above was in fact beginning to emerge towards the end of 1982. Whilst the final shift towards children's rights was reflected in a number of court decisions about 'unreasonable' withholding of parental agreement to adoption in the 1970s, two judgments in the Court of Appeal in 1982 appeared to have somewhat switched the balance towards greater recognition of parental rights. In future, and to allay public anxiety, the reception of children into care should preferably be decided by a panel who can also ask questions about the amount of preventive work carried out so far and why it has failed. The same panel would also hold periodic reviews of all children in care and enquire about the restoration work being done and any other plans on behalf of the child. Finally, the assumption of parental rights, usually a prerequisite to adoption placement, should form part of a judicial procedure. The safeguards suggested may not solve all the dilemmas, but at least the care authorities are likely to become much more conscious of their responsibilities. This process should also help to reduce the number of occasions when courts are faced with a *fait accompli*, because plans for a child cannot be held back on account of past mistakes.

Long-term fostering as an alternative to adoption has itself come under attack because of the element of 'insecurity' and impermanence it conveys to the foster family and the child. McKay (1980), for instance, questions the 'impermanency' involved in long-term fostering, though she still sees some role for it. Adcock (1980) goes further and argues that a child needs a permanent home which is intended to last, and should be given the legal security to make this possible. Children growing up in long-term foster care, she goes on, 'cannot be said to have permanent homes because they have no legal security against interference from either their own families or . . . from social workers.' Hussell and Monaghan (1982) suggest even more drastic measures, by arguing for a complete severance of the links between a child and his parents where the latter cannot fulfil all the tasks of parenthood. Visiting a child in care, the authors argue, is not sufficient to maintain him as part of his original family. The implication of the authors' view is that in contrast to fostering, adoption provides for greater permanency. Yet in spite of certain drawbacks, long-term fostering still has a lot to offer, including the placement of adolescents (see Triseliotis 1983). Zimmerman (1982) also found from a recent study that youngsters who grew up in stable foster care were currently functioning more successfully than those who were returned to their natural families. Planned permanency, through adoption or fostering, need not of course exclude interested parents or other relatives from playing a continuing part. Though this is an area in which practice experience is still very limited, it is bound to assume greater significance with the increasing number of older children now being placed. Some of the children have meaningful bonds which cannot be erased. These factors will inevitably necessitate a move towards more open or 'inclusive' adoptions. Provision may have to be made in suitable cases for access to children by parents and relatives who still have meaningful bonds with them. Again, this is an area in which more practice experience and knowledge are required to establish particularly how such arrangements can work out, and whether they affect the child's need for attachment to his new family. Keshet and Rosenthal (1980) provide some evidence which shows that children of divorced parents can relate positively to both their biological parents and to a step-parent. The very few children who retained some contact with a member of their birth family in our sample derived considerable satisfaction from it. As for long-term fostering, permanency when indicated should preferably be guaranteed by a form of legislation which approximates adoption, again with built-in access provision.

Turning to residential care, it is now apparent that the comments made by the Curtis Committee (1946) that some of the unsatisfactory practices they observed were past history were over-optimistic. Both Berry's (1975) and these findings still give reasons for disquiet as far as the quality of residential service is concerned. It cannot be claimed that what these studies have observed is again 'past history' until evidence is produced to the contrary. Harris (1981) made the point that 'comparing residential care in 1981 with residential care in 1961, we effectively have more of the same, and the developments that have taken place other than in size, have tended to be staff orientated rather than client orientated.'

There is no wish here to imply criticism of residential staff who are expected to carry out a very demanding job often without adequate training and support. Their relative isolation from the rest of the social services sets them and the children apart from others in the community. Whilst personal qualities appear to be most important, as evidenced by the residential people's comments, in the long run staff and residents become absorbed in institutional cultures with disabling results. Outsiders reading the former residential subjects' comments are likely to feel protectively towards them with consequent criticisms of staff. This would neglect the fact that insecure and deprived children who have been exposed to rejection, harshness and institutionalisation, can also be troublesome, difficult to control, sometimes 'nasty' and frequently rejecting, being unresponsive to attempts to help them. They can make staff feel helpless and hopeless. Perhaps the state of our knowledge of how to help is very limited, but enough is now known that should at least partially eradicate some of the more gross inadequacies found by the study. It cannot be sidestepped, for instance, that some of the reception and daily living routines and procedures can sometimes be insensitive to the children's feelings. Similarly the lack, in many cases, of direct involvement of the staff with the children contributes to the impersonal nature of institutional life. As in some other areas of life, activity as perceived by the children appeared to centre on the maintenance of the system. This absorbed such effort and attention that little was left for the children. Balbernie (1975) in his introduction to *After Grace – teeth* comments that 'residential treatment is an art, the art of consciously using oneself in relationship for others to create a healing culture.' Few relationships blossomed in the institutions where the study children grew up. Many respondents failed to identify with the institution and their carers and came to view it and them as rather punishing and uncaring. They tended to attribute their low self-image, insecurities and anxieties to the narrow and restricted life of the institutions with their routine, strict rules, their punishing approach and isolation from the outside community. The staff who were prepared and ready to listen to 'facts and feelings' were not as many as the time was usually spent in getting through the physical chores and arrangements. Though Barton's (1959) and Goffman's (1961) studies were based on observations of big institutions, their descriptions of the 'total institution' and of 'institutional neurosis' resulting from certain processes fit in with the descriptions of the residential people featuring in this study. Many of the residential people interviewed were psychologically and socially damaged. Not only did the system fail to meet their needs, but the evidence was that it contributed to their problems. Balbernie (1975: xiv) commenting again on the dangers of institutionalisation wrote:

> In child care almost any 'system' of socialisation will work provided those it serves and those who serve it feel themselves to actually be a part of it. Institutionalisation occurs when heart is lost and morale is gone, when love,

respect and enthusiasm are missing, when reliability is lost. It is from this that devaluation and depersonalisation spring.

It may be claimed that the kind of residential care examined here is no longer common practice and that few, if any, children now spend long periods of their lives in Homes. That, in effect, most residential care, with or without education on the premises, is now only for short periods of time until a child's difficulties are fully or partially resolved, or until such time as alternative plans are made. This may be a worthwhile objective to aim for, but studies by Rowe and Lambert (1973) showed that over a fifth of the children featuring in their study of 32 agencies in England, Wales and Scotland had been in care for 5 years or more, and 90 per cent of these were living in institutions. Newman and Mackintosh (1975) in a study of residential care provision in the South-East of Scotland found that a quarter of the children in residential institutions had been there for 5 years or more. A recent report by the Social Work Services Group (a longitudinal study of Children in Care 1981) showed that nearly a quarter of all children in care had been there for more than 5 years. About a third of those children were living in residential Homes mostly run by voluntary agencies. The report went on to add that there was little chance of these children leaving care before the age of 18. More interesting is the fact that 80 per cent of the long-term children had not been in care before. In effect their first admission to care proved to be for the remaining part of their childhood. A legitimate question is why alternative long-term plans had not been made after such long periods in care, and when it was evident that restoration was more of a dream than a reality.

Whilst it would be nice to think that no child who simply requires care should live in an institution, the reality suggests that such an environment may still be necessary for children for whom a family-type rearing may not be the answer. There is a body of opinion which supports institutions on the grounds that children are more likely to retain their connections with their natural families compared to fostering. However, residential establishments for long-term living, if required at all, have to be structured differently from other Homes to approximate as far as possible an ordinary family home. The caring staff too have to be selected for this specific job rather than simply be recruited to work as 'general' residential workers. The Homes we have in mind should provide 'good enough' caring unaffected by shift systems and staff changes, and guaranteeing stability and continuity. What is required in effect is a more discriminating approach to the needs of different children, with staff being selected for the specific job in mind. In this case, that of offering a 'parenting' type of experience.

For example, Triseliotis (1980a) has shown the higher levels of satisfaction expressed by those who were fostered on their own, or at least with one other child, compared to those fostered with a number of other children which included short and long stays. In the latter case the caring was experienced as more diluted. Harris in his review of MacVeigh (1982) (*Social Work Today* 14 November 1982 – a biography of Graham Gaskin who grew up in institutions) comments: 'Despite all our efforts since 1948, we can still fail individuals like Graham Gaskin, and none of us can feel satisfied until society's methods of caring for children who are disadvantaged and delinquent have improved beyond the experiences and feelings described in the book.' Besides a general improvement in the quality of care, the identity of children could be strengthened by their greater participation in the life of the Homes and the community, by access to updated personal records, and through active participation in their reviews. Reviews could become opportunities for involving children in discussions about their past and current circumstances and for an exploration of the future. Reinach and Roberts (1978) report somewhat more optimistic findings from their follow-up of children leaving an Observation and Assessment Centre by stating that 'in their relationships with staff children were moderately positive in the main and most felt they could confide in a staff member, at least to some extent.' Berridge (1983) also claims that his recent studies show that, compared to the past, there is now a significantly lower level of staff mobility in residential establishments.

The declining use of the conventional Children's Home is a good opportunity for investing more resources in supporting children leaving care to become independent. In a period of high unemployment and shortage of suitable housing, local authorities could develop affirmative policies towards teenagers who have been in their care.

A more immediate priority is the training of those working or aiming to work in residential units. Though the study demonstrated that the personal qualities of staff are important, respondents also tended to equate improvements in the institution and in their lives with the arrival of staff from 'courses'. It is estimated that something like 80 per cent of the staff of residential and day care units are untrained. In contrast almost 100 per cent of fieldwork staff in Scotland, and over 75 per cent in England and Wales are now trained. It is apparent that the residential and day care services lag significantly behind and that the training of their staff is long overdue. So is the need for the development of comprehensive support and consultancy systems for the staff in the front line. Currently those least equipped often find themselves performing some very demanding tasks. Notwithstanding the shortcomings found by this study, we would like to end by stressing the positive advantages of residential care as a method of choice and quote the Barclay Committee's (1982: para. 4.39) view that:

> It can lead a person to a significant re-evaluation of himself and his life, give him opportunities for trying out and learning new ways of relating to people at a level deeper than is possible in day provision, and it can provide someone who has had distressing and damaging experience of his own family not only with relief but also with joy and renewed hope.

Appendix

Table 1 Age of natural mother at child's birth

	Adoption N	%	Residential N	%
Below 21	12	32	5	16
21–25	14	38	8	25
26–30	5	13	9	28
31–40	5	14	9	28
41 and over	1	3	1	3
	37	100	32	100
Missing	7		8	
	44		40	

Difference index = 29%*

* The difference index ranges between 0 and 100. The higher the difference index the greater the difference between the two groups being compared.

Table 2 Marital status of natural mother at child's birth

	Adoption N	%	Residential N	%
Single	30	70	5	13
Married	7	16	23	59
Divorced/separated	6	14	11	28
	43	100	39	100
Missing	1		1	
	44		40	

Difference index = 57%

Table 3 Social class of family of origin by occupation[1]

Social class	Adoption N	%	Residential N	%
I & II	3	9	—	—
IIINM	8	24	—	—
IIIM	2	6	5	16
IV & V	20	61	26	84
	33	100		
Army	1			
	34	100	31	100
Missing[2]	10		9	
	44		40	

Difference index = 33%

[1] The classification of the adoption group is based on the occupation of the natural mother as most children were illegitimate. The classification of the residential group is based on the occupation of the father.
[2] Most parents for whom no occupation was given were described in the records as 'unemployed' or 'habitually unemployed'. It is unlikely that these parents held other than 'semi-skilled' or 'unskilled' occupations.

Table 4 Housing conditions of families of origin

	Adoption N	%	Residential N	%
Fairly stable	24	57	17	49
Precarious	14	33	1	3
Very precarious	4	10	17	48
	42	100	35	100
Missing	2		5	
	44		40	

$\chi^2 = 20.03$; d.f. = 2; $p < 0.001$
Difference index = 38%

Table 5   Economic situation of families of origin

	Adoption N	%	Residential N	%
Fairly stable	20	49	16	43
Precarious	18	44	14	38
Very precarious	3	7	7	19
	41	100	37	100
Not known	3		3	
	44		40	

$\chi^2 = 1.61$; d.f. = 2;
Difference index = 12%

Table 6   Quality of relationships in families of origin

	Adoption N	%	Residential N	%
Fairly stable	17	40	5	13
Disruptive	15	36	9	23
Very disruptive	10	24	25	64
	42	100	39	100
Missing	2		1	
	44		40	

$\chi^2 = 13.77$; d.f. = 2; $p < 0.001$
Difference index = 40%

APPENDIX

Table 7 Alcohol problems in family of origin

	Adoption N	%	Residential N	%
None	32	78	20	51
Some	1	2	2	5
Severe	8	20	17	44
	41	100	39	100
Missing	3		1	
	44		40	

$p < 0.001$ (based on combining 'none' and 'some')
Difference index = 27%

Table 8 Criminal convictions among the families of origin

	Adoption N	%	Residential N	%
Convictions present	7	17	20	51
No convictions	35	83	19	49
	42	100	39	100
Missing	2		1	
	44		40	

$p < 0.005$
Difference index = 34%

Table 9 Age at reception into care by sample

Age	Adoption N	Adoption %	Residential N	Residential %
Under 1	29	68	5	13
1–2 years	10	23	10	25
3–4 years	3	7	7	18
5–6 years	—	—	9	22
7–9 years	1	2	9	22
	43	100	40	100
Missing	1			
	44			

Difference index = 55%

Table 10 Gap between reception and final placement

Period	Adoption N	Adoption %	Residential N	Residential %
No gap	4	9	9	23
1 year and under	11	25	16	41
2–3 years	20	45	5	13
4–5 years	7	16	4	10
5 years and over	2	5	5	13
	44	100	39	100
Missing			1	

Difference index = 38%

Table 11 Time in family before legal adoption

	N	%
Under 1 year	19	46
1–2 years	15	37
3–4 years	3	7
5 years and over	4	10
	41	100
Missing	3	
	44	

Table 12 Periods in residential care before final placement (adoption only)

Period	Adoption N	%
Nil	4	10
1 year and under	13	32
2–3 years	18	45
4–5 years	5	13
	40	100
Missing	4	
	44	
Mean	25 months	

Table 13 Periods in foster care before final placement

Period	Adoption N	%	Residential N	%
Nil	34	77	30	75
1 year and under	7	16	4	10
2–3 years	2	5	3	8
4–5 years	1	2	3	7
	44	100	40	100

Difference index = 8%

Table 14 Age of adoptive parents at placement

Age	Adoptive father N	%	Adoptive mother N	%	Non-relatives* Adoptive father %	Adoptive mother %
Below 30	4	11	5	14	18	32
30–40	14	39	17	46	56	53
41–50	12	33	12	32	22	13
51 and over	6	17	3	8	3	1
	36	100	37	100	99	99
Missing	8		7			
	44		44			
Mean	40 years (s.d. 8.2)		41 years			

* Government Survey 1966.

APPENDIX

Table 15 House occupancy

	Adoptive parents N	%	General population* %
Owner–occupier	16	39	33
Local authority housing	16	39	54
Privately rented	—	—	13
Tied occupation	8	20	—
Other	1	2	—
	41	100	100
Missing	3		
	44		

* *Scottish housing: A consultative document* (1977), Cmnd 6552 London, HMSO. (The general population statistics include single people.)

Table 16 Number of all children present in the adoptive families (inc. study child)

	N	%
1	18	41
2	15	34
3–4	7	16
5 and more	4	9
	44	100
Mean	2.00	
	(s.d. 1.4)	

Table 17   Age at termination of formal education

	Adoption N	%	Residential N	%
Statutory school leaving age	12	27	21	52
1 year later	15	34	8	20
2 years later	6	14	5	13
3 years later	4	9	5	13
4 years or more	7	16	1	2
	44	100	40	100

Difference index = 26%

Table 18   Adoptees in social classes I and II contrasted with the social class of natural mother and adoptive father

Adoptees	Natural mother	Adoptive father
I	V	IIIM
I	IIINM	IIINM
II	IV	IIINM
II	IV	II
II	IV	IIIM
II	IV	IV
II	mother a minor	II
II	IV	IIINM
II	IV	IIIM
II	n/a	II
II	n/a	IIIM
II	IV	II
II	II	II

Table 19 Alcohol-related problems

	Adoption N	Adoption %	Residential N	Residential %	General population Scotland* %
No problems	32	74	26	65	55
Moderate	8	19	8	20	25
Severe	—	—	2	5	10
No drink	3	7	4	10	10
	43	100	40	100	100
Missing	1				
	44				

Difference index = Adoption & residential = 9%
Adoption & gen. pop. = 19%
Residential & gen. pop. = 10%

* Figures given by Dr Ritson at a seminar at University of Edinburgh, 25 November 1980, based on an unpublished study, 'Cultural aspects of alcoholism'.

Table 20 Sense of emotional well-being at interview

	Adoption N	Adoption %	Residential N	Residential %
Very good	29	65	13	33
Good	11	26	10	26
Uncertain	4	9	14	36
Poor	—	—	2	5
	44	100	39	100
Missing			1	
			40	

$p < 0.005$ (arrived at by collapsing the four ratings into two)
Difference index = 32%

Table 21 Capacity to cope with life by group

	Adoption N	Adoption %	Residential N	Residential %
Adequate	39	89	26	65
Uncertain	5	11	12	30
Inadequate	—	—	2	5
	44	100	40	100

$p < 0.05$ (based on combining 'uncertain' and 'inadequate')
Difference index = 24%

Table 22 Problems connected with being adopted or having grown up in a Home

	Adoption N	Adoption %	Residential N	Residential %
No problems	26	68	11	29
Moderate	12	32	22	58
Severe	—	—	5	13
	38	100	38	100
Missing	6		2	
	44		40	

$p < 0.001$ (based on combining 'moderate' and 'severe')
Difference index = 39%

Table 23   Anything missed by growing up adopted or in residential Homes

Missed	Adoption N	%	Residential N	%
Nothing	32	73	6	15
Uncertain	2	4	4	10
Yes – something	10	23	30	75
	44	100	40	100

χ^2 for l.t. = 27.32 (p<0.001)
χ^2 for deviation from l.t. = 1.01 (N = 5)
Difference index = 58%

Table 24   Current feelings of closeness to adoptive parents or house-parents

	Adoption N	%	Residential N	%
Very close to close	34	79	11	28
In-between	1	3	7	18
Distant or very distant	4	9	1	3
No contact	4	9	20	51
	43	100	39	100
Missing	1		1	
	44		40	

Difference index = 57%

Table 25 *The adoptees' perception of the adequacy of their income matched to the economic conditions of their families of origin**

		Income adequate or more so N	Adoptees Income inadequate N	Total N	%
Family of origin	Economic situation fairly stable	20	3	23	58
	Precarious or very precarious	12	5	17	42
		32 (80%)	8 (20%)	40	100

* Four adoptees could not be matched because of lack of information on the economic situation of their natural families

Table 26 *Criminal history among adoptees and in the families of origin*

		Criminal behaviour N	Adoptees No criminal behaviour N	Total N	%
Family of origin	Criminal behaviour	1	6	7	16
	No criminal behaviour	13	23	36	84
		14 (33%)	29 (67%)	43	100
	Missing			1	
				44	

Bibliography

Adcock, M. (1980), 'The right to permanent placement', *Adoption and Fostering* 99, no. 1, 21–4.
Ainsworth, M.D., Andry, R.G., Harlow, R.G., Lebovici, S., Mead, M., Prugh, D.G. and Wootton, B. (1962), *Deprivation of maternal care: Reassessment of its effects*, Geneva: WHO.
Advisory Council on Child Care (1970), *Care and treatment in a planned environment:* A report on the Community Homes Project, London: HMSO.
Aldgate, J. (1977), 'Identification of factors influencing children's length of stay in care', Ph.D. thesis, University of Edinburgh.
Allen, S. (1975), 'School leavers and the labour market', *Education Review* 4(3), 64–74.
Atkinson, A.B., Maynard, A.K. and Trinder, C.G. (1983), *Parents and children: incomes in two generations*, London: Heinemann Educational Books.
Balbernie, R. (1975), Foreword, in Millham, S., Bullock, R. and Cherrett, P., *After Grace – teeth: a comparative study of the residential experience of boys in approved schools*, Human Context Books.
Barclay Report (1982), *Social workers – their roles and tasks*, London: Bedford Square Press.
Barton, R. (1959), *Institutional neurosis*, Bristol: John Wright.
Beedell, C. (1970), *Residential life with children*, London: Routledge & Kegan Paul.
Berridge, D. (1983), 'Staff movement in community homes: some grounds for optimism', *Social Work Today*, vol. 14, 35, 7–10.
Berry, J. (1975), *Daily experience in residential life. A study of children and their care-givers*, London: Routledge & Kegan Paul, for Library of Social Work.
Bohman, M. (1970), *Adopted children and their families*, Proprius.
Bohman, M. (1971), 'A comparative study of adopted children, foster children and children in their biological environment, born after undesired pregnancies', *Acta Paediatrica*, Scand., suppl. 221.
Bohman, M. (1978), 'Some genetic aspects of alcoholism and criminality', *Arch. Gen. Psychiatry*, 35, 269–76.
Bohman, M. and Sigvardsson, S. (1980), 'Negative social heritage', *Adoption and Fostering* 101, no. 3, 25–31.
Borgatta, E.F. and Fanshel, D. (1965), 'Behaviour characteristics of children known to psychiatric outpatient clinics', Child Welfare League of America, monograph.
Bowlby, J. (1951), *Maternal care and mental health*, Geneva: WHO.
Bradburn, N. (1969), *The structure of psychological wellbeing*, New York: Aldine.
Brill, K. and Thomas, R. (1964), *Children in homes*, London: Gollancz.
Brown, M. and Madge, N. (1982), *Despite the welfare state*, London: Heinemann Educational Books.
Burgess, C. (1981), *In care and into work*, London: Tavistock.
Burns, J., Gregory, W. and Templeman, G. (1980), 'Residential care and adolescents', in Jones, R. and Pritchard, C. (eds), *Social work with adolescents*, London: Routledge & Kegan Paul.
Burt, C. (1943), 'Ability and income', *Brit. J. Educ. Psychol.*, 13, 83–93.

Cadoret, J. and Gath, A. (1978), 'Inheritance of alcoholism in adoptees', *Brit. J. Psychiatry*, 132, 252–8.
Campbell, A.E. (1979), 'The origins of implementation of sec. 12 of the Social Work (Scotland) Act, 1968', Ph.D thesis, University of Edinburgh.
Campbell, D.T. and Stanley, J.C. (1963), 'Experimental and quasi-experimental designs for research in teaching', in Cage, N.L. (ed), *Handbook of research in teaching*, Chicago: McNally.
Cass, L.K. and Thomas, C.B. (1979), *Childhood pathology and later adjustment: The question of prediction*, Chichester: Wiley.
Central Advisory Council for Education (1963), *Half our future*, (Newsom Report), London: HMSO.
Clarke, A.M. and Clarke, A.D.B. (eds) (1976), *Early experience: Myth and evidence*, London: Open Books.
Clough, R. (1982), 'Partners in care', *Social Work Today*, no. 7, 5 January, p. 15.
Clyde Report (1946), *Report of the committee on homeless children*, Cmnd 6911, London: HMSO.
Coffield, F., Robinson, P. and Sarsby, J. (1981), *A cycle of deprivation? A case study of four families*, London: Heinemann Educational Books.
Conway, E.S. (1957), 'The institutional care of children: a case history', Ph.D. thesis, University of London.
Cornish, D.B. and Clarke, R.V.G. (1975), *Residential treatment and its effects on delinquents*, London: HMSO.
Crowe, R.R. (1972), 'The adopted offspring of women criminal offenders: a study of their arrest records', *Arch. Gen. Psychiatry*, 27, 600–3.
Cunningham, L., Cadoret, R., Loftus, R. and Edwards, J.E. (1975), 'Studies of adoptees from psychiatrically disturbed biological parents: psychiatric conditions in childhood and adolescence', *Brit. J. Psychiatry*, 126, 534–49.
Curtis Report (1946), *Report of the care of children committee*, Cmnd 6922, London: HMSO.
Davis, A. (1981), *The residential solution*, London: Tavistock.
Davies, L.D. (1980), 'Countdown on drinking', in Family Doctor Booklet, BMA.
Dennis, W. and Najarian, P. (1957), 'Infant development under environmental handicap', *Psychology Monograph*, 71, 1–13.
Dinnage, R. and Kellmer Pringle, M. (1967), *Residential child care: facts and fallacies*, London: Longman.
Douglas, J. and Blomfield, J. (1954), *Children under five*, London: Allen & Unwin.
Erikson, E. (1968), *Identity: Youth and crisis*, London: Faber.
Eysenck, H.J. (1971), *Race, intelligence and education*, London: Temple Smith.
Eysenck, H.J. (1973), *The inequality of man*, London: Temple Smith.
Fanshel, D. (1962), 'Approaches to measuring adjustment in adoptive parents', in *Quantitative approaches to parent selection*, Child Welfare League of America.
Ferguson, T. (1966), *Children in care and after*, Oxford: Oxford University Press, for the Nuffield Foundation.
Field, F. (1974), *Unequal Britain: a report on the cycle of inequality*, London: Arrow Books.
Flint, B.M. (1967), *The child and the institution: a study of deprivation and recovery*, London: University of London Press.
Flint, B.M. (1978), *New hope for deprived children*, Toronto: University of Toronto Press.
Fogelman, K.R. (ed) (1976), *Britain's sixteen year olds*, London: National Children's Bureau.
Francis, S.H. (1971), 'The effect of own-home and institution-rearing on the behavioural development of normal and mongol children', *Child Psychol. and Psychiatry*, 13, 3, 173–90.
Gath, D., Cooper, B., Gattoni, F. and Rockett, D. (1977), *Child guidance and*

BIBLIOGRAPHY

delinquency in a London Borough, Oxford: Oxford University Press.
George, V. (1970), *Foster Care: theory and practice*, London: Routledge & Kegan Paul.
George, V. and Wilding, P. (1972), *Motherless families*, London: Routledge & Kegan Paul.
Goffman, E. (1961), *Asylums: essays on the social situation of mental patients and other inmates*, New York: Doubleday Anchor Books.
Goffman, E. (1963), *Stigma; notes on the management of spoiled identity*, Englewood Cliffs, N.J.: Prentice-Hall.
Goldberg, E.M. (1978), 'Social work since Seebohm: All things to all men?', Eileen Younghusband Lecture, National Institute of Social Work.
Goldberg, E.M. and Warburton, K.W. (1979), *Ends and means in social work*, London: Allen & Unwin.
Goldfarb, W. (1943), 'The effects of early institutional care on adolescent personality', *J. experimental education*, 12, 106–29.
Goodwin, D.W., Schulsinger, F., Hermansen, L., Guze, S.B. and Winokur, G. (1973), 'Alcohol problems in adoptees raised apart from biological parents', *Arch. Gen. Psychiatry*, 28, 238–43.
Goodwin, D.W., Schulsinger, F., Möller, N. Hermansen, L., Winokur, G. and Guze, S.B. (1974), 'Drinking problems in adopted and nonadopted sons of alcoholics', *Arch. Gen. Psychiatry*, 31, 164–9.
Goodwin, D.W., Schulsinger, F., Knop, J., Mednick, S. and Guze, S. (1977), 'Alcoholism and depression in adopted-out daughters of alcoholics', *Arch. Gen. Psychiatry*, 35, 751–5.
Gray, E. and Blunden, R.M. (1971), *A Survey of Adoption in Great Britain*, London: HMSO.
Grow, L.J. and Shapiro, D. (1974), *Black children – white parents*, Child Welfare League of America.
Haggstrom, W. (1964), 'The power of the poor', in Riesseman, F. (ed), *The mental health of the poor*, New York: Collier Macmillan.
Hall, J. (1976), 'Subjective measures of quality of life in Britain: 1971–1975. Some developments and trends', *Social Trends*, no. 7, 47–60.
Halsey, A.H., Heath, A.F. and Ridge, J.M. (1980), *Origins and destinations. Family, class and education in modern Britain*, Oxford: Clarendon Press.
Handler, J. and Hollingsworth, E. (1971), *The deserving poor*, Markham.
Harris, D. (1979), 'The nastiness of residential care', *Social Work Today*, vol. 10, 25, p. 33.
Harris, D. (1981), 'Painting a rosy picture of the future', *Social Work Today*, vol. 12, 40, p. 19
Hazel, N. (1981), *A bridge to independence*, Oxford: Basil Blackwell.
Henderson, A.S., Krupinski, J. and Stoller, A. (1971), 'Epidemiological aspects of adolescent psychiatry' in Howells, J.G. (ed), *Modern perspectives in adolescent psychiatry*, Edinburgh: Oliver & Boyd.
Heywood, J.S. and Allen, B.K. (1971), *Financial help in social work*, Manchester: Manchester University Press.
Hill, M. (1983), Unpublished paper on adoption allowances, Dept of Social Administration, University of Edinburgh.
Hill, M. and Laing, P. (1979), *Social work and money*, London: Allen & Unwin.
Holman, R. (1973), *Trading in children: a study of private fostering*, London: Routledge & Kegan Paul.
Holman, R. (1976), *Inequality in child care*, London: Child Poverty Action Group.
Humphrey, M. and Ounsted, C. (1963), 'Adoptive families referred for psychiatric advice. Part I: "The children"', *Brit. J. Psychiatry*, vol. 109, 599–608.
Hussell, C. and Monaghan, B. (1982), 'Going for good', *Social Work Today*, vol. 13, 47, 7–9.
Hutchings, B. and Mednick, S. (1974), 'Registered criminality in the adoptive and biological parents of registered male criminal adoptees', in Fieve, R.R. and Zubin,

D.A. (eds), *Genetics and psychopathology*, Cambridge, Mass.: Johns Hopkins Press.
Jacka, A.A. (1973), *Adoption in brief*, National Foundation for Educational Research.
Jackson, M.P. and Valencia, B.M. (1979), *Financial aid through social work*, London: Routledge & Kegan Paul.
Jaffee, B. and Fanshel, D. (1970), *How they fared in adoption: a follow-up study*, Columbia: Columbia University Press.
Jones, M. (1976), 'Reducing foster care through services to families', *Children Today*, November/December.
Jones, M.A., Neuman, R. and Shyne, A.W. (1976), *A second chance for families: evaluation of a program to reduce foster care*, Child Welfare League of America.
Jordan, B. (1974), *Poor parents: social policy and the 'cycle of deprivation'*, London: Routledge & Kegan Paul.
Jordan, W. (1981a), *Automatic poverty*, London: Routledge & Kegan Paul.
Jordan, W. (1981b), Talk given at a seminar organised by the British Agencies for Adoption and Fostering, June.
Joseph, K. (1972), Address to the Pre-School Playgroup Association, 29 June.
Kadushin, A. (1971), *Adopting older children*, 2nd edn, Columbia: Columbia University Press.
Kahan, B. (1979), *Growing up in care*, Oxford: Basil Blackwell.
Kenyon, W.H. (1977), *Alcohol and alcoholism in perspective*, Merseyside, Lancashire and Cheshire Council on Alcoholism.
Keshet, H.F. and Rosenthal, K.M., *Fathers without partners: a study of fathers and the family after marital separation*. Totowa, N.J.: Roan & Littlefield, 1980.
Kety, S.S., Rosenthal, D., Wender, P.H. and Schulsinger, F. (1968), 'The types and prevalence of mental illness in the biological and adoptive families of adopted schizophrenics', in Rosenthal, D. and Kety, S.S. (eds), *The transmission of schizophrenia*, Oxford: Pergamon Press.
Kirk, H.D. (1964), *Shared fate*, Glencoe, Ill.: Free Press of Glencoe.
Kirk, H.D. (1981), *Adoptive kinship*, London: Butterworth.
Knight, B.J. and West, D.J. (1977), 'Criminality and welfare depending in two generations', *Medicine, Science and the Law*, vol. 17, no. 1, 64–7.
Labouvie, E.W., Bartsch, T.W., Nesserroade, J.R. and Blates, P.B. (1974), 'On the internal and external validity of simple longitudinal designs', *Child Development*, 45, 282–90.
Lambert, L. and Streather, J. (1980), *Children in changing families*, London: Macmillan, for National Children's Bureau.
Lambert, R. and Millham, S. (1968), *The hothouse society*, London: Weidenfeld & Nicolson.
Lawder, E.A., Lower, K.D., Andrews, R.G., Sherman, E.A. and Hill, J.G. (1969), *A follow-up study of adoption: post-placement functioning of adoption families*, Child Welfare League of America.
Layard, R. Piachaud, D. and Stewart, M. (1978), *The causes of poverty*, Royal Commission on the Distribution of Income and Wealth, Background Paper no. 5, London: HMSO.
Leslie, S. (1974), 'Psychiatric disorder in the young adolescents of an industrial town', *Brit. J. Psychiatry*, 125, 113–24.
Lipset, S.M. and Bendix, R. (1959), *Social mobility in industrial society*, London: Heinemann Educational Books.
Maas, H. (1963), 'The young adult adjustment of twenty wartime residential nursery children', *Child Welfare*, 42, 57–73.
Mandell, B.R. (1973), *Where are the children?*, Lexington, Mass.: Lexington Books.
Martinson, R. (1974), 'What works? Questions and answers about prison reform', *Public Interest*, Spring, 22–52.
Mattinson, J. (1970), *Marriage and mental handicap*, London: Duckworth.
Mattinson, J. and Sinclair, I. (1979), *Mate and stalemate: working with marital problems*

in a Social Service Department, Oxford: Basil Blackwell.
McClintock, F.H. and Avison, N.H. (1968), *Crime in England and Wales*, London: Heinemann.
McDowell, L. (1982), 'Housing and inequality', Report to the SSRC, 1980, in Brown, M. and Madge, N.M., *Despite the welfare state*, London: Heinemann.
McKay, M. (1980), 'Planning for permanent placement', *Adoption and Fostering* 99, no. 1, 19–21.
MacVeigh, J. (1982), *Gaskin*, London: Jonathan Cape.
McWhinnie, A.M. (1967), *Adopted children: how they grow up*, London: Routledge & Kegan Paul.
Meacher, M. (1972), *Taken for a ride*, London: Longman.
Meier, E.G. (1962), 'Former foster children as adult citizens', unpublished Ph.D. thesis, Columbia University School of Social Work.
Miller, P. (1981), *A longitudinal study of children in care*, Social Work Services Group (Scotland).
Miller, E.J. and Gwynne, G.V. (1972), *A life apart*, London: Tavistock.
Millham, S., Bullock, R. and Cherrett, P. (1975), *After Grace – teeth: a comparative study of the residential experience of boys in approved schools*, Human Context Books.
Mortimer, J. and Blackstone, T. (1982), *Disadvantage and education*, London: Heinemann Educational Books.
National Child Development Study (1976), see Fogelman, K.R. (ed) (1976).
Newman, N. and Mackintosh, H. (1975), 'A roof over their heads?', Department of Social Administration, University of Edinburgh.
Oppel, W.G. and Royston, A.B. (1971), 'Teenage births: some social, psychological and physical sequelae', *Am. J. Public Health*, 61, 751–6.
Packman, J. (1968), *Needs and numbers*, London: Allen & Unwin.
Packman, J. (1975), *The child's generation*, Oxford: Basil Blackwell & Martin Robertson.
Page, R. and Clarke, G.A. (1977), *'Who cares?' Young people in care speak out*, London: National Children's Bureau.
Pappenfort, D.M. and Kilpatrick, D.M. (1969), 'Child-caring institutions, 1966: selected findings from the first national survey of children's residential institutions', *Social Service Review*, 43, 4, 448–59.
Parker, R.A. (1966), *Decision in child care*, London: Allen & Unwin.
Parker, R.A. (1980), *Caring for separated children*, London: Macmillan.
Parsloe, P. and Stevenson, O. (1978), *Social service teams: the practitioner's view*, London: HMSO.
Paterson, A. and Inglis, J. (1975), 'Intergenerational cycle of deprivation', in Brown, M. and Madge, N., *Despite the welfare state*, London: Heinemann Educational Books.
Plant, M. (1982), *Drinking and problem drinking*, London: Junction Books.
Plowden Report (1967), *Children and their primary schools*, Central Advisory Council for Education, vols 1 & 2, London: HMSO.
Pringle, M.L. Kellmer (1965), *Deprivation and education*, London: Longman.
Pringle, M.L. Kellmer (1967), *11,000 seven year olds*, London: Longman.
Pringle, M.L. Kellmer and Bossio, V. (1958), 'A study of deprived children. Part I. Intellectual, emotional and social development', *Vita Humana* 1, no. 2, 66–92.
Pringle, M.L. Kellmer and Bossio, V. (1960), 'Early prolonged separations and emotional adjustment', *J. Child Psychol. and Psychiatry*, 1, 37–48.
Prosser, H. (1976), *Perspectives on residential child care: an annotated bibliography*, National Foundation for Educational Research.
Raynor, L. (1980), *The adopted child comes of age*, London: Allen & Unwin.
Reinach, E. and Roberts, G. (1978), *A follow-up of children leaving an Observation and Assessment Centre after 3 years*, Dept of Social Study, Portsmouth Polytechnic.
Ripple, L. (1968), 'A follow-up study of adopted children', *Social Service Review*, vol. 42, no. 4, 479–99.
Ritson, B. (1980), Quoted at a seminar at University of Edinburgh, November, based on

unpublished data.
Roe, A. and Burks, B. (1945), 'Adult adjustment of foster children of alcoholic and psychotic parentage and the influence of the foster home', *Memoirs of the Section on Alcohol Studies*, no. 3, Yale University Press.
Rose, G. 1970, 'Penal reform as history', *Brit. J. Criminology*, vol. 10, 4, 348–71.
Rosen, A.C. (1971), 'The social and emotional development of children in long-term residential care', *Therapeutic Education*, Spring.
Rosenthal, D. Wender, P.H., Kety, S.S., Schulsinger, F., Welner, J. and Ostergaard, L. (1968), '"Schizophrenics" offspring reared in adoptive homes', in Rosenthal, D. and Kety, S.S. (eds), *The transmission of schizophrenia*, Oxford: Pergamon Press.
Roudinesco, J. and Appell, G. (1950), 'The effect of hospitalisation on the motor and psychological development of young children', *Semaine des Hôpitaux*, 26, 47, 2271–3.
Rowe, J. and Lambert, L. (1973), *Children who wait*, Association of British Adoption and Fostering Agencies.
Royal College of Psychiatrists (1979), *Alcohol and alcoholism*, London: Tavistock.
Rutter, M. (1972), *Maternal deprivation re-assessed*, Harmondsworth: Penguin.
Rutter, M. (1978), 'Early sources of security and competence', in Bruner, J. and Garton, A. (eds), *Human growth and development*, Oxford: Clarendon Press.
Rutter, M. and Madge, N. (1977), *Cycles of disadvantage*, 2nd edn, London: Heinemann Educational Books.
Rutter, M. and Quinton, D. (1980 and 1981), Reports to the SSRC, quoted in Brown, M. and Madge, N., *Despite the welfare state*, London: Heinemann Educational Books.
Sainsbury, E. (1975), *Social work with families*, London: Routledge & Kegan Paul.
Salo, R., quoted by Meier, E.G. (1962), in *Former foster children as adult citizens*, unpublished Ph.D. thesis, Columbia University.
Schaffer, H.R. and Schaffer, E. (1968), *Child care and the family*, London: Bell.
Schecter, M.D., Carlson, P.V., Simmons, J.Q. and Work, H.H. (1964), 'Emotional problems in the adoptee', *Arch. Gen. Psychiatry*, 10, 37–46.
Seglow, J., Pringle, M.L. and Wedge, P. (1972), *Growing up adopted*, National Foundation for Educational Research in England and Wales.
Sherman, E.A., Neuman, R. and Shyne, A.W. (1973), *Children adrift in foster care: a study of alternative approaches*, Child Welfare League of America.
Skodak, M. and Skeels, H.M. (1949), 'A final follow-up study of a hundred adopted children', *J. Gen. Psychol.*, 75, 85–125.
Specht, H. and Vickery, A. (1977), *Integrating social work methods*, London: Allen & Unwin.
Spence, J., Walton, W.S., Miller, F.J.W. and Court, S.D.M. (1954), *A thousand families in Newcastle upon Tyne*, Oxford: Oxford University Press.
Spitz, R.A. (1949), 'The role of ecological factors in emotional development in infancy', *Child Development*, 20, no. 3, 145–55.
Srole, L., Langer, T.S. and Rennie, A. (1962), *The mental health of the metropolis*, vol. 1, Midtown Manhattan Study, New York: McGraw-Hill.
SSRC (1975), Second report of the DHSS/SSRC Joint Working Party on Transmitted Deprivation, London: HMSO.
Stott, D.H. (1966), *Studies of troublesome children*, Tavistock Publications.
Sweeney, D.M., Gasbarro, D.T. and Gluck, M.R. (1963), 'A descriptive study of adopted children seen in a child guidance centre', *Child Welfare*, vol. 42, 345–9.
Szasz, T.S. (1973), *Ideology and insanity: essays on the psychiatric dehumanisation of man*, London: Calder & Boyars.
Theis, S. (1924), *How foster children turn out*, publication no. 165, New York Charities Aid Association.
Thoburn, J. (1980), *Captive clients*, London: Routledge & Kegan Paul.
Thoday, J.M. (1965), 'Geneticism and environmentalism', in Meade, J.E. and Parkes, A.S. (eds), *Biological aspects of social problems*, Edinburgh: Oliver & Boyd.
Thorpe, R. (1980), 'The experience of children and parents living apart: implications

and guidelines for practice' in Triseliotis, J. (ed), *New developments in foster care and adoption*, London: Routledge & Kegan Paul.
Tizard, B. (1977), *Adoption: A second chance*, London: Open Books.
Tizard, B. and Hodges, J. (1978), 'The effect of early institutional rearing on the development of eight-year-old children', *J. Child Psychol. and Psychiatry*, 19, 99–118.
Tizard, J. and Tizard, B. (1971), 'The social development of two-year-old children in residential nurseries', in Schaffer, H.R. (ed), *The origins of human social relations*, London: Academic Press.
Townsend, P. (1979), *Poverty in the United Kingdom*, Harmondsworth: Pelican.
Trasler, G. (1955), 'The effects of institutional care upon emotional development', *Case Conference* 4, 2, 35–40.
Trasler, G. (1960), *In place of parents: a study of foster care*, London: Routledge & Kegan Paul.
Triseliotis, J. (1969),'Evaluation of adoption policy and practice in Scotland', Ph.D. thesis submitted to University of Edinburgh.
Triseliotis, J. (1970), *Evaluation of adoption policy and practice*, Dept Social Administration, University of Edinburgh.
Triseliotis, J. (1973), *In search of origins*, London: Routledge & Kegan Paul.
Triseliotis, J. (ed) (1980a), *New developments in foster care and adoption*, London: Routledge & Kegan Paul.
Triseliotis, J. (1980b), *Growing up in foster care and after*, Report submitted to the SSRC.
Triseliotis, J. (1983), 'Issues of identity and security in adoption and long-term fostering', *Adoption and Fostering*, vol. 7, 1, 22–31.
Ward, P. (1980), *Quality of life in residential care*, Personal Social Services Council.
Wedge, P. and Prosser, N. (1973), *Born to fail?*, London: Arrow Books.
West, D.J. (1979), Report to the Joint Working Party on Transmitted Deprivation, quoted in Brown, M. and Madge, N. (1982).
White, K. (1977), 'I'd give 'em a clip round the earhole', *Social Work Today*, vol. 9, no. 16, 19.
Wilson, H. (1962), *Delinquency and child neglect*, London: Allen & Unwin.
Wilson, H. and Herbert, G.W. (1978), *Parents and children in the inner city*, London: Routledge & Kegan Paul.
Winnicott, C. (1961), *Child care and social work*, Codicote Press.
Witmer, H.L., Herzog, E., Weinstein, E.A. and Sullivan, M.E. (1963), *Independent adoptions – a follow-up study*, Beverley Hills: Russell Sage Foundation.
Wolkind, S.N. (1974), 'Sex differences in the aetiology of anti-social disorders in children in long-term residential care', *Brit. J. Psychiatry*, 125, 125–30.
Wolkind, S.N. (1977), 'Women who have been "in care" – psychological and social status in pregnancy', *J. Child Psychol. and Psychiatry*, vol. 18, 179–82.
Wolkind, S.N. and Renton, G. (1979), 'Psychiatric disorders in children in long-term residential care: a follow-up study', *Brit. J. Psychiatry*, 135, 129–35.
Wolkind, S.N. and Rutter, M. (1973), 'Children who have been "in care": an epidemiological study', *J. Child Psychol. and Psychiatry*, 14, 97–105.
Wolkind, S.N., Kruk, S.J. and Chaves, L.P. (1976), 'Childhood separation experiences and psychological status in primiparous women – preliminary findings', *Brit. J. Psychiatry*, 128, 391–6.
Wright, C.H. and Lunn, J.E. (1971), 'Sheffield problem families, a follow-up study of their sons and daughters', *Community Medicine*, 126, 301–7, 315–21.
Yule, W. and Raynes, N.V. (1972), 'Behaviour characteristics of children in residential care in relation to indices of separation', *J. Child Psychol. and Psychiatry*, vol. 13, 249–58.
Zimmerman, R.B. (1982), 'Foster care in retrospect', *Tulan Studies in Social Welfare*, vol. 14, New Orleans, Tulan University.

Index

Subject index

access to birth register 93, 101–2, 107, 183, 184
adjustment 6, 14, 30, 40–57, 60–61, 90–91, 97, 99, 112, 114, 130, 133, 134, 135–7, 147–9, 155, 156, 157, 160, 162, 169, 176–7, 180–2, 185, 186–7, 188–9, 200
adopted persons
   age at final placement 32–3, 87, 179
   age at interview 19, 179
   age at reception into care 31–2, 181, 206
   time between RIC and final placement 206
   time in family before legal adoption 207
   time in foster care before final placement 208
   time in residential care before final placement 207
adoption agencies policies and practices 3, 20, 25, 26, 33–4, 40, 41, 47, 93, 181, 195, 197
adoption of
   high risk children 3, 4, 26, 33, 39, 48, 180, 181
   older children 4, 8–9
adoption not acknowledged 95
adoptive parents 16
   house occupancy 209
   age at placement of child 50, 181, 208
   number of children in family 139, 209
   position of adopted child in family 139
age at revelation of adoption 93–5
alcohol
   abuse 28–9, 30, 129, 130, 131, 133, 171–3, 186
   consumption 129–32, 185
   problems 131, 132, 188–9, 211
allowances 195, 196

ambitions of
   adoptive parents 48, 71, 77–9, 181
   houseparents 77, 79–80
attachments 37, 38–63, 147–9, 180, 181–2, 190, 195, 197, 213

background of
   adoptees 6–7, 92, 93, 96–7, 98, 135, 179
   residential people 92, 96–7, 98, 179
bed-wetting 67–9

characteristics of
   adoptees 31–6
   families of origin 24–31
   residential people 31–6
Children's Act 1948 9, 10
   1963 191
   1975 93
children's moves before final placement 33, 36, 37, 87, 108, 135–6, 157, 181, 184
closeness to
   adoptive father 58, 59, 60, 113, 147–9, 181, 213
   adoptive mother 50, 58, 59, 60, 113, 132, 147–9, 181, 213
   housefather 58, 60–61, 147–9, 182, 183, 213
   housemother 58, 60–61, 132–3, 147–9, 182, 183, 213
communications
   with children in residence 96, 97, 98, 99, 100, 101, 102
   within family regarding adoption 93–7, 98, 99, 100
community attitudes towards
   adoptees 38, 139, 140
   residential people 38, 72, 141, 142, 143, 146, 147, 183, 184
composite variables
   disturbed family background 176
   disturbed respondents 133

INDEX

quality of life 31, 157–8
social disadvantage 29–31
conflict between
  adoptees and parents 70–1
  residential people and
    houseparents 71–4
coping with current life
  adoptees 134–5, 157, 186, 212
  residential people 134–5, 157, 186,
    189, 212
crime and delinquency 29, 30, 74, 86,
  110, 113, 127–9, 132, 133, 165, 173–5,
  185, 186, 188–9, 214

data collection
  from agency records 15, 16, 84–5, 180
  from respondents 15, 16, 180
deprivation 1, 2, 8, 9, 15, 29, 31, 73, 113,
  144, 145, 146, 157, 178, 190
disadvantaged 1, 2, 8, 9, 15, 29, 31, 73,
  113, 144, 145, 146, 157, 178, 190
discipline of children in
  adoptive home 63, 64–5
  residential establishments 63, 66–70
discontinuities 32, 33, 37, 87, 108, 135,
  136, 157, 181, 182, 184, 187, 188, 189,
  190
discrimination 82, 138, 140, 141, 144
disturbed people/background 30, 130,
  133, 155, 156, 160, 162, 169, 171,
  176–7, 185, 188–9
divorce 116–18, 169, 186

early adoptions 3, 4, 5, 39
economic situation of
  adoptees 108, 113, 156, 165–7, 168,
    185, 187–8, 214
  adoptive family 46–7, 181
  natural parents 27–8, 30, 165–8,
    187–8, 193, 204, 214
  residential people 108, 113, 156,
    165–7, 168, 182, 187–8
education 75–80
  schools attended 75–6
  age at end of formal education 75–6,
    210
education and attainment 49
educational qualifications 76–7, 110,
  114
educational qualifications and
  employment 111
emotional problems
  adoptees 35–6, 48, 50, 51, 82–4, 84–5,
    91, 107, 108, 110, 121–3, 135, 139,
    157, 184
  residential people 35–6, 82–4, 84, 85,
    91, 112, 118, 121–3, 135, 139, 157,
    184, 185
emotional well-being 118, 134, 136, 211
employment 28, 30, 31, 46–7, 108, 109,
  111–15, 116, 151–2, 156, 160–3,
  165–8, 185, 187–8, 204
environment and heredity 1, 2, 3, 7,
  24–31, 37, 92–3, 122, 138–40, 157,
  159–77, 179–89
extended family 61

families of origin 24–31, 92, 93, 101–7
  age of mother at child's birth 202
  alcohol problems 205
  criminal convictions 205
  economic situation 204
  housing conditions 203
  marital status of natural mother at
    child's birth 202
  quality of relationships 204
  social class by occupation 203
family relationships in the adoptive
  home 50, 58–61, 132–3, 147–9, 181,
  182, 183, 213
family size 29, 34, 50, 139
financial assistance in social work 191,
  193
foster care 6, 10, 12, 22, 33, 38, 59, 76,
  83, 112, 124, 128, 130, 163, 180, 194,
  196, 200
frequency of adoptive discussion 96, 97,
  98, 99, 100
friendship problems
  adoptee 132–3, 169
  residential people 132–3, 170–1

genealogy 37, 47, 92, 93, 102, 122, 138,
  139, 140, 184
genetic factors in explanations of
  behaviour 7, 157
  deprivation 2, 7, 157

hard to place children 3, 4, 8–9, 26, 33,
  39, 48, 180–1
health
  mental 12, 35–6, 84–90
  physical 34–5, 84, 127, 185
high risk children 3, 4, 5, 13, 26, 33, 39,
  180
homelessness 27, 164
housing circumstances
  adoptees 49, 114–15, 116, 133, 152,

156, 163–4, 187–8
adoptive families 49
natural families 27, 30, 163–5, 187–8
 residential people 114–15, 133,
  152, 154, 156, 164–5, 182, 185,
  187–8
identity formation 37, 92, 93, 101, 107,
 122, 138, 183, 184
identity problems in
 adoptees 140, 141
 residential people 183
illegitimacy
 adoptees 195
 residential people 87, 122
inclusive adoptions 197
income
 adoptees 108, 165–7, 168, 187–8, 214
 adoptive parents 46–7, 181
 natural parents 165–7, 187–8, 214
 residential people 108, 165–7, 168,
  182, 187–8
income and poverty 30, 31, 108, 113,
 115, 116, 133, 154, 156, 185
influence of past 117, 119, 120, 122, 124,
 127, 132, 134, 136, 137–47, 148, 149,
 157, 186
information, access to 92, 93, 98, 99,
 100, 101, 183
institutional neurosis 74, 198
intelligence 2, 29, 81
interviews 16, 17, 18

labelling 82, 138, 139, 141
late adoption 3, 5, 8, 9, 179
leisure activities of respondents 74–5
level of satisfaction with
 adoption outcome 3, 4, 5, 8–9, 18, 22,
  38–40, 41–9, 57–8
 residential outcome 11–14, 22, 38–40,
  51–7, 58, 182
lies or inaccuracies 94, 99, 103

marital problems among
 adoptees 116, 117, 133, 168–9
 residential people 113–14, 115, 116,
  117, 118, 133, 154, 169–70, 182
marital status
 adoptees 116–18
 natural parents 27
 residential people 116–18
memories of past 93, 94, 95, 105, 106,
 181
mental handicap

adoptees 87–90, 123–7, 133, 157,
 175–6
natural parent of adoptees 29, 175–6
natural parent of residential
 people 29, 175–6
residential people 87–90, 110, 119,
 123–7, 133, 135, 157, 172–6
methodology 15–18

occupations of
 adoptees 108, 109, 111–13, 156,
  160–2, 187
 adoptive parents 46–9, 79–81, 210
 natural parents 160–3, 187
 residential people 108, 109, 111–13,
  156, 162–3, 185, 187
outcome of
 adoption 3, 4, 5, 8–9, 14, 18, 22, 77,
  81, 95, 107, 156, 181
 residential care 11–14, 22, 77, 182

parental rights 196
parental tasks 196
parenting qualities of
 adoptees 118–21, 187
 residential people 118–21, 187
personal social services 11, 24, 25, 29,
 182, 189, 190, 191, 193, 194, 195, 196
predictions 2, 5, 194
prejudice 83, 140, 141, 143, 184
preparation for independence
 employment 151–2, 155
 general 72, 149–51, 155, 186, 200
 handling money 152–3
 housekeeping 153–4, 155
 parenthood 154–5
pre-placement experiences
 adoptees 31–2, 181, 206, 207, 208
 residential people 31–2, 89, 184, 206,
  208
presence of
 affection 5, 8, 37, 40, 41, 42, 44, 53,
  57, 59, 148, 181, 182, 190
 love 5, 37, 40, 41, 42, 44, 52, 53, 57,
  59, 62, 73, 119, 145, 146, 148, 149,
  181, 182, 190
 warmth 5, 37, 40, 41, 42, 44, 57, 59,
  147, 148, 154, 180, 181, 182, 190
preventive policies 190, 191, 192, 193,
 194, 195
psychiatric referral
 adoptees in adult life 123–7, 133, 157,
  175–6, 185, 186, 188–9
 adoptees in childhood 87–90, 125,

INDEX

175-6, 184
  and natural family background 90
  natural parents 29, 175, 176, 188-9
  residential people in adult life 119,
    123-7, 133, 135, 157, 172-3, 175-6,
    185, 186, 188-9
  residential people in childhood
    87-90, 110, 125, 126, 175-6
punishment
  emotional 64-5, 66-70
  physical 56, 63, 64-5, 66-70

qualifications 20-2, 24, 29, 30, 158, 189
qualitative data 15-18
quality of relationships in
  adoptive home 37, 40-51, 181
  residential home 37, 51-7, 181, 182,
    197
quantitative data 15-18

reaction to revelation of adoption 94,
  95, 97, 99
reception into care 16, 24, 25, 28, 164,
  194, 195
reception into care panel 196
Register House 93, 101, 102, 103
rehabilitation 191, 194, 195
relationship problems among
  adoptees 38, 39, 90-1, 94, 180, 186,
    188-9
  natural parents 28, 30, 188-9
  residential people 38, 39, 51, 90-1,
    180, 186, 188-9
remarriage 116, 117
residential care 9-14, 177, 179, 182, 183,
  186, 198, 199, 200, 201
residential nursery children 7, 12
residential persons
  age at interview 19, 179, 189
  age at main residential placement
    32-3, 87
  age at reception into care 31-2, 89,
    184, 206
  gap between reception and final
    placement 206
  time in foster care before final
    placement 208
reunions
  of adoptees with relatives 101, 104
  of residential people with
    relatives 102, 106
revelation of adoption 93-5
rigid institutional rules 63, 66-70, 72,
  73, 139, 142, 146, 182

sampling 3, 18, 19, 20, 36, 159, 189
  sample loss 20-21, 22, 179
  selection criteria 19, 20
satisfaction with life 112, 114, 135-7,
  156, 157, 180, 181, 185, 186, 187, 200
  211
school
  attendance 75-6, 110
  leaving age 75-6, 210
self-rating 15-18, 37, 38, 58, 90, 108,
  121, 134, 180
separation experiences 15, 29, 37, 87,
  120, 186, 195
sex difficulties 169, 170
siblings
  adoptive 50, 61, 209
  natural 34, 61, 62, 63, 114, 182, 183
single parents 25, 29, 190, 191
social class
  adoptees 81, 109-11, 160-62, 187,
    210
  adoptive parents 47, 48, 49, 79, 81,
    181, 210
  natural parents of adoptees 27, 81,
    109-11, 160-62, 187, 210
  natural parents of residential
    people 27, 162-3, 187
  residential people 109-10, 162-3,
    187
social policy 3, 11, 20, 25, 26, 33, 34, 40,
  41, 47, 93, 181, 182, 190, 191, 192,
  193, 194, 195, 196, 197
social security benefits
  adoptees 113, 156, 165-6, 167, 168,
    185
  natural parents 30, 165-6, 168
  residential people 113, 156, 165-6,
    167, 168
social work/social workers 24, 25, 29,
  189, 190, 191, 192, 193, 194, 195
social work intervention 11, 182
standard of living among
  adoptees 113, 167, 168
  residential people 113, 167
statistics 22-3, 202
stigma
  adoptees 138, 140
  residential people 122, 138, 141, 143,
    144, 183, 190

training of residential staff 10, 52, 73-4,
  183, 197, 199, 200
transmissions from parents to
  children 1, 2, 178, 179, 187-9

alcohol abuse 1, 2, 159, 171–3, 177
criminality 1, 2, 159, 173–5, 177
housing 1, 2, 159, 163–4, 163–5, 177
income 1, 2, 159, 160–3, 165–7, 168, 177
psychiatric conditions 1, 2, 159, 175–6, 177
relationships 1, 2, 159, 168–71, 177
travelling families 156

truanting 82
twins 2

unemployment among
  adoptees 112
  residential people 112

women and alcohol 186
women and crime 186

Author index

Adcock, M. 196
Advisory Council on Child Care 52
Aldgate, J. 194, 195
Allen, B.K. 191, 192
Allen, S. 75
Andrews, R.G. 4
Appell, G. 12
Atkinson, A.B. 189
Avinson, N.H. 129

Balbernie, R. 198
Barclay Report. 200
Barton, R. 74, 198
Bartsch, T.W. 22
Beedell, C. 52
Berridge, D. 200
Berry, J. 52, 57, 72, 154, 155, 197
Blackstone, T. 76
Blates, P.B. 22
Blomfield, J. 84
Blunden, R.M. 50
Bohman, M. 7, 16, 128, 129, 172, 174, 188
Borgatta, E.F. 88
Bossio, V. 12, 13
Bowlby, J. 12, 33
Bradburn, N. 17
Brill, K. 9
Brown, M. viii, x, 113
Bullock, R. 88, 151
Burgess, C. 9, 75, 82, 111, 151
Burks, B. 6
Burns, J. 52
Burt, C. 2

Cadoret, J. 7, 172
Campbell, A.E. 190
Campbell, D.T. 22
Carlson, P.V. 88
Cass, L.K. 185
Central Advisory Council for Education 83

Chaves, L.P. 120
Cherrett, P. 88, 151
Children's Act 1948 9, 10
  1963 191
  1975 93
Clarke, A.D.B. 3, 8, 37, 136
Clarke, A.M. 3, 8, 37, 136
Clarke, R.V.G. 11
Clough, R. 194
Clyde Report 9, 10
Coffield, F. 159
Conway, E.S. 13
Cooper, B. 89
Cornish, D.B. 11
Court, S.D.M. 84
Crowe, R.R. 7, 174
Cunningham, L. 7
Curtis Report 9, 10, 197

Davies, L.D. 130
Dennis, W. 12
DHSS vii, 1, 68, 192
Dinnage, R. 11, 12, 14
Douglas, J. 84

Edwards, J.E. 7
Erikson, E. 92
Eysenck, H.J. 2

Fanshel, D. 4, 16, 18, 88, 94
Ferguson, T. 13, 128
Field, F. 2
Flint, B.M. 8, 12
Francis, S.H. 13

Gasbarro, D.T. 88
Gath, A. 7, 172
Gath, D. 89
Gattoni, F. 89
George, V. 10, 195
Gluck, M.R. 88
Goffman, E. 74, 138, 198
Goldberg, E.M. 191, 192

INDEX 227

Goldfarb, W. 12
Goodwin, D.W. 7, 171, 172
Gray, E. 50
Gregory, W. 52
Growm, L.J. 5
Guze, S.B. 7, 171, 172
Gwynn, G.V. 146, 147

Haggstrom, W. 2
Hall, J. 17
Halsey, A.H. 76
Handler, J. 188
Harris, D. 73, 197, 200
Hazel, N. 11
Heath, A.F. 76
Herbert, G.W. 190
Hermansen, L. 7, 171
Herzog, E. 4, 7,
Heywood, J.S. 191, 192
Hill, J.G. 4
Hill, M. 193, 195
Hodges, J. 37
Hollingsworth, E. 188
Holman, R. 83
Humphrey, M. 88
Hussell, C. 196
Hutchings, B. 7, 174

Inglis, J. 157

Jacka, A.A. 5
Jackson, M.P. 193
Jaffee, B. 4, 16, 94
Jones, M.A. 194
Jordan, B. 1
Jordan, W. 190, 193
Joseph, K. 1

Kadushin, A. 5, 8, 16, 17, 33, 37, 39, 50
Kahan, B. 192
Kenyon, W.H. 129
Kety, S.S. 7
Kilpatrick, D.M. 13, 87, 88
Kirk, H.D. 40, 41
Knight, B.J. 165
Knop, J. 7, 172
Kruk, S.J. 120

Labouvie, E.W. 22
Laing, P. 193
Lambert, L. 49, 195, 199
Langer, T.S. 123
Lawder, E.A. 4
Layard, R. 76

Loftus, R. 7
Lower, K.D. 4
Lunn, J.E. 188

Maas, H. 7
McClintock, F.H. 129
McDowell, L. 164
McKay, M. 196
Mackintosh, H. 199
MacVeigh, J. 200
McWhinnie, A.M. 4, 40, 101
Madge, N. vii, x, 2, 113, 175, 188
Mandell, B.R. 48
Martinson, R. 11
Mattinson, J. 185, 192, 193
Maynard, A.K. 189
Meacher, M. 141
Mednick, S. 7, 172, 174
Meier, E.G. 6
Miller, E.J. 146, 147
Miller, F.J.W. 84
Millham, S. 88, 151
Möller, N. 7, 171
Monaghan, B. 196
Mortimer, J. 76

Najarian, P. 12
National Children's Bureau 74, 76, 82, 83
Nesserroade, J.R. 22
Neuman, R. 194
Newman, N. 199

Oppel, W.G. 121
Ostergaard, L. 7
Ounsted, C. 88

Packman, J. 24
Pappenfort, D.M. 13, 87, 88
Parker, R.A. 10, 21, 191
Parsloe, P. 192
Paterson, A. 157
Piachaud, D. 76
Plant, M. 132
Plowden Report 75, 82
Pringle, M.L. Keller 11, 12, 13, 14, 84, 89
Prosser, H. 12
Prosser, N. 2, 29

Quinton, D. 118

Raynes, N.V. 13, 87
Raynor, L. 5, 16, 20, 39, 48, 74, 76, 81,

87, 88, 94, 102
Reinach, E. 200
Rennie, A. 123
Renton, G. 87
Ridge, G. 76
Ripple, L. 4
Ritson, B. 129, 211
Roberts, E. 200
Robinson, P. 159
Rockett, D. 89
Roe, A. 6
Rosen, A.C. 13
Rosenthal, D. 7, 197
Roudinesco, J. 12
Rowe, J. 195, 199
Royal College of Psychiatrists 130
Royston, A.B. 121
Russell, J. viii
Rutter, M. 1, 2, 13, 14, 37, 88, 90, 118, 175, 188, 189

Salo, R. 6
Sarsby, J. 159
Scheter, M.D. 88
Schulsinger, F. 7, 171, 172
Scrole, L. 123
Seglow, J. 5, 16, 48, 50
Shapiro, D. 5
Sherman, E.A. 4, 194
Shyne, A.W. 194
Sigvardsson, S. 128, 188
Simmons, J.Q. 88
Sinclair, I. 192
Skeels, H.M. 7
Skodak, M. 7
Specht, H. 192
Spence, J. 84
Spitz, R.A. 12
SSRC vii, 2, 17, 22
Stanley, J.C. 22
Stevenson, O. 192
Stewart, M. 76
STOPP 68, 69

Stott, D.H. 83
Streather, J. 49
Sullivan, M.E. 4, 7
Sweeney, D.M. 88
SWSG 199
Szasz, T.S. 141

Theis, S. 6
Thomas, C.B. 9, 185
Thorpe, R. 195
Tizard, B. 8, 9, 12, 37, 48, 49
Tizard, J. 12
Townsend, P. 2
Trasler, G. 10, 12, 13
Trinder, C.G. 189
Triseliotis, J. viii, 18, 26, 38, 40, 47, 48, 59, 76, 92, 93, 101, 107, 109, 112, 124, 130, 163, 180, 197, 200

Valencia, B.M. 193
Vickery, A. 192

Walton, W.S. 84
Warburton, K.W. 192
Ward, P. 17
Wedge, P. 2, 5, 16, 29, 48, 50
Weinstein, E.A. 4, 7
Welner, J. 7
Wender, P.H. 7
West, D.J. 129, 165
White, K. 68
Wilson, H. 83, 190
Winnicott, C. 52
Winokur, G. 7, 171
Witmer, H.L. 4, 7
Wolkind, S.N. 13, 88, 90, 118, 120
Work, H.H. 88
Wright, C.H. 188

Yule, W. 13, 87

Zimmerman, R.B. 197